Science Fiction Film

Film Genres series

Edited by Mark Jancovich and Charles Acland

ISSN: 1757-6431

The *Film Genres* series presents accessible books on popular genres for students, scholars and fans alike. Each volume addresses key films, movements and periods by synthesizing existing literature and proposing new assessments.

Published:

Fantasy Film: A Critical Introduction
Teen Film: A Critical Introduction

Forthcoming:

Historical Film: A Critical Introduction
Anime: A Critical Introduction
Documentary Film: A Critical Introduction

Science Fiction Film

A Critical Introduction

Keith M. Johnston

B L O O M S B U R Y
LONDON • NEW DELHI • NEW YORK • SYDNEY

Bloomsbury Academic
An imprint of Bloomsbury Publishing Plc

50 Bedford Square
London
WC1B 3DP
UK

175 Fifth Avenue
New York
NY 10010
USA

www.bloomsbury.com

First published in 2011 by Berg
Reprinted by Bloomsbury Academic 2013

British Library Cataloguing-in-Publication Data
A catalogue record for this book is available from the British Library.

ISBN: HB: 978-1-8478-8477-0
PB: 978-1-8478-8476-3

Library of Congress Cataloging-in-Publication Data
Johnston, Keith M., 1973-
Science fiction film: a critical introduction/Keith M. Johnston.
p. cm. — (Berg film genres series)
Includes bibliographical references and index.
ISBN 978-1-84788-476-3 (pbk.) — ISBN 978-1-84788-477-0 (cloth) —
ISBN 978-1-84788-478-7 (individual e-book)
1. Science fiction films—History and criticism. I. Title.
PN1995.9.S26J45 2011
791.43'615—dc23
2011028876

Typeset by JS Typesetting Ltd, Porthcawl, Mid Glamorgan.

To my mum and dad.

Contents

Illustrations

Acknowledgements

Many thanks to the editors and publishers of this series for giving me the opportunity to contribute to scholarship on the science fiction film, and the extra time needed to complete it.

Thanks to colleagues at the University of East Anglia who have supported me during the writing of this book; and to my friends, particularly Alan Colquhoun, who has an innate ability to find a different perspective on a range of debates and ideas, from three-dimensional film to parallel universes. As ever, my main source of inspiration and support has been my wife, who has put up with eighteen months of our lives being cluttered with science-fiction detritus.

However, this book is dedicated to my mum and dad, two people without whom I would never have become a science fiction fan or scholar. They took me to see my first science fiction film (*The Humanoid*, 1979: because *Star Wars* was sold out), bought me my first action figure (R2-D2), took me to my first science fiction-themed restaurant (Buck Rogers' Burger Bar in Glasgow), searched for back issues of my favourite science fiction comic (*2000AD*), escorted me to my first science fiction convention (*Doctor Who: A Celebration*, Longleat 1983), and helped steer my brief science fiction career as a Dalek, trundling awkwardly up the Royal Mile in Edinburgh.

Without knowing it, they laid the groundwork that led to this very book ... and I couldn't have done it without them.

Introduction

H. G. Wells preferred the term 'fantasias of possibility', which would 'take some developing possibility in human affairs and work it out for as to develop the broad consequences of that possibility' (Wells 1967, 7). John Wyndham felt it presupposed 'a technology, or an effect of a technology, or a disturbance in the natural order, such as humanity, up to the time of writing, has not in actual fact experienced' (Wyndham 1968, 7). Theodore Sturgeon thought it was about 'a human problem, and a human solution, which would not have happened at all without its science context' (Sturgeon, quoted in Sobchack 1988, 19). Kingsley Amis described a hypothesis 'on the basis of some innovations in science and technology ... whether human or extraterrestrial in origin' (Amis 1960, 18); while editor John W. Campbell Jr. said it was 'an effort to predict the future on the basis of known facts' (Campbell, quoted in Telotte 2001, 3). Within these five different definitions of the science fiction narrative there are recurring notions of what all science fiction contains, regardless of medium. A potential future development within science or the natural world, caused by human or unknown force, which has to be understood, tamed or destroyed. Technology is key to many of these definitions, a suggestion that science fiction is as reliant on the 'science' element as the 'fiction'.

Book-length discussions of science fiction often tie themselves in knots trying to come up with a workable definition of the science fiction genre, what elements are important and how that can be applied across examples from the past century. This book is less concerned with such a concrete, unyielding definition, because it does not see the science fiction genre as fixed and unchanging. Rather, the book will demonstrate that the genre is as notable for its flexibility and genre hybridity as it is for a series of conventions around developing technology or science. For now, it is enough to say that this book intends to treat science fiction film as a popular fictional genre that engages with (and visualizes) cultural debates around one or more of the following: the future, artificial creation, technological invention, extraterrestrial contact, time travel, physical or mental mutation, scientific experimentation, or fantastic natural disaster. Science fiction films are traditionally dramas about these topics, usually with thrilling and romantic elements and often reliant upon state-of-the-art special effects techniques to create a new, or expanded, worldview. In recent years, sci-fi themes, backdrops or narrative devices have been more dominant in Hollywood blockbusters, but those are only one thread of the current science fiction tapestry.[1]

Science fiction does appear to be linked to change, mutation or evolution: few science-fiction narratives are about stasis. Yet attempts to define the science fiction film prefer the genre to remain static, as though genres are not capable of transformation or variation. The term is first used within US pulp magazines (appearing in *Amazing Stories* around 1926); it becomes more commonly applied to films in the 1950s genre expansion and features prominently in mainstream and independent cinema from the mid-1970s on. Such a master narrative ignores the ebbs and flows of the genre, however, and exploring the historical specificity of the genre in particular time periods is one of the aims of this book: replacing the search for the genre's 'unconscious structure' with a focus on 'the historical development of those cultural codes' that underpin the popularity of science-fiction films (Jancovich 1992, 16). To give one specific example of cultural discourse here, and its relationship to generic knowledge, the term 'Frankenstein' has become a catch-all term for cultural concerns around the dangers of biological or mechanical creation in the years since the publication of Mary Shelley's original novel in 1818. Debates over genetically modified (GM) food used terms such as 'Frankenstein food' or 'Frankenfood', while the UK government's proposed Human Fertilisation and Embryology Bill was denounced as an 'endorsement of experiments of Frankenstein proportion' (Toke 2004, 88; Gledhill and Lister 2008). The fictional character of Dr Frankenstein still exerts a potent influence on cultural perceptions of scientists and the genres in which they feature. Understanding such historical and cultural spheres and tracing how science fiction films operate within them will allow the book to explore the genre's changes and mutations, as much as any similarities.

This focus on the larger cultural understanding or awareness of genre does not preclude a focus on the textual elements of the film, their use of innovative stylistic or narrative elements. Indeed, one of the difficulties in writing a book such as this is how to comment on, or talk about, the great science fiction films. Many of these images and films are so familiar: the art deco-influenced robot body in *Metropolis* (1927); Michael Rennie striding out of a flying saucer in *The Day the Earth Stood Still* (1951); the glorious jump cut from flying bone to floating space station in *2001: A Space Odyssey* (1968); the kinetic space battles of *Star Wars* (1977); or the balletic 'bullet time' sequences of *The Matrix* (1999). The book will offer a survey of work done on those films, as well as the link between the 'Red Menace' and the 1950s invaders from Mars (and elsewhere), or the problems of artificial humanity in *Blade Runner* (1982); but the book must, of necessity, also expand the discussion of science fiction films beyond those recurring examples. It aims to be more than a compendium of the known films, the expected academic discussions, and therefore (where relevant) it will move beyond American films, to Britain, Japan, Russia, Germany and others, to consider the lesser known global genre products alongside the dominant canon.

The historical side of the project throws up other issues. It is almost impossible to approach these films with the fresh eye that a contemporary audience might have had, watching Leslie Nielson romance Anne Francis in *Forbidden Planet* (1956), or queuing round the block for tickets to a new film called *E.T.: The Extra Terrestrial* (1982). Yet part of the project for this book is to try to find a fresh perspective on such films, to think about what is meant when such films are described as belonging to the science fiction genre. The very notion of genre suggests an unspoken yet shared assumption of agreed terms and conventions that reach across global audience members, an unwritten belief system that can identify what a science fiction film (or book, or comic, or television series) is. This book will challenge some of those preconceptions, and investigate how the science fiction genre has grown on film, how it has changed and developed over the years.

To accomplish these aims, and to guide the individual reader, *Science Fiction Film: A Critical Introduction* is split into three distinct sections. Part I, 'What is Science Fiction?' offers an overview and intervention into debates around the science fiction film genre. After a brief discussion on the competing foci of genre theory, a broader cultural approach (favoured by writers such as Andrew Tudor, Mark Jancovich, Jason Mittell and Lincoln Geraghty) is applied to the science-fiction genre, considering both the textual and extra-textual elements that might influence audience opinion on the definition of a genre film. Chapters 2 and 3 then focus on specific elements of academic work on science fiction: how other academic theories around psychoanalysis, feminism, or postmodernism have been applied to the genre and how the emphasis on the technological spectacle of the science fiction film has dominated critical discussions of the genre. This section aims to provide readers new to the genre with an understanding of past and present critical debates around science fiction in cinema.

Part II, 'Genre History' is a response to Alan Williams' belief that a new approach to genre studies would involve a return to film history. Williams stated that such an approach would explore 'a genre's pre-history, its roots in other media … studying all films, regardless of perceived quality, and … going beyond film content to study advertising, the star system, studio policy, and so on' (Williams 1984, 124). Applying such criteria, Part II covers the historical development of the science fiction film, highlighting the roots and prehistory of the genre, exploring the breadth of films produced (including lesser known areas such as exploitation and animation) and complicating existing notions of periodization by expanding the range of films both internationally and across generic borders. Chapters 4 through 7 are not designed to create a master narrative for the science fiction film, but are an attempt to think about the wider historical and industrial context within which these films were developed, released and received by audiences.

Part III offers a further development of that historical focus and picks up specifically on the last element of Williams' call for a new approach to genre: a move beyond the textual quality of the films to study how such films were marketed and what that reveals about studio policy towards genre products. While writers such as Steve Neale and Rick Altman have made some inroads in this area, there remains a lack of focus on the specific advertising of the science-fiction genre. Chapters 8 and 9 examine two different forms of studio advertising, the pressbook and the 'coming attractions' film trailer, and explore the placement of generic iconography, star imagery and rhetorical language within these promotional materials. Chapter 10 shifts to the post-'digital turn' world of the Internet, to consider how production companies have adapted to an online environment, and how this has made fan participation with marketing materials more visible and contested.

This combination of academic theory, historical and cultural discourse and awareness of extratextual influences provides a complex introduction to the science fiction film but one that (due to length) must remain partial. Writing as much as a fan of the genre as a genre theorist, the hope of the author is that this book functions as a gateway (stargate, hyperspace jump point, time portal) to the larger universes (utopian, dystopian, parallel) of science fiction and opens up new areas of genre exploration. As this book was being written, a newspaper article questioned the future of the science-fiction genre, claiming that the genre had splintered into a series of subgenres (citing niches such as biopunk, space opera, clockpunk, time travel, military sci-fi and steampunk) and noting that tenets of the science-fiction genre had grown outside the genre and invaded the Hollywood mainstream (Irvine 2008, 50). Such an approach elides the tangled history of the science fiction film, which grew out of multiple types of film in the silent period, has never had constant genre borders that can be defined (or policed), and remains as hybrid now as it did in 1977, 1951 or 1927. This book hopes to demonstrate that, rather than splintering into subgenres, the science-fiction film has always been complex, multiple, contested and distinctive. And that academics and fans should not want it to be any other way.

Part I
What is Science Fiction?

–1–

Genre, Theory and Science Fiction

A definition of the science fiction genre from an academic perspective might focus on thematic areas around technology, science, futurism or the figure of 'the Other'. An equally valid definition might come from popular identification of iconographic elements such as flying saucers, robots, ray guns and aliens. A third discussion of the term, from an industrial perspective, might focus on special effects or spectacle. Any attempt to understand the genre must engage with all three and accept that further viewpoints would be equally valid. However, academic and popular criticism, as well as individual audience groups, often desires limitations on genre, a set of rules or conventions within which films are, or are not, contained. Yet genres do not exist *a priori*; they are not a natural phenomenon that can be precisely catalogued and labelled. Rather than pre-existing forms, genres are cultural creations that are formed and reformed on a regular basis, prone to shifts in emphasis and meaning. A genre definition such as 'science fiction' can be used regularly in film production (directors, producers or actors might refer to their project in generic terms); by film audiences (discussing whether they want to see a specific genre); within advertising materials (promoting elements that are seen as intrinsic to the genre); or by critics or academics reviewing or writing on the film or genre. In each instance, the exact definition of what each individual means by the term 'science fiction' is more fluid than traditional genre boundaries allow. Equally, their definition will be different from what a producer, audience member or critic might have meant by the term 'science fiction' ten, thirty or fifty years ago. Defining the links between these disparate groups, historical meanings and the industrial and cultural backgrounds that such genre films are produced (and discussed) within is the aim of this current chapter, although it is an approach that will echo through the rest of the book.

It may be possible to say that everyone knows what a science fiction film is to them, within their own definitions and experience, but there is no guarantee that those opinions would coalesce into a more rigid definition (Neale, 1990). Many genre theorists look to (contemporary and historical) industrial discourses, or to the film text itself, to identify generic definitions or, at least, some generic common ground. Within science fiction, stories based around advanced technology, robotics, space exploration or time travel are likely candidates of such standard genre narratives. Yet such selections are continually open to challenge: the story of *S1m0ne* (2000) was built around advanced technology creating a virtual actress, but the film is more concerned with romance and Hollywood satire; *Short Circuit* (1987) features a central robotic character but shares many similarities with broader family films of the period. Equally, space exploration is at the heart of *Apollo 13* (1997) and *The Right Stuff* (1978), but these films make claims to biographic and dramatic status; time travel, perhaps the most likely candidate, features as a plot device for romance-based films such as *Kate & Leopold* (2000), *The Lake House* (2005) or *The Time Traveller's Wife* (2009).

This chapter will begin the process of exploring text- or discourse-based definitions of the science-fiction genre, establishing what traits and elements these approaches use, and how generic categories have historically been defined and applied. If genre is a collective exercise (Tudor 1974, 135), a cultural construct that draws from more than simply a series of films (and books, and television shows) that have been identified (and canonized) as something called 'science fiction', then it is important to consider how such shared understanding is created and how it has been investigated academically. Such genre studies have, historically, been overly reliant on an exclusive notion of genre as text: if the study of films within a genre need not look beyond genre films then 'genre histories further the notion that genres are reducible to lists of texts' (Mittell 2002, 30). Expanding genre history beyond the text is a crucial function of modern genre study and, while this book will be concerned with the visual, textual and thematic analysis of films that could be construed as science fiction, it will be equally aware of the popular discourse surrounding science fiction. As such, the book contributes to recent investigations of how such discursive networks have historically shaped perceptions of 'science fiction' as much as the films that are produced and marketed to audiences (see, for example, Geraghty, 2009). However, before moving into a debate about the path for future genre study, it is important to first consider why genre has been so important within both Film Studies and Hollywood.

Describing a film as being 'Science Fiction' is, to paraphrase Andrew Tudor, to state that the film shares something – 'an indefinable "X"' – with other films called 'science fiction' (Tudor 1974, 15). The quest to isolate that unknown 'X' has been at the core of genre studies since it became institutionalized within Film Studies in the late 1960s and through the 1970s. The move towards genre theory has been described as a move away from the auteur theories of the 1950s and 1960s, where the director was identified as a film's main creative force (Hutchings 1993, 60; Hollows et al. 2000, 82). Film authorship studies had been used to identify and define the artistic merits of a sole author who could exploit the rigid production practices of Hollywood to create individual film art, thus claiming higher cultural value for such films and directors. Developed partially in opposition to this (although there has been work on how auteurs used generic conventions; see Kitses [1969] 2004; McArthur 1972), genre theory offered a way to think about wider industrial practices in Hollywood – to investigate culture, history, ideology and the generic evidence of the films themselves. Early academic genre studies were dominated by textual and formalist analysis designed to identify (what were seen as) self-contained generic categories (the Western and Gangster film were dominant examples of this trend: Kitses [1969] 2004; Warshow 1970; McArthur 1972). Film-genre analysis began, therefore, as an attempt to analyse the codes and conventions of a series of films, with the underlying assumption that those films were connected in some way, often around iconographic and thematic traits that were identifiable to 'all' viewers. The Western film was seen as repeating key visuals (the cowboy, the six-shooter and the frontier town) while thematically representing larger cultural and historical oppositions built around the American frontier myth: wilderness and civilization, nature and culture, the West and the East.

Science fiction was not a central example in this initial flourish of genre studies. Although there is no clear reason for its exclusion, issues around juvenilia and cultural superiority may have acted against it. In the mid-to-late 1960s, when genre analysis was popularized, science fiction films were split between larger action blockbusters (*Fantastic Voyage,* 1966; *The Time Machine,* 1960) and lower budget independents (*The Beach Girls and the Monster,* 1965; *Santa Claus Conquers the Martians,* 1964), but both varieties were predominantly popular with youth audiences. Science-fiction films had been tagged with juvenile characteristics since the early 1950s, and this critical reputation has echoed through the decades since. Many critics have attempted to avoid this tag by canonizing certain 'adult' texts (*2001: A Space Odyssey, Blade Runner,* and *District 9* (2009) would be pertinent examples here) ahead of those with more popular leanings. Making such distinctions is not a purely academic or critical move: individual audience groups also identify and police their own genre boundaries, chastising others who do not recognize similar borders (Jancovich 2002). These assumptions of superiority around the classification of genre texts are as potent today as they were in the 1960s when the initial work on film genre elided the role of science fiction.

The absence of science fiction from this initial round of genre theory may also have been linked to its lack of auteur figures, its existence in small pockets of production activity across multiple companies and (despite its apparent interests in the Cold War and atomic bombs) a lack of academic interest in exploring its connections to deeper social mythologies.[1] There was also a concern over genre boundaries, most notably between the science fiction and horror genres, with films such as *The Invisible Man* (1933) or *The Thing from Another World* (1951) blurring clear lines where one genre ended and another began. With genre studies preferring stricter border control (as seen in the early success of work on the Western, gangster film or *film noir*), science fiction offered a more challenging case study. Yet, barring the work of Susan Sontag, the absence of science fiction from early genre theory is striking, particularly given its strong visual and thematic content. There is an argument (at least in the 1950s films) for a shared iconography of missile-shaped rockets, flying saucers, and the ubiquitous star field seen in films such as *Destination Moon* (1950), *Conquest of Space* (1955) or *Missile to the Moon* (1958). Equally, like the Western, many science fiction films are fascinated with the idea of a frontier (the 'final' frontier of space would become a common generic reference) and contain a similar thematic opposition between wilderness (desert) and civilization (urban city): it appears in *Earth vs. the Flying Saucers* (1956), *Them!* (1954) and *The War of the Worlds* (1953). With recurring interest in the role of technology, and the figure of the alien/robotic/created 'Other', the genre would present fertile ground for such genre-based criticism from the 1970s on, but remained largely absent from this first moment of theory.

Many of these elements are, of course, situated within the film and assume more than a passing knowledge of a series of film texts. Challenging the belief that the film was the sole location of genre, Andrew Tudor demonstrated that most genre work actually assumed the pre-existence of a generic category, into which critics could place their favourite examples of iconography or thematic similarity. Isolating those films for detailed study required a list of characteristics that could only be discovered after the analysis has been carried out: 'we are caught in a circle that first requires that films be isolated, for which purposes a criterion is necessary, but the criterion is, in turn, meant to emerge from the empirically established common characteristics of the films' (Tudor, 1974, 136). Breaking with the established tenets of genre study, Tudor offered two solutions: accept *a priori* criteria (borrowed from literature, or other sources), or consider the 'cultural consensus' around individual genres (Tudor, 1974). While the former may offer a useful expansion of conventions and iconography, it simply replaces the circular logic of film criteria with earlier criteria from literature. The suggestion of activity outside of the generic film, in the wider culture and audiences, is a more compelling development, but genre theorists have subsequently struggled to quantify how to measure or identify this 'cultural consensus' effectively (indeed, the idea that there is a dominant consensus, rather than multiple positions, is also problematic).

More recent attempts to develop genre studies have investigated the industrial use of genre categories, particularly around production and promotional discourses (Altman 1999; Neale 2000). Films were being produced and specifically marketed as individual types or narratives from at least 1909: *Bioscope* trade posters from the time include the 'Selig Melodrama' *The Witch's Cavern*, Lubin's 'Trick Comic' *Rubber Man* (*Bioscope* 1909b, 22), the Cines-Films' 'Detective Story' *A Treacherous Maid* (*Bioscope* 1910c, 58) and Essanay's *A Western Girl's Sacrifice*, 'one of our best recent Western subjects' (*Bioscope* 1911b, 16). The pre-existence of such industrial and popular categories presents a unique challenge within genre theory. Unlike authorship, which stressed high cultural artistic merit, which stood in opposition to the studio system (and which was decoded by intellectual effort), genre study necessarily embraced the industrialized Hollywood system, populist films and the audience. Genre has often been the means by which Hollywood studios produce, and reproduce, successful products, and 'greenlight' new projects. Financial success brings more products in similar generic categories: the success of *Star Wars* can be linked to the production of *Battlestar Galactica* (1978), *Starcrash* (1979) or *Battle*

Beyond the Stars (1979), for instance; or the growth of family science fiction films in the 1980s after *E.T.: The Extra Terrestrial.* Popular, and recurring, genre success also suggests that audiences are aware of generic categories, and perhaps gain particular enjoyment from the presentation of known pleasures (be they visual or story based). Given the pre-existence of genre as a known quantity, popular mainstream success and the potential multiplicity of audience response are seemingly intrinsic to any understanding of how genre works.

This shift towards understanding genre as a larger cultural construct, not simply residing in the films (or television series, or books, or video games), is necessarily seen as a constantly adaptive process and one that foregrounds the historical nature of any generic claims. (Altman 1999; Neale 2000; Mittell 2002). Genres are not fixed, set categories; they are flexible, changing concepts that can be better understood by appreciation of the discursive network surrounding them. If genre is a nexus for culture, audience, and filmmakers, or how 'particular definitions, interpretations, and evaluations ... play out within the various realms of industry, audience, text, critics, policy makers, and broader social context' (Mittell 2002, 30) then the need for a specific 'X' factor is replaced by a fluid notion of a range of different influences, shifting and malleable. Science-fiction films cannot be understood simply as a series of films that feature rocketships; equally, they are about more than visual display and effects spectacle. Like every other genre, the science fiction film needs to be placed within a larger network of influences (including films from other genres). The move away from a strict definition of a genre film (with preconceived borders and conventions) has created a wider appreciation that genres almost always function as hybrids: the detective-science fiction films *Minority Report* (2002) or *Soylent Green* (1973); the war film-science fiction hybrids *Them!* or *Aliens* (1986); the animated science fictions *Wall-E* (2008) and *La planète sauvage/Fantastic Planet* (1973).

This discussion of academic genre theory, and the notion of genre as a wider cultural construct, where producers and audiences draw on a far greater (and diverse) range of influences, should not suggest that it is impossible to define a genre – simply that we need to be alert to the shifting nature of genre, particularly over different periods of time (Geraghty and Jancovich 2008; Geraghty 2009). There is now no assumption that such categories are set, or ahistorical. Genre is at once shaped by interactions with culture and society, and a force that can be applied within culture. Depictions of space travel on film were closely tied up with the 'real-world' science fact of NASA's Apollo and Gemini missions (as well as the USSR's own space achievements). Meanwhile, reports or commentary on recent scientific breakthroughs (for example, the large hadron supercollider) regularly use terms like 'mad scientist', or 'science fiction' to talk about 'real-world' science and scientists. There is no easy causal link here, but it is clear that generic conventions and developments draw from contemporary culture and feed back into it.

Adding this cultural-based perspective to genre analysis does not mean abandoning a text-based approach; it means finding a balance that borrows from the best of both worlds. Textual work has defined the field of genre study since the 1970s and has provided many useful and challenging readings of films and television programmes. Genre films are as capable of challenging ideologies or belief systems as they are of supporting them, having offered potent explorations of contemporary culture, racism, gender politics and nationality. To present its discussion of the development of the science fiction film, and how such films interrelate with genre theory, this book will, of necessity, begin to map out and analyse the possible narrative, iconographic and thematic characteristics of science fiction films. Given that these films rely on intertextual references to each other, to other genres, and to influences drawn from literature, television and other media, understanding those textual characteristics is an essential stage in categorizing one element of how genre works. Yet other elements deserve equal analysis. Rather than see genre studies as beginning and ending with the viewing of a wide range of films, a broader discursive and cultural analysis demonstrates that science-fiction films do not reproduce generic meaning on their own. Instead, it is possible (and desirable) for analysis to illuminate a relationship between text, industry, culture and audience: a relationship that promulgates and promotes genre.

The very notion of a term like 'science fiction' in everyday language demonstrates that genre remains an essential tool for communicating something about a series of films (and other media). Hollywood has always relied on visual imagery, rhetoric and reference to known pleasures as key generic triggers within film marketing. The continued success of many such films, and the ability of other national cinemas to claim or subvert such triggers for their own productions, supports a wider industrial and cultural importance of genre. The very dominance of genre in so many avenues of criticism, audience choice, academic research and institutional work supports the continuing desire to explore it, understand it and investigate how individual films make use of that cultural knowledge. The rest of this chapter, and the next two chapters, will begin that exploration, with specific examples from the science fiction genre that will unpack what that term implies, what assumptions underlie its use, and what associations it might be constructing.

Defining the Science Fiction Genre: *Moon* (2009)

Genre can be a contested arena because producers, audience members and academics all have variations on what a genre should contain, either visually or thematically. Investigating a modern genre film demonstrates how the cultural and textual components of one science fiction film can raise debates around other generic examples, expanding out to encompass both historic and modern conventions. *Moon* (2009) was produced as science fiction (director Duncan Jones described it as 'grown up science-fiction,' a deliberate homage to 1970s genre films *Silent Running* (1970) and *Alien* (1979), advertised as science fiction (posters focused on

Figure 1.1 The teaser poster for *Moon* (2009) suggests generic status through elements such as Sam Rockwell's astronaut costume (Sony Pictures Classics/Photofest)

Sam Rockwell in astronaut outfit (Figure 1.1); trailers displayed the moon landscape and technology), and reviewed as science fiction (Roger Ebert talked about it as 'hard sci-fi'; MTV noted it was a 'terrific sci-fi space film' – *Moon* website 2009). This discourse will inevitably play some part in shaping audience expectations and definitions of *Moon* as belonging to the science fiction genre. An investigation of the film's *mise en scène* (including, but not limited to the notion of iconography) and narrative structure (including themes and characters) also point towards its place within the science fiction genre.

Moon is set in the mostly automated lunar mining base Sarang, where one human astronaut, Sam Bell (played by Sam Rockwell), and a robot servant-cum-administrator (Gerty, voiced by Kevin Spacey) maintain a series of huge harvesting machines that roam the Moon's surface, collecting and processing moon rock into a clean source of energy for Earth. Injured towards the end of his three-year contract, Sam spends several days in Sarang's sickbay before tricking a seemingly sinister Gerty into letting him back out onto the lunar surface. There he finds the body of another Sam, battered but alive. After a period of distrust and conflict, the two Sams discover they are simply the latest corporation-designed clones to operate this base, that their memories are implanted rather than real and that they will be killed after three years. The discovery that the family of the real Sam Bell lives on Earth, though much older than their memories or the video messages they've been watching, leads them to plan an escape from the Moon before corporate hit-men arrive to restart the programme.

There are certain textual elements of *Moon* that might be identified as science fiction. The narrative fulfils both (literal) requirements of that term: it is a fiction based around scientific or technological advances, though one that is firmly rooted in contemporary understanding. Spacesuits are required on the Moon, robots are only a few steps removed from current industrial machinery, travel to and from the Moon is by rocket propelled vehicles, while working on the moon is akin to long shifts on oil rigs or some equally remote Earth-bound outpost. This desire for a possible realism is not a requirement of science fiction, but most genre films relate aspects of their *mise en scène* to realistic traits. Although early filmed science fiction made guesses about what a trip to the Moon would be like (in *Frau im Mond*, 1929, the astronauts walked around the lunar surface with no suits on), many films show the absence of gravity in space travel, or make reference to artificial gravity and air (*2001: A Space Odyssey* is the obvious example here but similar ideas can be seen in *Phantom Planet*, 1961, and *Rocketship X-M*, 1951). Even those films set in a distant part of the universe (often described as 'space opera') rely on certain realistic or naturalistic traits that audiences can relate to: most of *Star Wars*' characters speak English, breathe oxygen, have families, build houses, fight wars and fall in love. While much filmed science fiction may be predicated on scientific advances (or change brought about by alien technology), there are few films that do not make some claim to a recognizeble verisimilitude.

Set design is a key element in any science fiction film that ties in to these notions of near future realism. In *Moon*, Sarang base is a combination of smooth sleek interiors and human presence, advanced technology but with the sheen of human use and habitation. Away from the sterile corridors, there are Post-It notes stuck to surfaces, Sam counts down the days by drawing smiley faces on the bathroom wall, his bedroom is a mess of clothes and papers. The outside of the base is utilitarian, grey, sunk into the surrounding rock; the harvesters are large machines, squat boxes that trundle across the lunar surface like giant trucks or threshers. Designing such near (or far) future habitats, vehicles and weaponry is an important way that fantastic science fiction concepts can be at once iconographic and rooted in the familiar, the known. *Minority Report* portrayed a fantastic yet familiar world where cars had become oblong pods, security systems (and advertising) relied on iris identification, and jet-packs were in use; yet those pods continued to move along freeways, CCTV cameras remained fallible, and helicopter-style vehicles were still more efficient than rocket-packs. Set design also has strong ties to the genre's claims for iconography. Design elements can become iconic in themselves, from the bullet-shaped rocket of

Le Voyage dans la lune/A Trip to the Moon (1902) to the svelte Art Deco-inspired robotic figure of Maria in *Metropolis*. Science fiction is also visualized on a larger scale than many generic films. The immense skyscraper cities of *Blade Runner* and *Kôkaku kidôtai/Ghost in the Shell* (1994); the sweeping desert plains of Tatooine (*Star Wars*) and Arrakis (*Dune*, 1984); the dystopian future Earths of *The Terminator* (1984) and *Wall-E*: despite the varied cinematic technologies involved in creating them, these all contribute to the epic, fantastic spaces of science fiction. Yet set design is as intimately involved in the small design elements of the future as the large: the communicator from *Star Trek*, the moving video pages of the newspapers in *Minority Report*, or the BFG from *Doom* (2006). These contribute to a fantastic iconographic view of the future while linking such futurity to existing devices as the radio, the newspaper and the gun.

Closely linked to set design is costume, the idea of what future clothing and apparel might look like. In *Moon*, Sam's costumes match the lived-in look of the base, from the basic scruffier clothes he wears around the base to the bulkier spacesuit (similar to existing astronaut design) he dons to go out on the surface. Audience knowledge of Sam is partly guided by what he wears and how he looks in those clothes. The spacesuit links him to existing knowledge of the space programme, but also acts as his uniform, a reminder of his job.[2] As in *Moon*, costume in science-fiction films is a marker for character: for all the technological set design elements of *Minority Report*, for example, people still shopped in Gap for khakis and shirts. Equally, the uniforms of that film's Pre-Crime Unit mimic many science fiction films in their focus on a professional, often military, group: the colour-coordinated crew costumes of *Star Trek*; the utilitarian combat outfits of the future soldiers of *Aliens* or *Soldier* (1998); even the matching clothes of superhero teams the *Fantastic Four* (2005) and the *X-Men* (2000). In two early examples of this trend, both *High Treason* (1929) and *Things to Come* (1936) depict future societies through a simple, cohesive fashion statement. While the application of one costume to the whole of human culture is unusual in science fiction it is more common with the creation of alien societies (the warlike Klingons of the *Star Trek* universe are almost always seen in battered leather and armour). It is more common to find a scattering of different costumes for different purposes: to create the rambling culturally chaotic future of *Blade Runner*, or to suggest the varied personalities of the *Nostromo* crew in *Alien* (where the crew, while asleep, are in matching outfits, but quickly choose their own, disparate, clothing styles). Costume functions to suggest the future but also remains tied to the known, creating a world that is different but familiar enough to be recognizable.

Costume and set design in many science fiction films are often enhanced by special effects techniques. *Moon*'s self-contained moon base is an impressive practical set inside, with its exterior and the surrounding lunar landscape all computer generated. Equally, when Sam discovers an immense chamber of clone capsules beneath the base, only the first few pods are practical, the rest of the background is added digitally. Matte paintings, stop-motion animation, miniatures, back-screen projection and computer-generated imagery all add new elements to existing material. This can range from the creation of entire digital worlds and characters in the more recent *Star Wars* trilogy to simple background work to add dimension or remove elements in *Children of Men* (2006). Special effects in science fiction films again tread the line between realism and fantasy, wanting to create amazing vistas but often attempting to make them appear possible. While early cinema was content with the tricks that could be achieved through effects, by the time of *The Lost World* (1925) the filmmakers wanted to root the special effect (stop-motion dinosaurs) in relation to live action elements, either actors or locations. The combination of real and unreal can be seen in films as diverse as *Earth vs the Flying Saucers, Jurassic Park* (1993) and *Transformers* (2007); a desire for photo-realistic shots that aim to fool the audience into believing in such fantastic imagery. This complicates the creation of generic iconography (flying saucers, spaceships, robots, etc.) and the use of visual effects to suggest a potential reality for such imagined technology.

Set design and effects are combined to create these future technologies and to make them appear plausible, but the narrative meaning behind such technology has shifted over the years. The technology of *Moon* includes the robotic Gerty – a combination of squat rectangular bodies and related appendages that moves around the base on roof-mounted rails; it contains all the necessary tools to help run the base and its main 'face' is a screen on which a series of smiley faces are displayed, ostensibly to match his mood or message (the masculine pronoun is suggested by Gerty's voice). Like many future SF technologies Gerty is not always a positive presence, functioning instead as generic reference and narrative puzzle. From his initial appearance, Gerty echoes another space-based computer, HAL 9000 (*2001: A Space Odyssey*): flat, inflectionless voice; slow, deliberate statements; an obsession with his human co-worker; and the suggestion that he is hiding something sinister. The film playfully baits any viewer who brings this generic knowledge to the film, ultimately taking Gerty in another narrative direction, but the presence of a potentially unreliable computer does tie the film in with larger genre depictions of technology.

Robots and computers often bear the brunt of science fiction's uncertainty about new technology. Gerty is simply the latest in a line that stretches from *The Mechanical Mary Anne* (1910) through Robby the Robot in *Forbidden Planet* to the super computer networks of *The Terminator* and *The Matrix*. The issue with technology is often human control – the underlying belief that technology will either go wrong (of its own accord), be taken over, be misused by its creator, or become self-aware and want to destroy the human race. Although rooted in various non-cinematic stories (from the Jewish Golem legend to Mary Shelley's *Frankenstein*), science fiction films have been able to visually depict this myth of automation and its destructive potential. There are few technologies in science fiction that are not ultimately used for negative purposes. New scientific formulas or machines to turn people invisible

(*Hollow Man*, 2000), increase their brain power (*The Lawnmower Man*, 1992), or to induce an evolutionary leap (*Altered States*, 1980), inevitably lead to the test subject going mad or indulging in a god complex. The creation of more advanced computers causes them to turn against their creator, attempt to reproduce, and either enslave or destroy humanity (*The Invisible Boy*, 1957; *Colossus: The Forbin Project*, 1970; *Demon Seed*, 1977). Robotics, as suggested with the example of Gerty in *Moon*, can be seen as a more optimistic field. While many automatons are destructive (*Devil Girl From Mars*, 1954; *Westworld*, 1973; *Eve of Destruction*, 1991) there are cases where the humans are untrustworthy compared to their creation (*The Stepford Wives*, 1975; *Android*, 1982) or where the robotic figure is as heroic as the humans (*Wall-E*, *Silent Running*; *Cherry 2000*, 1987). Machines such as the robot in *Metropolis* have become iconic within the genre, becoming attractive images that are the source of visual pleasure outside of their destructive narrative role. Several have even achieved a star status, with posters, models and guest appearances for Robby the Robot (Figure 1.2), C3-PO and the Transformers. These robotic stars offer a balance of technology and reliability, they can be comic as well as a source of narrative tension and this balance works to complicate their appeal. Even counting these latter illustrations, however, technology in science fiction film narratives is often an active force within the diegesis.

Technology is also a key narrative element of Sam's mission and job at Sarang base. Technology literally keeps him alive, allows him out to travel across the

Figure 1.2 Robby the Robot, one of the science fiction genre's first robotic stars (MGM/Photofest)

moon's surface and to escape the satellite and journey to Earth. Unlike Gerty, many of these technologies are inherently neutral and the film makes little or no effort to present them as destructive (although the chamber where clones are atomized does contain echoes of that notion). This is one of the contradictions within science fiction films. Exploration narratives necessarily rely on such background technologies: spaceships, space stations, advanced habitats. Such spaces are traditionally coded as positive/negative or simply neutral, a mode of travel (Sobchack 1988). Ships such as the *Millennium Falcon* and the starship *Enterprise* are seen as positive, slicing through space, fighting battles and (notably) controlled by human (or humanoid) pilots. The *Nostromo*, by contrast, is a neutral space at the beginning of *Alien* but is increasingly infected by its alien intruder (or the robotic traitor among the crew) into a dark, unsafe space. Between these poles, many genre films use their ships simply as neutral transport options. The construction of ships such as the *Excelsior* (*Himmelskibet*, 1919) or the *Luna* (*Destination Moon*) suggests a central dramatic status, yet once they have launched the drama is external (normally from space phenomenon such as meteor showers). Events happen to, or around, the ship, not because of anything inherent to it, or its structuring technology. Space stations or colonies have similar fates: the mining base of *Outland* (1981) moves from neutral to dangerous, again because of the arrival of outside influences; while the space station of *Marooned* (1969) is neutral, simply another working environment.

Not all technologies are based around computers, automatons or habitats, however. Many science fiction films contain a desire to portray new screen technology. In *Moon*, computer and video screens are the only interfaces Sam has available for communication and interaction; he watches videos from his wife on a screen, he receives instructions via a screen; his conversations with Gerty are directed at a screen. Like the viewing audience, he only receives information via this visual interface. The reflexive nature of the science fiction film towards future screen technologies has been described as film vividly imagining 'the technologies that would outdo it' (Stewart 1998, 129). Cinema has been fascinated with cinema projection and exhibition since its earliest days (*The Countryman and the Cinematograph*, 1901, showed film clips on its screen within a screen). Proto-science fiction films between 1910 and 1940 investigated the possibilities of new visual technologies such as the television (*Murder by Television*, 1935) and the videophone (*Love and Science*, 1912), while *Videodrome* (1982) painted a horrific vision around the proliferation of television and video technology. The emphasis on mechanical vision recurs throughout the genre: viewscreens are used for communication in films from *Barbarella* (1968) to *The Hitch-Hiker's Guide to the Galaxy* (2005); surveillance cameras record and display activity in *THX 1138* (1971) and *The Truman Show* (1998). Several films also discuss the next generation of visual entertainment, the technologies that threaten to replace cinema: virtual reality in *Tron* (1982), *The Lawnmower Man* and *The Matrix*, or the addiction caused by downloading and experiencing other people's memories and emotions in *Strange Days* (1997). This fascination with interfaces and screens has fuelled science-fiction films for almost a century and seems set to continue, with *Inception* (2010) suggesting a technological way to enter and change people's dreams.

Screen technologies have been relied upon to structure narratives and present special effects, and represent one way in which cinematography can be represented within the science fiction genre. Camerawork is an essential part of *mise en scène*, but is often overlooked within science fiction films because of the emphasis on the creation of special effects, or the impressive set design being filmed. While there is not enough room here to cover all science fiction camerawork techniques, it is worth pointing out several useful recurring devices. Mobile and agile cameras are frequently utilized, often exploring sets, areas or effects images that would be impossible for normal human sight. *2001: A Space Odyssey* initiated one element of this trend, with slow methodical camerawork that tracked round, past or through spaceships. *Alien* and *The Empire Strikes Back* (1980) developed this work: a mobile camera creeps through the *Nostromo* while its crew sleeps, and then later sweeps through those self-same corridors and hatches; while the kinetic camera of *The Empire Strikes Back* twists and follows the *Millennium Falcon* through an asteroid field. This latter example, putting the camera in the midst of a special effects sequence, has become more dominant in genre films, particularly CGI effects-based blockbusters such as *Armageddon* (1998) and *Iron Man* (2008). The rootless, mobile camera has also become a recent signifier of reality across many Hollywood films: within the genre, *Cloverfield* (2008) and *Children of Men* offer compelling examples of mobile camerawork, while *Moon* returns to the more contemplative option of *Alien* or *2001*. Much science fiction necessarily relies on shot-reverse shot structures, particularly to introduce narrative information, but the reliance on, and interest in, new technology, means it is also the genre most likely to take chances or experiment with new camera techniques: for example, the motion control system for special effects in *2001: A Space Odyssey* or the development of 'bullet time' for *The Matrix*.

All of these elements of *mise en scène* largely focus on the settings and trappings of the science-fiction universe being created, and how that world is captured on film. There are two further aspects of the science fiction film that are often overlooked: performance and soundtrack. One of the key elements in the technology of Gerty in *Moon* is the vocal performance of Kevin Spacey, yet performative issues are rarely discussed in relation to genre studies (De Cordova 1995, 129). Within science fiction, this may be related to the genre's relationship with both popular cinema, and modern Hollywood blockbusters (and their ancillary products): areas not commonly discussed in relation to acting or performance styles. Science fiction is rarely described as an actor's cinema, despite the genre being host to performances from actors as diverse as Robert Duvall, Kate Winslet, Charlton Heston, Sigourney Weaver and Ralph Fiennes. Critics often focus on how such actors escape the conventions of science fiction acting – the repetition of words such as melodramatic, cold, or stiff, alongside an expectation of wooden or robotic acting styles, most commonly associated with genre stars such as Arnold Schwarzenegger ('about as well suited to movie acting as he would be to ballet': Maslin 1984) or Keanu Reeves (a 'wooden talent … does some of his most interesting acting with a piece of latex covering his mouth' – Morris 1999). This tendency to diminish the work of genre actors, however, can overlook the more subtle work done by actors such as Sam Rockwell in *Moon*, who ultimately performs three different versions of Sam and keeps them distinct and identifiable. Performance styles in science fiction cannot be reduced to simple notions of melodramatic gestures and wooden acting; further work on this area of the genre would, of necessity, need to engage with the different requirements that generic production places on performance styles, not least the ability to act with, and in relation to, special effects technologies (Cornea 2007 offers a compelling move in this direction).

The science fiction soundtrack is also something that can be overlooked by critics. It is never subject to the kind of analysis that visual information regularly receives. Soundtrack refers to more than simply the style of music being used in the film, but covers everything from the sound effects of the technology (robots, spaceships, ray guns) to effects applied to dialogue or alien languages (Sobchack 1988, 146–222; Whittington 2007). In *Moon*, music and silence counterpoint Sam's initial loneliness; the lack of silence and the change in music once his clone appears matches the more dissonant tone of the character's relationships. Music is perhaps the strongest signifier of a particular kind of science fiction film: *2001: A Space Odyssey* set a strong example of how orchestral classical music could be used to suggest grandeur and awe to special effects imagery. *Star Wars*, *Stargate* (1994), and *Predator* (1987) offer variations on that theme, although with music by composers such as John Williams, Danny Elfman and Alan Silvestri, which recalls a particularly ornate period of classical music. A more science-fiction-specific soundtrack element occurs in the use of the theremin, an early electronic instrument that presaged the now commonplace use of musical motifs or themes for particular characters. Many 1950s genre films (including *The Day the Earth Stood Still* and *Forbidden Planet*) used the theremin only when alien figures were on screen, creating an indelible association between the theremin and the 'voice of the extraterrestrial Other' (Wierzbicki 2002, 130). The importance of the aural element – of creating alien language, music, or performance cannot be underestimated: *Close Encounters of the Third Kind* (1977), for one, would be reduced in impact without John Williams's score and the now infamous five musical notes used as a basic communication system.

Set design, costume, special effects, screen technologies, camerawork, performance and soundtrack are all aspects of the science fiction *mise en scène* that are essential to understand how a film such as *Moon* can be seen, purely on a textual basis, as part of the science-fiction genre. Its interest in technology as part of its narrative progression also links it to existing traits from other generic products in film, television and literature. Yet none of those examples exist in a vacuum: each one depends on an intertextual relay of existing conventions, ideas and recurring motifs from within the discursive strategies of science fiction media more generally, and the wider cultural sphere. It is important to acknowledge the textual basis of science fiction film when analysing individual cases, but any understanding of how the films function as generic texts necessarily involves linking the genre to wider cultural debates, industrial discourse and popular knowledge. Such discourse can be seen as an influence on genre films: German interest in rocket technology in the 1920s fuelled the production of *Frau im Mond*; the series of Mars-based films in 2000–1 can be read as a reaction to the successful Pathfinder mission of 1997 (the first robot probe to land on Mars since 1976), and the images that were beamed back. Yet real-world science is only one of the ways in which genre can be affected by contemporary events, particularly when it comes to how audiences perceive genre and are guided towards specific popular definitions of generic knowledge.

Popular Definitions of Genre

> Whether it's a flying saucer whirling through space or a gleaming city on a distant planet, at the core of all science fiction is the provocative question, 'What if …?' Science fiction represents stories and situations that tap our brightest hopes and darkest fears about what might, one day, turn out to be true. (AFI 2008c, 35)

To demonstrate how genre reproduction can occur through discourse and across multiple connections, the chapter will move on to consider several non-textual perspectives on the science fiction genre. Rather than the textual elements that may appear in a science fiction film, this approach considers other discursive networks that influence definitions of science fiction that circulate within culture. Many extratextual sources of genre information have a close relationship with the genre text: the marketing that aims to lure in new viewers to see new genre films, the critical reviews that appear when they are released, or the exhibition sites for viewing them. Yet these are not the only external influences that impact on definitions of the term 'science fiction'. Since the advent of home video, DVDs, and the Internet, the multimedia landscape has expanded the range of locations where audiences are exposed to definitions of what 'science fiction' is: not least, shelving systems at video stores such as Blockbuster, descriptions on television electronic programme guides, and Internet Web pages ranging from shopping sites (Amazon), encyclopaedia (Wikipedia) and social network (Facebook quizzes that rank science fiction films, or reveal what *Star Wars* character contributors are). Societal changes also expand the definitions of this genre: advances in science and technology appear to mimic earlier science 'fictions' (heart transplants, genetic manipulation, mobile phones, space travel), and new scientific discoveries are often referred to in generic terms. These different stimuli help shape modern definitions of what genre is, what is meant by the term 'science fiction' and what films and television programmes can be conveniently categorized within that genre.

Identification of films as science fiction occurs within sites for video and DVD viewing and purchasing. Genre films are grouped together either physically (in a Blockbuster store) or electronically (Amazon, Lovefilm): a commercial-based approach to genre definition that contributes to a popularization of film and television titles in specific categories. These conglomerates do not act alone, of course. The promotion of genre definitions is shaped both institutionally and industrially, by film societies and production companies, through press releases, events and marketing. The promotion of the science fiction genre will be covered in more detail in section three, but a recent example of institutional genre definition will help clarify some of the points being made here. In 2008, the American Film Institute published 'AFI's 10 Top 10', a series of Top Ten lists described as 'America's 10 Greatest Films in 10 Classic Genres' (AFI 2008a). The ten 'classic' genres selected by this institution were: animated, fantasy, gangster, science fiction, western, sports, mystery, romantic comedy, courtroom drama and epic.[3] The AFI explained that the films that made the final list were judged on their critical recognition, award achievement, popularity over time, cultural impact and historical significance ('A film's mark on the history of the moving images through visionary narrative devices, technical innovation, or other groundbreaking achievements' – AFI 2008b, 4).[4] Yet nowhere in the publicity material surrounding this event is there ever any questioning of why genre is a suitable form in which to present a list of classic films: genre is presented as a *fait accompli*, a term audiences are comfortable with, producers work within, critics acknowledge, and everyone accepts as a useful classification system. As such, the list represents an institutional approach to genre definition: a 'top down' selection process of generic canon; a continued focus on texts (and textual content) as the purveyor of generic information; and a relegation of popular audience response in favour of production and critical opinion. Such choices mirror the academic frameworks covered earlier in this chapter, suggesting similar shaping policies at work in the larger cultural field.

These policies are clearly seen in the AFI definition, and selection, of science-fiction genre films. The list continues many of the long-running debates over what a science-fiction film is, what it should contain, what themes it should explore, and how it should look. The AFI definition of SF is 'a genre that marries a scientific or technological premise with imaginative speculation' – distinct from their definition of 'fantasy' as 'a genre where live action characters inhabit imagined settings and/ or experience situations that transcend the rules of the natural world' (AFI 2008b, 3).[5] As we have seen, critics and academics have been trying to create and impose strict genre demarcations for decades, and these two sentences fall prey to the same problems: many of science fiction's technological premises 'transcend the rules of the natural world'; equally, live action characters can inhabit 'imagined settings' in animated films – *Avatar* (2009) is an obvious example here; while the marriage of scientific premise and imaginative speculation can provide the basis of true stories such as *Apollo 13* or *The Right Stuff*. The pitfalls of such attempts to categorize films into one genre can also be seen by the AFI 'fantasy' top ten containing *King Kong* (1933), *The Wizard of Oz* (1939) and *Groundhog Day* (1996); films that other writers/institutions/audiences might want to claim for the action-adventure, children's, romantic comedy, or science fiction genres. Rather than open up debate, it is possible to see the AFI list as policing specific generic borders.

The AFI top ten of science fiction films reveals other issues. The list comprises *2001: A Space Odyssey, Star Wars IV: A New Hope, E.T.: The Extra Terrestrial, A Clockwork Orange* (1971), *The Day the Earth Stood Still, Blade Runner, Alien, Terminator 2: Judgment Day* (1991), *Invasion of the Body Snatchers* (1956) and *Back to the Future* (1985). Representing a specific definition of what the SF genre is, this list reveals the current cultural value of the genre in the early twenty-first century and its canonization within the American film establishment. Some narrative similarities can be seen: six of the ten films feature extraterrestrial threats or visitors, six films deal with future societies, while two films directly involve time travel. Historically, the list privileges the years 1968–82, ahead of the 1950s (a key era in academic writing) or the recent past (only one entry from the last two decades). This potential institutional or critical revisionism repositions the science fiction genre away from 1950s black-and-white science fiction towards more recent contributions to the genre, both artistic (directors Stanley Kubrick and Ridley Scott feature twice in the list, suggesting a preference for auteurist-tinged visual stylistics) and commercial (films from popular directors George Lucas, Steven Spielberg, Robert Zemeckis and James Cameron). The two pre-1968 films that make the list are already culturally regarded, canonized within histories of the science fiction genre and (perhaps importantly) recently remade within the current Hollywood production system. The inclusion of these older films fulfils the AFI's interest in presenting a diverse range of American film but equally distracts attention from the popular 'creature features' of the 1950s that are unlikely to feature on such a Top Ten list.

The AFI list is problematic but it is also useful. Like the Amazon or Blockbuster examples listed above, it is an attempt by an institution to impose a particular generic identity on a series of films. There is no compulsion for audiences to agree with the choices, or the definition, but such large institutions do have a role to play in boundary setting. The list also throws open the issue of generic hybridity: *Groundhog Day* could be seen as both romantic comedy and science fiction (reliving the same day has a tangential link to time travel narratives), while *Frankenstein* (1931) represents an early Hollywood studio attempt to marry a scientific or technological premise (the reanimation of dead tissue) with an imaginative speculation (would such a reanimated creature be monster or man). The AFI, in placing *Frankenstein* within the science fiction genre, also appears to challenge the dominant generic identity that Universal Studios promotes for the film. Universal began the process of defining *Frankenstein* within the horror pantheon in the 1930s (linking it with *Dracula*, 1931;

The Invisible Man and *The Mummy*, 1933) and continued to do so with recent DVD releases of these films (and their sequels). Packaged as 'The Legacy Collection,' each DVD set had matching shiny metallic green covers, clear plastic panels that placed an image of the central 'monster' in relation to a generic image (a mountaintop castle for *Dracula*, a laboratory for *The Invisible Man*, pyramids for *The Mummy*, a tower struck by lightning-bolts for *Frankenstein*), and a black-and-white Universal 'seal' that used an image of the Boris Karloff 'Frankenstein's Monster' and the legend 'Universal Studios Home of the Original Monsters.'

Claims for *Frankenstein* as a horror film, like many genre studies, rest on textual and thematic issues: specifically how the film fits within the Universal horror style (traditionally seen as a combination of European talent and stylistic approaches borrowed from German Expressionism). Yet the textual evidence of *Frankenstein* could be equally applied to make an argument for its science fiction status: the film dramatizes the story of a scientist's experimentation with the reanimating properties of electricity, and contains an overt focus on Dr Frankenstein's laboratory and scientific equipment. Discursively, like other proto-science fiction films that owed a debt to Shelley's story, the film fits within contemporary cultural concerns about scientific progress within medicine, including artificial replacement of limbs and the possibility of organ transplants. Yet cultural knowledge of Frankenstein tends to revolve around the classic Boris Karloff makeup, and the intertextual relationship that Universal has set up around its horror classics. Here, genre is a contested borderland, with no clear-cut division. Indeed, horror has been described as science fiction's 'evil twin', both genres interested in 'the question of difference, typically posed as that of the difference between human and non-human' (Penley 1991a, vii). Despite this claim that the science fiction and horror films are closely interrelated, the examples from the AFI and Universal suggest that institutional and industrial efforts are attempting to separate them out into strict and distinct genre camps.

As this chapter has argued, it is more useful to think about science fiction as a flexible, potent genre that borrows and utilizes other generic corpuses when needed, yet contains enough similarities to remain distinct in its own right. If we reconsider the AFI list of the Top Ten genres, it is possible to pick out science fiction films that crossover with all but one of the selected genres: science fiction-animation (*Fantastic Planet, Wall-E*), science fiction-fantasy (*Avatar, The Fountain*, 2006), science fiction-gangster film (*Sky Racket*, 1936; *The Adventures of Pluto Nash*, 2002), science fiction-Western (*Wild Wild West*, 1999; *Serenity*, 2005), science fiction-sports (*Rollerball*, 1975; *Space Jam*, 1996), science fiction-mystery (*Soylent Green, Minority Report*), science fiction-romantic comedy (*Eternal Sunshine of the Spotless Mind*, 2004; *Multiplicity*, 1996), and science fiction epic (*2001: A Space Odyssey, Dune*).[6] There are equally strong options if the list expands to other genres not covered by the AFI: science fiction-comedy (*Men in Black*, 1997; *The Hitch-Hiker's Guide to the Galaxy*), the science fiction-drama (*Contact*, 1997; *Gattaca*, 1997), the science-fiction musical (*Just Imagine*, 1930; *The Rocky Horror Picture*

Show, 1975), the science fiction-film noir (*Blade Runner, Dark City*, 1998), or the science fiction-war film (*Enemy Mine*, 1985; *Wing Commander*, 1999). This all confirms J.P. Telotte's claim that 'broadening the potential field for ... films in the genre ... [is] an instructive and valuable experience for the larger practice of genre thinking' (Telotte 2001, 10). Setting a strict definition for the science fiction film works to limit the possibilities of the genre: not because the films do not draw from a common set of similarities and ideas, or even because audiences have differing opinions on what a science fiction film is, but because the genre is constantly shifting and adapting. Genre cannot be collected, sealed in amber, and admired as a never-changing entity. It is flexible, hybrid, and multiple: to move forward genre theory must necessarily engage with this tendency towards variation and mutation, to understand genre both as a historically distinct entity, and a volatile contemporary discourse.

In that vein, the following two chapters of this book are attempts to position and understand the theoretical claims that have been made for science fiction films, being alert to their assumptions around generic conventions, themes and iconography. That work begins with a consideration of science fiction as a masculine genre, and feminist responses to science fiction films, before exploring academic criticism around the genre as revelling in special effects-fuelled destruction. Many such approaches move beyond textual detail to consider the social or cultural role that science fiction films might play. As this chapter has demonstrated, the science fiction genre comes with a set of expectations, assumptions, and conventions. Understanding those elements will enhance any analysis done on textual characteristics of the various films identified as science fiction: fusing those together offers the strongest route to examine and understand the aesthetic, thematic and critical development of the science fiction genre throughout the last hundred years.

–2–

Reading Science Fiction

Chapter 1 discussed various attempts to define and categorize what critics, academics and audiences mean by the term 'science fiction' but it is important to note that many studies of the science fiction film make little or no reference to larger definitions of generic identity (this is most apparent in edited collections or individual articles – for example, Penley et al. 1991; Kuhn 1999; Rickman 2004). These works assume that the reader has a broad understanding of the term 'science fiction' and focus on particular elements from specific genre films. Such work offers an important evolution in how aspects of science fiction have been critically discussed (beyond the generic terminology of iconography or thematic devices), while often expanding out to a wider range of texts than those found in generic meditations. Articles are as likely to focus on *Eternal Sunshine of the Spotless Mind*, *The Truman Show* or *Dick Barton Strikes Back* (1948) as they are to analyse the traditional canon of *Metropolis, Alien, Blade Runner* and *The Terminator*. By summarizing and applying some of the more dominant critical approaches within science fiction studies, this chapter will consider what these disparate reading positions reveal about the generic themes, ideas and ideologies contained within the science fiction film. A useful starting point, and one that informs the structure of this chapter, is Annette Kuhn's division of these academic approaches to the science fiction film into five areas: reflections, ideologies, repressions, spectators, and intertexts (Kuhn 1990, v–vi). Exploring and developing these disparate areas of academic interest, as well as more recent interests in film history and cultural studies, will demonstrate how different approaches to the science fiction film complicate notions of what such genre films are capable of, how they create meaning and what audiences can do with them.

One dominant recurrence across these individual approaches is gender, and Richard Maltby's claim that, as early genre critics were male, more attention was given to 'male' genres (Western, gangster, *film noir*) that valorized 'patriarchal and masculine concerns'. Such criticism moved analysis away from mainstream Hollywood genre production (which has historically attempted to attract women with female-oriented films) by focusing on authentic, masculine culture over-popular, feminized culture (Maltby and Craven 1995, 132–5). The place of science fiction within this gender/genre debate is uncertain. There was a critical reluctance for writers in the 1960s and 1970s to engage with science fiction films as a coherent genre, given its perceived overlap with horror films, the assumed populist, immature audience and the related cultural stereotype of *Flash Gordon*-style comic strip/pulp magazine heroics. The latter association with juvenilia and an interest in fantastic possibilities (rather than the historical 'reality' of gangsters and cowboys) may have prevented critics from seeing science fiction as a potent genre that played out similar notions around patriarchy and masculinity. These gender issues become more complex given that the cultural perception of science fiction films and audiences is largely male (the 'geek' or 'nerd' stereotype predominates here), yet much of the dominant academic work on the genre has come from female critics.[1] Susan Sontag wrote the first critical theorization of the genre (Sontag 1965), while writers such as Vivian Sobchack (1988), Constance Penley (1991; 1997), Annette Kuhn (1990; 1999), Barbara Creed (1993), Aylish Wood (2002) and Christine Cornea (2007) have followed in her footsteps. If genre criticism of the Western and the gangster film does betray a gender specific practice, then science fiction genre criticism may redress that balance, opening up debates as to how the genre discusses and dramatizes masculine and feminine issues.

Female critics were enthusiastic adopters of certain critical strategies applied to film studies in general, and science fiction more specifically, from the 1970s on. Employing Marxist, psychoanalytic, feminist, and ethnographic methodologies in relation to the science fiction genre such critics posited a deeper understanding around what such films said (or left unsaid) about social events, gender politics, the unconscious, or the audience. These different and disparate approaches are represented in Annette Kuhn's five categories of reflection, ideology, repression, spectator, and intertext, and their application within science fiction criticism. While there are obvious echoes of other critical concepts in these five examples, particularly their analytical focus on aspects of *mise en scène*, narrative, and spectatorship, the theoretical roots of all five reflect different tensions and methodological pathways. Few of these approaches begin with the intent of defining the science fiction genre, or its limits, but all offer a suggestion of generic pleasures and textual repetitions that are useful when applied to the larger questions of genre covered in chapter one, and through the book as a whole. Considering those five approaches, and recent developments in cultural studies and film history-led writing, allows a wider sense of how science fiction cinema has been discussed and read in the past five decades.

Reflection

Minority Report was remarkably on target for America's mood in 2002, which is probably why it was so well received. (Rickman 2004, 290)

Reflection is perhaps the most traditional theoretical example, where a film, or series of films, is regarded as (unproblematically) reflecting social or cultural issues: for example, the recurrent reading of all 1950s science fiction as 'Cold War' paranoia, or the terrestrial focus of 1970s SF portraying an isolationist America (Kuhn 1990,

16). Such readings largely take place at the level of narrative, finding ideas or images that repeat across multiple films, and assume all audiences will easily recognize this dominant encoding. Thus, it is possible to suggest that American science fiction of the 1980s is imbued by Ronald Reagan's presidency and its focus on American values, particularly around masculinity: *The New Barbarians* (1983), *Masters of the Universe* (1987), and *Predator* all contain dominant narratives about male-centric power and the display of (supposedly) masculine qualities of fighting, patriarchy and normative sexuality. Such a reading sees these films as a reflection of existing social and political movements within American culture: a more recent example, as demonstrated by the opening quotation, would be the period after the terrorist attacks of 11 September 2001. Cultural commentators and critics saw this as a moment when all media (including film, television, literature and comic books) had to decide how to discuss or 'reflect' those recent events. A series of genre films released after 9/11 can be read as reflections on how such home-grown terrorist attacks could occur within America: *War of the Worlds* (2005), *Transformers,* and the remake of the television series *V* (2009) all refer to alien threats that come from within, threats that (as advertisements for *War of the Worlds* claimed) were 'already here'. Analysis of such films might claim they were reflecting a post-attack social anxiety over whom to trust in this new century.

While such readings are tempting, they tend to rely on a series of false assumptions. First, whether films are able to reflect the thoughts and opinions of everyone in society (or even a convincing sample). Second, and related, that the audience will take the same meaning from each film, or recognize their culture being reflected back at them. Third, the suggestion that all films will present the same attitude towards aspects of society: the notion of masculinity in 1980s science fiction, for example, has to ignore genre films such as *Lifeforce* (1985), *Cherry 2000* or *The Terminator* where masculinity is questioned, or where femininity has its own powerful presence. The example of 9/11 must, of necessity, assume all films contain this reflection: yet many contain little if any overt commentary on the issue, while the idea of aliens secretly visiting the planet, and living among us, has been present within films since the 1910s. The crucial issue with reflection as an analytical tool is its methodology, particularly the notion that there is no mediating presence between 'real' social events and the fictions created on screen. Given the multiple input involved in most genre film creation, the complex series of negotiations and influences through production and the varied audiences who watch the finished product, the idea that there is one dominant social perspective that the film reflects is simplistic (if occasionally tempting). Film analysis necessarily accepts that film has a relationship with world issues, societal concerns and cultural totems, but that relationship includes a complex process of construction and representation, not a simple reflection.[2]

That said, certain films are created with a distinct political or social intent. Hollywood and other national film industries occasionally produce films that act as a direct commentary on wider social or political issues. *Enemy Mine*, with its 'buddy movie' narrative of alien and human enemies forced to work together (and ultimately becoming friends), reworks *Hell in the Pacific* (1968, where the enemies were World War Two American and Japanese soldiers) and can be read as a rather blunt allegory for acceptance and tolerance (arguably in relation either to racism or the US-USSR relationship of the mid-1980s). *Alien Nation* (1988) and *District 9* commented on apartheid and racism within their narratives, while *The Man in the White Suit* (1951) offered a comic look at industrial relations and the ominous power of capitalist companies. Crucially, however, these films are not simple reflections of their time, or the interests of their audiences; they are deliberate fictional constructions that engage with political or social elements. The audience may accept those ideas, or reject them, or may not think about them at all, but in such cases there is a definite intent to link generic content with a political position. Such overt statements are uncommon in genre productions, particularly given that Hollywood studios see partial or partisan positions as a barrier to mass-market and international success. Yet a second branch of criticism, particularly applicable to genre films, claims to find political and social meaning underneath the surface, revealing a hidden ideological subtext within all science fiction films.

Ideology

Ideological criticism moves on from reflection to consider how films construct and create meanings as part of a network that portrays dominant conventions, practices and structures as normative. Ideology is 'the shared set of meanings and values through which a society makes sense of its own structures and processes and their relationship to the material world' (Thornham and Purvis 2005, 74). These meanings are most often embodied within social institutions and state apparatuses like religion, education, family and the mass media, and often appear as 'common-sense' assumptions about the world. This social, cultural and ideological matrix represents and conveys influential images or ideas, a process whereby certain beliefs become enmeshed as part of everyday life, unquestioned and often unseen (or unheralded). *Aliens in the Attic* (2008), for example, features a comic alien invasion plot that could be read as a paean to male dominance (the main humans and aliens are male, while Bethany (Ashley Tisdale) accepts a subordinate position to Tom (Carter Jenkins), despite the fact he is her younger brother), patriarchy (Tom realizes his father's teachings and opinions were correct all along) and family (Tom, Bethany and their younger relations learn to work together to defeat the aliens). Rather than a reflection of social concerns or events, ideological criticism tends to look beyond surface meanings, investigating the deeper structures that films and television shows may be supporting. The process of ideology within entertainment has been called 'the maintenance of consent' (Maltby and Craven 1995, 393) because of the way that media products (narrative-based items such as films and television shows, but also including news broadcasts or reality television) implicitly reaffirm the ideological principles of the society that produced them (and the dominant structures that such positions support).

Film studies, borrowing from linguistic theory, had to contend with an early assumption that there was one ideology (an 'Ideology-in-general' in Althusarian terms; see Jancovich 1995, 123–50), rather than a series of ideologies that needed to be recognized, identified and analysed. For the purposes of this chapter, it is enough to note that ideological systems are affected by historical period, country, and possibly by individual circumstance: despite the theoretical simplicity of an overarching ideological network to which everything belongs, ideological analysis must, of necessity, be aware of the wider historical, social and cultural systems that film production existed within. Much ideological criticism also worked only at the level of narrative and character, eliding the role of *mise en scène* elements such as editing, camerawork, or set design. In terms of the science-fiction genre, ideological criticism was most commonly seen in relation to Marxist and feminist critiques of films and filmmakers, and ideas around patriarchy, heterosexuality and colonialism (see, for example, Dadoun 1991; Penley 1991b; Creed 1993) Such criticism has tended to focus on the depiction of women within science fiction, such as the divisive figure of Ellen Ripley (Sigourney Weaver) in the *Alien* series, Sarah Connor (Linda Hamilton) in *The Terminator*, or the female scientists of 1950s science fiction.

Feminist approaches to science fiction are useful in opening up existing narratives, showing how films produced in the Hollywood system can be read both in support of dominant ideology but also how other audiences could offer an oppositional viewpoint, challenging existing reflection-based readings. This idea of 'reading against the grain', of finding an alternative viewpoint that challenges the representation of dominant ideology, has been particularly influential in allowing critics to engage with science fiction films from different decades, cultures, and production contexts. *Cat-Women of the Moon* (1953), for example, does not fit easily into a standard reflection approach to 1950s science fiction, only tenuously connected to a narrative around atomic fears, Cold War concerns or suburbanization. Instead, the film offers an exploration narrative that relies on certain established themes: the team includes elder scientist Laird (Sonny Tufts), military man Kip (Victor Jory), and female navigator Helen (Marie Windsor). Visiting the moon, they discover a matriarchal society of alluring female warriors with plans to invade the Earth, and ultimately defeat them. Traits of a particular 1950s American ideology can be seen in the film: Kip is a stalwart, masculine military man who asserts his position within the group, rescues a brainwashed Helen, wins her affections from Laird and plots against the cat-women. The reestablishment of military and heterosexual normality by the end appears to curtail any oppositional reading. Equally, the cat-women are attractive Hollywood models and actresses in tight-fitting black leotards, seemingly cast more for their looks than any strong dramatic purpose. The feminine contribution appears to be as stunning set dressing rather than rounded psychological characters.

Yet the film also lingers on key issues that challenge that ideological reading. The bulk of the film pictures a female-only society with powerful mental abilities, who are able to control and manipulate Earthmen to do their bidding. Looking beyond the cheesecake elements of the Cat-women costumes, they are presented as strong and commanding, easily a match for the largely apathetic male astronauts. While Kip is proven right not to trust the moon women, and his desire to conquer and destroy them is highlighted within the film, it is not his direct action that defeats the Cat-women. Their plans are only foiled through the betrayal of Lambda (Susan Morrow), a Cat-woman who has fallen in love with the team's engineer.[3] At the end, although the Earth rocket escapes, the lithe, powerful and sexually attractive cat-women remain dominant, their society largely unchanged despite the visitors from Earth. It is also relevant to any reading that the film was produced in 3-D, with staging and photography that suggests the female form was also a spectacular attraction within the film, supporting the notion of female dominance within the narrative.

Ideological analysis is not limited to debates around feminism. Films such as *Avatar, Renaissance* (2006) and *Jetsons: The Movie* (1990) raise questions around capitalism and colonialism as normative. Despite its status as a children's cartoon, *Jetsons: The Movie* (a feature length animated adaptation of the 1960s Hanna Barbera television series) concerns the Jetson family, particularly dad George. A traditional middle-class salary man, Jetson works at Spacely's Sprockets, a large corporation run by Mr Spacely, an unrestrained capitalist who is only interested in profit. The Jetsons are sent to an asteroid mining facility (which comes complete with its own consumerist shopping mall), unaware it is being sabotaged by the Grungees, a race of cute teddy-bear aliens who are trying to save their underground city from the mining machinery. In a curious echo of *Metropolis*, George Jetson mediates between capitalist boss Spacely and new working-class labourers, the Grungees. The outcome is ideologically dubious: Spacely employs the Grungees, and succeeds in his goal of creating an off-world mining operation (to produce sprockets cheaply). Although the Grungees' terrorist activities are successful, that success is measured in capitalist terms: they become workers, consumers, part of the Spacely Sprockets' machine. From committing an ideological crime against capitalism (sabotage) they become an integral part of the capitalist enterprise. Equally, Spacely admits knowing the Grungees were the original inhabitants of the asteroid but his expansionist aspirations remain unchecked at the end: the colonial and capitalist power of Earth wins out, a victory represented by Spacely's mine, the consumer paradise of the shopping mall, and, by extension, Spacely and the Jetsons themselves.[4]

Despite the potency of such ideological approaches, some of the criticisms of reflective analysis remain applicable. Reflective work prefers to find a general social movement that can be easily expanded across a range of films but, in attempting to offer a wide commentary, runs the danger of missing what makes each film unique.

Ideological criticism, by contrast, is often more specific, looking at individual films, but the ability to identify the ideological workings and then offer an alternative reading, inevitably suggests further, multiple, interpretations of those films. That is not to deny the important role that ideological criticism has had to play in science-fiction studies, particularly from feminist writers eager to claim new ground for films within the genre, but to point out that its strength (revealing dominant and convergent readings) can also reveal the limitations of such an approach. It is also important to note that many ideological readings assume the kind of 'Ideology-in-general' approach noted above, rather than considering the historical specificity of the ideological systems in place when a film was produced. Recent work in cultural studies that suggests a combination of ideological analysis with historical and cultural research may suggest a potent way to move this debate forward.

Repression

Similar to ideology in that it aims to unveil previously unseen or hidden qualities within media texts, repression applies psychoanalytic methods to enhance or develop the socio-cultural models used in ideological studies. Using a variety of approaches drawn from psychoanalysis (including, but not restricted to, the theories of Freud, Jung and Lacan), these critics aim to unearth unconscious meaning through the close reading of texts, including a broader sense of how elements of *mise en scène* could impact on the creation of meaning. Theoretical work explored the unconscious elements of film texts 'as much for what they displaced, condensed, or censored as for what they said' (Maltby and Craven 1995, 427). Science fiction films were seen as sharing a particular interest in 'the primal scene and the mysteries of conception and birth, sexual drives and the desire for forbidden objects, the Oedipal scenario and sexual difference' (Kuhn 1991, 93). This approach gained relevance given the genre's interest in artificial and genetic creation, seen in films as diverse as *Lola* (1916), *The Perfect Woman* (1949) and *Species* (1995), as well as a fascination with time travel narratives that revisited scenes of conception and birth, such as *The Terminator, Back to the Future* and *The Time Traveller's Wife*. This use of psychoanalysis focused on how films and narratives were structured by, or represented, these particular unconscious systems. Psychoanalytic theory also continued a larger move within film studies towards how the individual viewer used or was affected by/positioned by texts.[5] This latter interest in the interaction of viewer, audience and film would have a direct impact on more cultural and ethnographic models of audience spectatorship that will be discussed in the next section.

Psychoanalytic techniques, although identifying broader unconscious traits, were often applied to specific science fiction films, creating a compelling cinematic canon around genre and repression: most notably *Alien, The Terminator,* and *Metropolis*.

Articles on these films offer more than simple narrative analysis, with an emphasis on elements of *mise en scène*, and their potent representative links: the repeated vaginal openings in *Alien*'s set design and special effects (Creed 1986, 129–30), the 'tech noir' sets and backgrounds of *The Terminator* (Penley 1991c, 64–6), or the masturbatory rings that stroke up and down the metallic body of the robotic Maria in the transformation scene in *Metropolis* (Dadoun 1991, 144 (Figure 2.1)). Part of this work has obvious links to ideological readings, in positioning sexual difference (notably masculine/feminine roles) as a key element within such films, and providing oppositional readings (against the grain) of perceived masculine or patriarchal dominance. Yet psychoanalysis goes beyond ideology by stressing sexuality and gender as a structural component of science fiction genre as a whole. Psychoanalysis of cinema as an institution has claimed film is a potent medium because of its link to dreams and unconscious states: within that, science fiction film can be seen as a central exploration of the fantastic and unusual, a genre predicated on the display of bizarre and incredible vistas and illusions. The science fiction genre is, in this reading, literally one of dreams and possibilities. Psychoanalytic criticism offers a route to explore the layers of repressed meaning contained across such genre films.

As with ideological analysis, psychoanalysis has produced some fascinating and important readings of key genre films. Yet the approach can be seen to contain

Figure 2.1 The creation scene from *Metropolis* (1927) has been the focus of both feminist and psychoanalytical genre criticism (Paramount Pictures/Photofest)

many of the same issues as ideology and reflection. Despite many articles that focus on the analysis of sequences and images from one film, others make claims about what genre films do that never move beyond generalizations. The idea that all space exploration narratives are about autonomy may be a useful starting position, but it ignores the historical and textual specificity of space travel as seen in *Himmelskibet*, *Rocketship X-M* and *Apollo 13*. The multiple examples of penetrative imagery in all science fiction may indeed infer a 'primal scene ambiance' (Dervin 1991, 97–8) but the preference for psychoanalytic writing to link all films back to these same concepts ultimately feels like a limitation on the critical ability to discern what the films themselves are doing that is unique, not repetitive. Equally, by focusing on the unconscious (and unfalsifiable), psychoanalysis lays itself open to the accusation that it is 'opposed to people's experiences of film texts' (Jancovich 1995, 147). As with the theories discussed above, there remains an assumption with readings around repression that the viewer is simply a spectator to these events; that, despite the possibilities of reading against the grain, individuals do not bring their own unique perspective to a film (everyone responds based on a pre-existing unconscious network that they are rarely aware of). The concept of a spectator remains an ideal viewer, not the socially distinct individual who watches the film in a particular context that helps shape their interaction with the text.

Spectator

Ideological and repressed readings rely on the ability of a critic to peel away the surface level of a film to reveal the 'true' meaning underneath. Both offer a complication of the assumed relationship between audience member and film, or spectator and text. From early 'hypodermic' models where all spectators took in the desired message put there by the producers, to the possibility of texts positioning a viewer in a particular way, through to the more open notion of multiple viewing positions, these approaches began to assign some agency to the spectator: the viewer became the site where meaning was generated, albeit with help from the text. This begins to privilege the broader cultural awareness of film, and genre, that chapter one discussed, and moves academic work towards the reception of genre films as much as their textual content. Questions about a spectator-led approach to science fiction films necessarily revolve around who is watching, what knowledge they bring to the film, and what they do with the text. One subset of psychoanalysis considered cinema in relation to notions of voyeurism and scopophilia, but ultimately returned to generalizations about an ideal viewer rather than a distinct and aware audience member. More recently, academics have turned to historical and ethnographic approaches to spectatorship and film reception, trying to understand how audiences interacted with specific texts, and what that reveals about wider audience interaction with genre films.

Interest in academic reception and audience studies has been dominated by the science fiction and fantasy genres, from *Judge Dredd* (Barker and Brooks 1998) and *The X-Files* (Wooley 2001) to *Star Wars* (Will Brooker 2002; Matt Hills 2002) and *Doctor Who* (Tulloch and Jenkins 1995). *Star Trek* and *Star Wars* were early pivots for such work, largely because of the size and diversity of their fan cultures. Key works on science-fiction audiences explored the relationship between *Star Trek* and fan audiences, focusing on how audiences can create subcultures of their own, sharing and expanding the fictional universe they watch, producing their own stories, videos, and art that reworks elements of the original film and television series (Lamb and Veith 1986; Jenkins 1988; 1992; Penley 1997).[6] Will Brooker has suggested that continuing fan love for genre texts such as *Star Wars* is a large part of what keeps them feeling fresh and relevant in the early twenty-first century, rejuvenating them and keeping them alive, rather than relegating them to a particular decade or subsection of film history (Brooker 1999).[7] Genre fandom is a continual process of negotiation, not just with the original texts, but with the expansion of textual properties into sequels, computer games, books, comic strips, Internet sites, mobile phones and across other merchandising opportunities.

The move from textual analysis to analysis of how viewers interact with their favourite genre texts also engages with the other theoretical positions discussed above. Jenkins notes how female fans of *Star Trek* used printed fanzines to debate whether the show presented a masculine ideology, or if there was space within both the episodes and the larger fan culture, to make a claim for sexual equality. Fans have also challenged the show's elision of homosexual characters and created fictional works that explore their own (oppositional) readings that include a homosexual bond between Captain Kirk and Spock (known as slash fiction, or K/S – Jenkins 1988). Created almost exclusively by female *Star Trek* fans, this incarnation of fandom challenges the larger cultural assumption that science fiction fans are predominantly male; an assumption that the growth of the Internet has further exploded. More than half of all Internet users are now female, and the growth of social networking sites such as Facebook, MySpace and Twitter has increased the virtual possibilities of discussing fan texts such as *Star Trek, Star Wars* and *The X-Files*, as well as opening up new portals for sharing fan-produced videos, stories or artwork (Rogers 2009). However, while the notion of a more female-oriented genre fandom subverts expectations, it does not fully explain the fascination with a genre still largely controlled by men and aimed (as many Hollywood films are) at a masculine teenage audience.[8]

The growth of the Internet has both expanded and complicated studies of fandom and reception. Official and fan Web sites compete for attention, revealing exclusive news or 'spoiler' information about forthcoming narratives; fans produce unique videos that repurpose existing footage into new forms; and thousands of blogs allow individuals to post comments on any genre media product, or to contribute to larger generic discussions. Studying such complex interrelationships is a challenge to existing ethnographic methodologies, borrowed from television or cultural studies, which previously privileged interviews, embedded observation and surveys to try to ascertain general audience response (Hills 2002). The Internet presents a challenge in terms of available data and selection, particularly the discussions of fans on forums and social networking sites and the use of such commentaries. Such work becomes its own form of textual analysis, where the analyst has to perform a reading of the accumulated data, translating it into more academic language and potentially losing aspects of that discourse in the process. This can lead to charges of generalization but it does allow mediated access to what genre audiences are thinking: those audiences can only be partial, one online element of a larger picture but they do allow some conclusions to be drawn.

Studying the audience and reception of genre films is a different methodological endeavour than the narrative and textual analysis that dominated the initial three approaches. Yet such studies reveal that the ideal (or normal) viewer that those earlier techniques relied upon is a myth. A fuller understanding of what audiences do when they view science fiction films, whether they are swayed by particular generic advertising or marketing techniques, or how they engage with the existing cultural understandings of genre, reveals the potential for alternative and innovative readings of films and other generic products. The emphasis on historical or modern audience activity necessarily connects to the wider range of texts and materials that surround a spectator's understanding of the film, television show, or book they have chosen. To explore that wider cultural understanding of texts, society and individual, involves turning to studies of the larger intertextual world of the science fiction genre.

Intertext

Theories of intertextuality are a central pillar of any presumption of genre, stating as they do that films necessarily relate to other films, as well as other texts. Given the basic tenet of genre studies is that a genre film shares some indefinable 'X' with other genre films, then an intertextual relay is a necessary ingredient. It has become a crucial area of modern genre theory and cultural studies, exploring how genre films rely on a range of generic texts (film, television, DVD, books, video games, the Internet) to create or enhance meaning, as well as engaging with wider discursive networks around art, commerce, politics and culture. Films do not exist in a vacuum but in a constantly shifting sphere of influence: some influences are written into the text (either in subtle or overt ways), with the expectation that audience members can identify the homage, while others are elements that viewers can bring in based on their own larger generic or discursive network. Although theories of intertextuality have developed since the 1980s, it is not a new element of genre production or criticism. Intertextual references can refer to textual evidence or larger cultural knowledge. The futuristic city of *Just Imagine* is a riposte to *Metropolis*' visuals, which was itself a response to the mechanistic and Modernist skyline of Manhattan; *Le Voyage dans la lune* was playing on knowledge of Jules Verne and H. G. Wells' moon exploration stories, which were themselves part of a nineteenth-century fascination with astronomy; reviews of *Metropolis* in 1927 noted the debt it owed to H. G. Wells and Carel Capek's robot play *R.U.R.* (1922); while the 1977 trailer for *Close Encounters of the Third Kind* not only made reference to the 'UFO-logy' terms of first, second and third 'kinds' of close encounter but also linked itself to *2001: A Space Odyssey*. In all these cases, audiences were not required to have this knowledge themselves but a percentage of audience members would be able to understand the intertextual reference.

The growth of academic interest in concepts of intertextuality began during the 1980s, and links this aspect of genre to debates around postmodernism. The term 'postmodern' may be one of the most misapplied in the wider cultural sphere, particularly the way that the self-referential qualities of early texts such as *Blade Runner* (with its blend of advanced futurism and world-weary 1940s *film noir* aesthetic) are now taken to infest every cultural product.[9] For the purposes of this chapter, postmodernism challenges the realist belief that films can ever capture a real world, claiming that instead of reflecting or mirroring the world, visual representation is always a simulacra, a series of images that relate only to themselves, not some substantive external reality. Critics have used postmodernism to deride recent Hollywood productions as a cinema obsessed with recycling images of itself through remakes, sequels and prequels; an aesthetic bricolage of existing elements welded together rather than the production of anything new or innovative (Tasker 1993). This view of bricolage bears a resemblance to the Frankenstein monster or cyborg of science fiction narratives, cobbled together from spare parts, borrowed ideas and leftover aesthetic devices. Yet the critical claim that postmodern theory reveals how modern Hollywood has become aesthetically and thematically bereft ignores a crucial historical element: Hollywood has always privileged a system of bricolage. Films with science fiction premises have, since the early twentieth century, featured a patchwork of elements borrowed from other media, other films, and larger cultural concerns. As Chapter 1 explored, science fiction is, and always has been, a hybrid genre – and therefore one that engages in intertextual references.

Since the popularization of theories around postmodernism, self-referentiality, and intertextuality the American film industry has embraced the idea of the intertext as part of the modern merchandising machine, turning critical theory into capitalist conglomeration. This has particular relevance to the science fiction genre, given the dominance of science fiction narratives within modern blockbuster filmmaking and promotion. Blockbuster films (and even those lower down the financial pecking order) are regularly accompanied by the near-simultaneous release of adaptations (book, comic book), soundtracks, video games, toys, Web sites, clothing, and deals with other related corporations (fast food restaurants, soft drinks, mobile phone companies, car manufacturers). These major film releases appear intent on creating their own intertextual networks. Intertextual references between media products, merchandise and nostalgia now fuel much modern blockbuster filmmaking: *Transfomers* is an adaptation of a line of toys, *Lost in Space* (1998) and *Mission Impossible* (1996) recycled 1960s television for modern big-screen audiences, *Mars Attacks!* (1995) was based on a series of 1950s bubblegum cards, while *Eight Legged Freaks* (2005) makes textual references to a wide range of 1950s science-fiction films (Geraghty 2009). For the purposes of genre studies, it might be more useful to think of these intertextual relays as genre extensions, fuelling perceptions both of one innovative generic product as well as larger generic qualities and conventions. Textual (or aesthetic) bricolage has been augmented by industrial bricolage and the role of the consumer in finding new information, discovering intentional links but also creating their own connections between texts, genres and media.

Conclusion

These distinct approaches, with different methodologies and outcomes, represent dominant ideas around how to talk about and analyse science fiction films. Unlike the history of genre theory laid out in Chapter 1, which has tended to develop away from a purely textual-based system towards a broader cultural understanding of genre, these are not historically diverse, or critically disparate approaches. Studies of science fiction films are still being published that take reflectionist, ideological or psychological approaches to their source material and they continue to provide fascinating perspectives on both canonical and new entries into the science fiction genre. Ethnographic and intertextual studies are moving away from the strict focus on the text as the site of meaning, developing an audience or reception studies focus to the creation of genre within individual audiences, or through the extratextual materials that exist alongside science fiction film releases, or the many alternative genre screens that exist in television, videogames, on the Internet, or on mobile phones. Each approach has its own adherents, and its own strengths but the latter focus on the wider network of generic influences is the one that this book will develop and explore.

There is as much that binds these approaches together as makes them distinct: they are all interested in how the genre creates meaning, whether that is as a reflection of societal fear, ideological position, psychological intent, spectatorial interest or intertextual referent. They also have an assumption that science-fiction films represent a coherent genre (even if they do not define the characteristics of that generic identity) and that it can be explored through textual or extratextual means. Beyond that, however, all five analytical approaches have touched on one dominant idea: the role of technology within the genre. Technology is a central conceit within science-fiction analysis: whether reflecting a societal uncertainty over new developments (cloning in *Gattaca*; surveillance techniques in *The Truman Show*), considering how consumer technologies might portray capitalist ideology (the Gap advertisements in *Minority Report*; fashion in *High Treason*), or using spaceship-based exploration to investigate repressed areas of human consciousness (*Event Horizon*, 1997; *Sunshine*, 2007). On the level of production, technology has been key to how films are able to depict these science fictions and, in terms of dissemination and exhibition, new devices have fuelled an interest in how viewers use technology and how media technologies have fuelled theories around intertextuality. While Chapter 1 made reference to the narrative role of technology, Chapter 3 will move on from these different approaches to consider a production element that appears across multiple analyses of the science fiction film. From the genre's first theorist to work in the early twenty-first century, the place of the special effects spectacle and its function within these films has continued to fuel debates over the content and influence of the science fiction genre.

–3–

Science Fiction and Technology

The science fiction film has long been discussed in terms of its role as the main producer and purveyor of special effects imagery. From the first depiction of cinematic space travel in *Le Voyage dans la lune* through stop motion alien invaders in *Earth vs the Flying Saucers* to computer generated robots in *Transformers*, new technology has fuelled the genre's ability to display new worlds, new life-forms, and new spectacles of destruction. Despite the place of computer-generated imagery in almost all branches and genres of modern filmmaking, the science fiction genre continues to be a nexus where effects technology and spectacular visual imagery interact (Pierson 2002). Given the international success and dominance of Hollywood blockbusters such as *Iron Man*, *GI Joe: The Rise of Cobra* (2009) and *Inception*, films that feature a high proportion of special effects and at least a partial science fiction premise, the link between the genre and visual effects seems unlikely to recede. Yet the critical dismissal of effects as 'empty' (Allon, Cullen and Patterson 2002, 542) or 'stupefyingly silly' (Ropfkopf 2009) suggests that spectacular imagery remains a controversial element of modern filmmaking practice, particularly the recurring (and limiting) claims that spectacle stands in opposition to and disrupts (or diminishes) narrative. With audiences seemingly eager to embrace spectacular images, and worldwide film and television production engaged in producing (and marketing) computer-generated and three-dimensional imagery, the debate remains central to any understanding of generic spectacle past, present and future.

Spectacle, Technology and Narrative

'We are merely spectators; we watch' (Sontag 1965, 45). Susan Sontag's description of the role of the viewer in relation to science fiction spectacles has been mirrored in later academic commentary that links spectacle and special effects technologies. It is echoed in the description of such films as a 'showcase … [for] innovations in production design and special effects' (Thompson and Bordwell 1994, 715) and the identification of special effects as 'grand displays of "industrial light and magic"' (Sobchack 1988, 282). Spectators or watchers of a showcase or a grand display: the emphasis here suggests a gap between viewer and image, an urge to spectate rather than participate. The science fiction film has been at the centre of discussions around the place of spectacle in cinema, with visual spectacle described as a medium-specific element of its success, particularly in comparison to science fiction television (Pearson and Messenger-Davies 2003, 103) or science-fiction literature (Kuhn 1990, 6). Indeed, the ability of the genre film to visualize the alien, the unusual or the nonexistent is seen as a central tenet of its continued success (Sobchack 1988; Kuhn 1990).

This emphasis on spectacle as a medium-defining quality is problematic, not least because it states that the dominant purpose of such spectacle is simply to be gazed at, looked upon or admired. This suggests a reduction in the variety of viewer positions towards such spectacle but also separates spectacle (something to be observed) from narrative (something to be drawn into, immersed within). Film narrative is traditionally seen as inclusive, pulling viewers into (and leading them through) a coherent diegetic world. Spectacle, in the terms used above, is not immersive, it is obvious, overt, something audiences are aware of watching, a spectacular visual element that exists in its own right, possibly separate from narrative. Generic spectacles that fulfil such a criteria might include the dinosaurs of *Jurassic Park*, the superpowers of the *Fantastic Four*, or the natural disasters of *2012* (2009). In all these cases, though, the generic spectacle exists within a narrative structure and cannot be separated from it easily. Rather than limit this debate to a simple narrative/spectacle dichotomy (which is ultimately self-defeating), this chapter will argue that any understanding of such films needs to engage with a wider understanding of what audiences find spectacular in these generic texts. This necessarily involves an awareness of the shifting balance of *mise en scène*-based visual spectacle and film narrative in individual films, the contribution of technology, soundtrack and star performance to definitions of spectacle, and a greater appreciation of the role of critical reviews, marketing materials and (more recently) DVD special features within the larger discourse around spectacle and special-effects technologies.

This debate is also the latest iteration of a larger historical and cultural discourse that links film history, spectatorship, technologies of vision and science fiction with spectacular visual display. Spectacle, spectator and spectatorship are all linked by a root Latin word, *spectare,* meaning 'to watch'. A spectacle is, therefore, something that is out of the ordinary, impressive in some unusual or unexpected way. Watching a spectacle is normally to view an event designed for mass spectatorship, not for individual pleasure: it exists to affect a wide range of viewers. The presentation of visual spectacle through technological means has never been a purely film-based phenomenon. Architecture and art have created spectacle for millennia and technologies that replicated moving, or changing, vision (the likes of magic lantern shows, or camera obscura) have existed for hundreds of years. The nineteenth century featured an intensification of interest in using new technologies to capture movement and reality: the thaumatrope and phekanistoscope animated static drawings into a sequence of movement and various photographic processes from the 1840s onwards successfully froze images of street scenes, people and still lives. The road from photography to motion-picture cinematography has been covered elsewhere (see, for example, Chanan 1996) but the changing nature of visual spectacle in Victorian culture is a crucial element in the convergence of such technologies.

In the nineteenth century, the simple act of photography was considered spectacular, but viewing photographs was an individual (or small group) experience. Visual spectacle in the Victorian era was developed by a series of artistic, cultural and economic factors, most notably the panorama and diorama, and the series of Great Exhibitions, Expositions, and Worlds Fairs. Panoramas and dioramas were huge painted and staged canvases and scenes erected in specially constructed buildings in city centres across Europe and the US. Designed to dwarf the viewers, people were ushered in, through darkened passages, to emerge in the middle of a circular room where the immense painting had been hung and specially lit. The scenes being pictured could be a contemporary local scene or an historical event (an exciting or famous battle, the might of Rome during Caesar's reign) (Comment 1999, 7–8).[1] Creating a visual spectacle, these vistas were something to be gazed at, explored visually, and experienced viscerally.[2] With their emphasis on large audiences, specially constructed communal viewing rooms and immersive widescreen spectacle, the panoramas offer compelling connections to later notions of spectacular cinema presentation. They also presented a different world, or a different view of a known world, similar to the unique visual perspectives offered by cinematic special effects such as matte painting, miniatures or CGI landscapes. Popular throughout the nineteenth century, both panoramas and dioramas existed well after the advent of cinema: as Tom Gunning points out, they remained a key attraction at Expositions into the twentieth century (Gunning 1994).

From London's Great Exhibition of 1851 to the 1904 St Louis World Exposition (and beyond), such shows conformed to similar, spectacular patterns. They were designed to be modern, technologically advanced and futuristic: small cities that sprang up on vast tracts of land either in the centre of capital cities (Hyde Park in London) or on the outskirts (as in the case of St Louis). These immense projects were sites of visual fakery and illusion, an impermanent hyper-real landscape that was constructed quickly, lasted six to nine months, and was then gone again (a useful correlation with the futuristic world building and set construction seen in genre films such as *Blade Runner* and *Batman* (1989), or the movie-based theme parks at Disneyland and Universal Studios). Essential to any understanding of the growth of visual spectacle, these exposition sites encouraged people to gaze at spectacular images and illusions, to enjoy and immerse themselves within the activity of watching and looking and to acknowledge that activity (therefore preventing any notion of 'total' immersion). Such fairs were 'one of the great training grounds and laboratories for a new community-based visual culture … [they] raised the act of spectating to a civic duty and technological art' (Gunning 1994, 423).

These expositions merged early consumer culture, an interest in visual communication (early moving pictures were shown at expositions from 1893 on), the possibilities of new transport, and technological advances. The later expositions also offered compelling links between this visual spectacle and early attempts to visualize the spectacle of futuristic science, technology and travel. The 1901 Pan-American Exposition, held in Buffalo, New York, included a simulated voyage to the moon. One of the main attractions on the Midway (the popular commercialized entertainment sector), 'The Trip to the Moon' offered its paying customers an experience that claimed to recreate a fantastic trip into space. Relying on moving panoramas, purpose built sets, and costumed actors, the ride placed viewers in a large 'ship' that flew to the moon (the ship remained largely static, as painted and photographic backdrops of the exposition, the sky above Buffalo, and the vacuum of space moved past it to create the illusion of movement). On reaching the lunar landscape, people would walk through specially constructed moon caves, meet the Selenites (the moon inhabitants of H. G. Wells' recent story *The First Men in the Moon*), attend a pageant at the Palace of the Man in the Moon, and sample 'moon cheese' before departing. Although similar to other shows at expositions (recreations of earthquakes, river rides, foreign street scenes) the 'Trip to the Moon' ties together the nineteenth-century interests in spectacle, vision, new forms of transport and a growing fascination with the fantastic possibilities of technology (all equally prevalent in the 'scientific romances' of novelists such as Wells and Verne). The advent of a moving picture industry between the 1890s and the 1910s can be seen as an extension of such elements, as they coalesced around a form of mass entertainment that foregrounded visual spectacle and encouraged spectatorship.

The Victorian obsession with spectacle and vision seen in these exhibitions, also informed the creation and expansion of early film, particularly what Tom Gunning has identified as the 'cinema of attractions': from the initial spectacle of visually recording movement, to capturing reality, and the increasing interest in cinema trickery. Crucially for the debate over genre and spectacle, this cinema of attractions highlighted a 'conscious awareness of the film image engaging the viewer's curiosity. The spectator does not get lost in a fictional world and its drama, but remains aware of the act of looking' (Gunning 1994, 121). This historical example is an essential step in understanding how the cultural interest with visual spectacle first interacted with cinematic narratives. George Méliès' discovery and utilization of trick effects developed a particular brand of spectacular cinema, one that would prove influential for later generic filmmakers. Often described as the first science fiction filmmaker (for his work on *Le Voyage dans la lune*, among others), Méliès is more accurately described as a filmmaker who relied upon visual spectacle across a variety of genres. His most famous work, a trip to the moon that borrows liberally from Wells and Verne (and may be a satire of their narratives – Cornea 2007, 13), features a series of spectacular images: a bullet-shaped rocket exploding off a ramp, flying through space and crashing into the eye of the moon; umbrellas planted in the soil grow into space plants; the hostile natives explode on contact. Here, narrative progression (takeoff, landing, exploration, return home) is balanced with attractions and special effects. This collection of spectacular fantastic images, effects work (including miniatures, stop motion, and double exposures) and nascent generic ideas around futuristic travel, exploration and destruction would fuel not only later proto-science fiction but also the first serious academic work on the science fiction film.

Susan Sontag's 'The Imagination of Disaster' has, in many ways, been as influential theoretically as Méliès' film was generically. The article offers a breakdown of several recurring narrative traits of the 1950s and early 1960s science fiction film, and describes the genre's reliance on special effects-derived destruction in phrases and words that resonate to this day. Science fiction films are not about science, they are about 'disaster ... the aesthetics of destruction ... the peculiar beauties to be found in wreaking havoc, making a mess' (Sontag 1965, 44). Sontag's discussion of moments of special effects-fuelled disaster and destruction is largely focused on wide-screen Technicolor genre entries such as *War of the Worlds* and *Sora no daikaijû Radon* (*Rodan*, 1956) but can also be applied to *The Day the Earth Caught Fire* (1961), where miniatures and matte effects show the impact of earthquakes and global warming on the cities of the world, or the stop-motion demolitions of New York, Washington DC and Rome, in (respectively) *The Beast From 20,000 Fathoms* (1953), *Earth vs the Flying Saucers* and *20 Million Miles to Earth* (1957). Yet these potent moments of destruction, admittedly spectacular in their own right, are about more than the reflection of 'world-wide anxieties ... about contemporary existence ... [or] the individual psyche' (Sontag 1965, 42–7). By not engaging with the issue of how such moments of spectacle exist within each film's narrative structure, and by assuming that they all represent a common (global) audience perception, Sontag does not reflect on the specificity and the unique attributes of such images and films.

Sontag's work also struggles when covering lower budget genre examples, where the widescreen special effects spectacle is less overt, if featured at all. Given the relative scarcity of colour and widescreen in science fiction films of this time period, the theory needs to apply to smaller projects to retain its potency. Here, Sontag refines the notion of disaster so that it moves away from the spectacle of large-scale physical destruction to smaller notions of mutation and deformity. This move allows her to consider a film such as *Invasion of the Body Snatchers*, but without the sense of destructive spectacle the argument is less well defined. Sontag regards this film, and others with a similar narrative, as the physical destruction of self and the imposition of regimented order: but the argument does not engage with the very lack of the effects spectacle that had been so important in earlier examples. *Invasion of the Body Snatchers* is a potent illustration of a film that relies on tone, mood and performance over any effects-created visual spectacle: this treatment matches its narrative of an insidious takeover, where people do look exactly the same, not visually different, unusual or spectacular. Sontag does not explore this visual element and, despite a convincing argument around how such films may represent contemporary ideas around depersonalization ('the very model of technocratic man, purged of emotions, volitionless, tranquil ... turned into a machine' – Sontag 1965, 47), the reliance on destruction as a central visual motif is never convincingly applied beyond the initial strong examples.

Sontag does, however, make explicit that such visual spectacle works within a narrative framework: her examples are all about locations, monsters or model work, elements that contribute to a particular narrative effect. Here, visual spectacle plays a psychological role for the audience, a release that allows them to fantasize about worldwide destruction, or the ability of special effects to tame the sublime and produce 'cognitive mastery' of the panoramic and visually spectacular (Bukatman 1999, 250). While Sontag offers a brief comparison between spectacle in science fiction and spectacle in horror and Biblical epics, it might be more illuminating to consider the difference between the spectacle offered in non-genre and genre films, and whether it 'lies in their "excuses," the narratives they employ' (Rickman 2004, xv). What Rickman suggests here is that the difference between all special effects spectacles, whether in genre films or otherwise, may be located not simply in their narratives, but in their larger use (thematic, aesthetic, ideological) within the film being viewed. Rather than follow Sontag's initial notion of an effects spectacle fulfilling the same function across a whole genre (the idea of destruction, fuelled by contemporary fears of actual nuclear disaster), it may be more useful to think about how spectacle functions within an individual film.

Geoff King has offered a move in this direction, part of a project that also criticizes a series of academic assumptions that claimed an increased special effects spectacle would lead to an imminent demise in Hollywood cinema (King 2000, 2). King usefully historicizes elements of this move towards the spectacular within culture and cinema, correctly placing cinematic spectacle not as a modern development but as a result of studio strategies to retain (or regain) audiences, then a more recent cross-platform convergence around computer games and theme park rides (King 2000, 2). The recent reintroduction of 3-D and the continued push towards IMAX cinemas within genre filmmaking would support the necessity to understand the industrial context of spectacle-led sequences within generic films. This understanding of the roots and uses of spectacle deepens the examination of specific case studies where there is an interplay of spectacle, narrative, aesthetics, and production history: most notably, *2001: A Space Odyssey* and *Star Wars*. Unfortunately, the identification of *2001* as more spectacle than narrative, and *Star Wars* as an example where special effects are relied upon to visualize narrative events, not be spectacular in their own right, raise the concern that *Star Wars* is somehow the benchmark and that *2001* is incorrect or unusual in its approach.

In fact, many science fiction films fit somewhere between these two poles of *2001* and *Star Wars*, even with the genre's increased use of CGI and the expansion into blockbuster filmmaking. Some sequences of *Blade Runner*, for example, linger on the effects work (most notably the ziggurats that loom over the future city) while other uses (the police hover cars) are driven by narrative or hybrid generic requirements; in *The Day After Tomorrow* (2004) the CG storms, tidal waves and vast frozen landscapes look spectacular but are essential ingredients to illustrate the disaster-laden story of extreme global warming. Unlike the early cinema of attractions, genre narratives remain coherent and largely work within established 'three-act' structures that are familiar from notions of the classical Hollywood cinema and screenwriting classes. When special effect sequences appear within such a structure, they rarely dominate to the detriment of the narrative (indeed, there is a potent industrial argument around the use of CG to create realism: the epic images of films such as *Gladiator* (2000) and *Alexander* (2005) utilize special effects to suggest the historically 'real'). While audiences may be aware of the special effects image (largely because of the marketing of such imagery, as Chapter 9 will investigate), modern Hollywood spectacle, to borrow King's language, appears more interested in visualizing narrative events than overwhelming them.

Part of this concern over the placement of spectacle and narrative is a cultural worry over films 'dumbing down' of Hollywood (and, to a lesser extent, other world cinemas) offering lesser products that cater to (and encourage) a less intelligent audience. This is a key reason why certain genre texts become canonical, while others are often overlooked or, as in chapter one, why bodies such as the AFI choose to focus attention on to *The Day the Earth Stood Still* rather than *Them!*, or *Blade Runner* over *Spacehunter: Adventures in the Forbidden Zone* (1983). This creation of a cultural hierarchy within genres (and within audiences, who are equally likely to create and enforce their own generic conventions) has led many science fiction blockbusters of the 1980s and 1990s to be derided as 'rides ... less narrative than they used to be and more spectacular, with their spectacles more compressed one atop another ... [while] theme park rides and attractions became more narrative than, say, roller coasters had been' (Bukatman 1998, 266). Yet, it is equally clear that such concerns are equally about what audiences will make of such films amid fears that entertainment is outpacing artistic innovation: *2001* is acceptable spectacle, because it is artistic and led by a recognized auteur, while more recent blockbuster spectacle is commercialized and led by populist producers such as Jerry Bruckheimer.

This discussion of spectacular special effects imagery is necessarily limited if it only sees such effects as the sole source of possible spectacle: it is important to recognize that effects work is simply one aspect of how spectacle can function within film. Film studies often expands (and necessarily complicates) the term beyond the industrial technology that has created special effects such as stop-motion animation, motion control cameras, matte paintings, optical effects, or computer-generated elements. The very notion of what individuals find spectacular can vary – a particular star image, for instance, a musical sequence, or an array of fantastic costumes – suggests a range of imagery that different audience members might choose to linger over (and be aware of the joy of looking that such spectatorship implies). Star images may be less common in the science fiction genre (partly due to actors reluctant to be typecast in one particular role or genre) but Charlton Heston in *The Omega Man* (1971) and *Soylent Green*, or Will Smith in *Independence Day*

(1996), *Men in Black* (1997), *I, Robot* (2004) and *I Am Legend* (2007) suggests a certain spectacle around masculine performance may be at work in such generic texts. Other films, such as *Hellboy: The Golden Army* (2008), *Brazil* (1985) or *The Fountain* (2006) feature complex set design or costumes that lure the eye away from the narrative: these elements have the potential for spectacle, existing as areas that may attract audience attention. Equally, although the genre offers a much smaller sample, musical sequences can be found in science fiction films and offer a different pleasure and opportunity to the spectacle of special effect-based visuals. The musical sequences in *Just Imagine* are relatively staid, but generic films such as *The Rocky Horror Picture Show*, *Spaceballs* (1987) and *The Hitchhiker's Guide to the Galaxy* feature musical numbers that arguably stand out from (or pause) the narrative flow. The growth of aesthetic influences from music videos could also signify another source of viewer pleasure; visual and musical editing techniques contribute to spectacular sequences in *Thunderbirds* (2004) and *Aeon Flux* (2005), while science fiction imagery has been used to add spectacle to music videos for Jamiroquai, Michael Jackson and Queen.

There are, of course, cinematic technologies other than special effects that have been used by Hollywood (and other film industries) to enhance spectacular elements of the screen. The coming of synchronized sound offered a new audio spectacle of dialogue, soundtrack and sound effects: the crackle and hum of electrical equipment in the scientific labs of *Frankenstein* and *The Invisible Ray*; or the deafening roar of creatures from *Gojira* to the *Predator*. Colour cinematography offered new pictorial opportunities to the *mise en scène* of genre films *Destination Moon* (where primary-coloured spacesuits were set against the barren rock of the Moon), *War of the Worlds* (the pulsating green Martian war machines) and *Dr Who and the Daleks* (an array of coloured Daleks as opposed to the black-and-white options of the BBC television show). The latter film also made use of the new widescreen formats developed in the 1950s, which introduced the longer, thinner screens that the flying saucer of *Forbidden Planet* flew across, which opened up the vast scale of the Krell civilization in the same film, or which were filled with the post-apocalyptic scenes of *On the Beach* (1959). In each case, the technological innovation offered new visual or aural aspects to the genre, which were used to enhance both spectacle and narrative.

The reappearance of three-dimensional photography within Hollywood films has become an important intersection in this discourse around spectacular imagery. Yet the discourse around 3-D has tended to privilege claims around realism and verisimilitude as much as spectacle: a discourse that recalls the short-lived 3-D bubble of the 1950s which, according to film posters of the time, offered not spectacle, but 'startling realism, dazzling depth, life-like action, and excitement.' Despite posters that stressed the visual excitement of elements that leapt off the screen (a lion erupts from the screen in *Bwana Devil*'s 1953 poster; a chorus-line high kicks off screen in *House of Wax*'s, 1953); the competing discourses around

3-D (whether in the 1950s, 1980s or the 21st century) revolve around claims of realism and immersion as much as spectacle. The tagline for *Second Chance* (1953) emphasized it was 'SO REAL – every girl will feel like she's in the arms of Robert Mitchum' while adverts for the 3-D short of a 1953 Rocky Marciano fight noted that 3-D was 'better than ringside'. Realism and immersion are as important as the spectacle of images leaping off the screen. Meanwhile, one film critic described *It Came from Outer Space* as having '3-D dimensional photography ... [that] gave impressions of depth and true vastness ... the over-all illusion seemed natural and unobtrusive' (A.W. 1953). Depth as illusion and natural, spectacle and realism but also working in support of the narrative, with 3-D elements of *It Came from Outer Space* stressing the size of the interior of the alien spacecraft, and presenting alien and human characters on individual layers of the image (Johnston 2008b).

The recent return of 3-D production and exhibition, first through IMAX cinemas and then in more mainstream digital conversions, has been helped by genre successes such as *Monsters vs Aliens* (2009) and *Avatar*. The critical reaction to the latter film, given its (uncertain) claims to live action status (rather than the now accepted computer animated world of *Monsters vs Aliens*) has conformed to the earlier discourse around realism, immersion, solidity and nature. Some British newspaper critics described the film as 'immersive ... approaching the organic' (Romney 2009); 'the crystal clear 3-D makes it feel as if you could simply reach out and let your hand brush against a fern or catch a floating firefly' (Hunter 2009); or described the film's characters as 'reach-out-and-squeeze-'em real' (Collin, 2009). Not all British film critics made such claims, with Peter Bradshaw and Tom Huddleston defining the film in relation to visual spectacle rather than realism or immersion. Yet it is clear that the discourse around spectacle and realism, and the ability of special effects and cinematic technology to provide elements of both, is a central tenet to current (and potentially future) discussions of new developments in filmmaking.

Stars, sound, colour, widescreen and 3-D: the expansion of elements that are capable of offering generic spectacle appears to confirm that spectacle can offer 'a range of pleasures associated with the enjoyment of "larger than life" representations, more luminous or intense than daily reality' (King 2000, 4). In this respect, spectacle is not a fixed or easily transferable set of expectations. Critical reviews of science fiction films will traditionally focus on special effects as the source of spectacle and audience research does seem (at least in part) to support the belief that viewer expectation of spectacle is also located around those technologies and processes (Barker and Brooks 1998). Despite historical and more recent examples of spectacle in other branches of visual entertainment (the availability of cheaper special effects technologies has increased the level of effects-based spectacle that can be utilized in genre television: most notably in twenty-first century revisions of *Battlestar Galactica* (2004–9) and *Doctor Who*, 1963–present) there remains an assumption that spectacle remains a factor of cinema itself, something that only the big screen experience can truly offer (Pearson and Messenger-Davies 2003). Despite DVD, television and mobile media technologies changing the average screen size for film viewing, the association of spectacle (particularly special-effects-created spectacle) with the blockbuster cinematic experience seems unlikely to disappear. Spectacle (in whatever form) remains a moment of cinematic excess, a popular draw among audiences, and is as potent now as it was in the Victorian era, the early years of film, or the 1950s.

Given the prevalence of effects work within most science fiction films and the increasing presence of science fiction narratives within modern blockbusters, this discourse around spectacle, narrative and realism will continue to develop. As the book moves on to consider genre history, however, it will become even clearer that this is not a new debate. It occurs and recurs at various points in the historical periods that will be covered in Part II, and has continually impacted on popular conceptions of what the genre was, what it looked like, and what form it could take next. The reliance of film studios on the latest technology, be it wider screens or home video, computer games or the Internet, stop-motion animation or computer-generated imagery, is always at the heart of science fiction filmmaking and narratives. As the following chapters will demonstrate, however, modern technology may be used to create such compelling visual images, but technology and scientists are rarely neutral or positive elements of these science fiction narratives.

Part II
Genre History

–4–

1895–1950: Origins of a Genre

Scientific romance. Thriller. Trick film. Comic short. Fantasy. Scientific melodrama. Horror. These are some of the most common terms applied by industry, critics and trade press to films produced between 1895 and 1950, many of which have been retrospectively labelled as 'science fiction'. These generic descriptions all contain within them elements that audiences would become familiar with as the science fiction film developed. In the sixty-five year time period covered here, the reliance on tricks (special effects) that began with Georges Méliès soon grew to encompass advanced model work (*20,000 Leagues Under the Sea*, 1916; the 1936 *Flash Gordon* serial), stop-motion animation (*Prehistoric Poultry*, 1917; *King Kong*), set design (*First Men in the Moon*, 1919; *Aelita*, 1924; *Things to Come*), and optical effects (*Metropolis*, *The Invisible Man*, 1933). Narrative fantasies encompassed journeys into space (*The '?' Motorist*, 1902), alien visitation (*A Message From Mars*, 1913), visions of the future (*Just Imagine*) and time travel (*It Happened Tomorrow*, 1944). Films as diverse as *Das Brilliantschiff* (*The Brilliant Ship*, 1920) and *Murder by Television* offered a hybrid combination of melodramatic and thriller conventions; while romance and humour could be seen in a range of films, from *Mechanical Husband* (1910) to *The Perfect Woman*. Later generic entries combined many of these elements, but in the years before the science-fiction film genre was named or categorized, they could be found in individual features, shorts and serials. Examining how early films developed these conventions, alongside other influences on fantastic filmmaking techniques from books, popular science and world events, will demonstrate how science-fiction filmmaking arose from these proto-generic beginnings.

Underrepresented within academic study, this period is often telescoped into the traditional, albeit brief, canon of *Le Voyage dans la lune*, *Aelita*, *Metropolis*, *Things to Come* and the first *Flash Gordon* serial. That narrow selection elides hundreds of other films that dealt with narrative issues surrounding automation, advanced technology, space travel, scientific progress, invisibility, fantastic explorations, body snatching, radiation anxiety and transformation (Benson 1985). While these elements are identified and analysed in 1950s science fiction films, the fertile ground of the previous half-decade is largely unknown, a cinematic lost world. Useful explorations of other work by Méliès, early transformation-based films, and international contributions to generic conventions from France, Germany and the Soviet Union exist but are more interested in how cinema represented the increased mechanization of society (Telotte 1999, 2001). Reducing many fantastic or trick films between 1895 and 1920 to an expression of 'the amazing properties and, in most cases, the humoresque products of a variety of machines' (Telotte 2001, 81) privileges depictions of this 'machine age' over the wealth of other areas that would coalesce under the heading of science fiction.

To explore this period, and its suggestive links to future generic conventions, narrative and thematic trends from the films need to be considered alongside larger social, cultural and political influences from the time period. If the history of science-fiction films does not reside solely in textual details but in the assumptions and discursive networks that surround them, then genre history must explore the 'various realms of industry, audience, text, critics, policy makers, and broader social context' (Mittell 2002, 30). What follows therefore is not a complete record of all films that contain early generic markers but a selection and analysis of influences and opportunities that presage the film genre's identification in the 1950s. This work necessarily engages with elements of generic prehistory from other media: theatrical productions, magic shows, photography and scientific experimentation (Williams 1984, 124). Yet the main narrative, thematic and allegorical influence stemmed from literature. As examples from these decades of fantastic film production will demonstrate, early experiments within the genre were indebted to the work of equally fantastic (and scientifically informed) authors such as Mary Shelley, Jules Verne, Robert Louis Stevenson, and H. G. Wells. The cultural impact of their work can be traced through these films, and provide a series of potential generic threads around the artificial creation of life, mechanization, bodily transformation, alien invasion, fantastic travel and futurity.

Invention and Creation

Scientific experimentation and innovative technological marvels reached popular heights during the nineteenth century. New inventions such as gaslight, photography, the machine gun, steam trains, dynamite and x-rays impacted on public awareness of scientific progress. Each new invention appeared to enshrine scientists and inventors as the pinnacle of modern achievement, pushing forward the boundaries of human knowledge. Yet such brilliance also contained within it the possibilities of misuse, or destructive power. The machine gun and the stick of dynamite were new creations whose power was inevitably destructive; fast transportation via steam trains led to numerous pedestrian deaths. New political and scientific theories were also problematic, from the still resonant revolutions in late eighteenth-century France and America to Charles Darwin's theory of evolution. Both challenged existing religious doctrine by suggesting humans were individuals, in charge of their own destiny, and not controlled by a higher power. The rise of science through the nineteenth century, and its contribution to popular discourse, promised a world open to reason and debate, not beholden to tradition and superstition. Confronting or questioning a higher power was at the heart of one of the key literature texts of the period, Mary Shelley's *Frankenstein*: her tale of artificial man-made creation added scientific knowledge, biological experiments and natural electricity (the lightning storm) to existing myths and legends. At the same time, the novel's obsessive (often blinkered) protagonist became a figure around whom debates around the use of scientific knowledge would coalesce. While other sources impact on the 'mad' scientists that inhabit the film genres of science fiction and horror, Shelley's depiction of a dominant, driven scientist (and his monstrous creation) inform many early films with a fantastic or futuristic premise.

The first short films of Thomas Edison and the Lumiere Brothers focused on recording reality: vaudeville acts, location scenes, country and urban life. Such realistic scenes also formed the bulk of Georges Méliès early film career, until he discovered the ability of the film camera to create unsettling substitutions and fantastic special effects. Méliès' work defies genre, offering a mixture of fantasy, supernatural, science, horror, fairy tale and political satire. Yet his most famous works contain strong narrative elements of scientific experimentation, creation and transformation that would be developed in later genre films. As early as 1897, Méliès' *Chirurgien Americain* (*A Twentieth Century Surgeon*) was depicting a surgeon who experiments on a tramp by replacing his legs and body. The same year saw Méliès using a scientist's mechanical creation to confound and confuse a clown in *Gugusse et L'Automate* (*The Clown and the Automaton*). At the same time, partially influenced by Méliès, other filmmakers showed scientific figures experimenting with X-rays and baby incubators (both new technologies in the time period), elixirs to increase life and special potions that enabled the drinker to reach unbelievable speeds. The scientist-inventor was depicted as a modern magician, both creator of the moving camera and star of many of its first attractions and narratives.

Unlike Shelley's doctor, few of these early cinematic scientists were depicted as dangerous or morally questionable figures. Most of the films are comic notions about current or future inventions, based around the ideas of creation and transformation: the incubator that ages a baby into an old man, x-rays appear to turn people into skeletons, serums that devolve men into apes, or make them invisible. The figure of the scientist in this period has more in common with magical characters that appear in early films such as *The Magician* (1897), performing unusual feats with the help of camera trickery. While supernatural shorts could depict magicians as spiteful or demonic figures, the scientist or doctor character remains hapless but rarely devilish. The only uncertain note about the scientist (and another link back to Shelley's *Frankenstein*) is the recurring conceit that they have little or no control over their invention, as in *The Electric Goose* (1905) where one scientist's discovery (harnessing and using electricity) accidentally reanimates a family dinner. Like most scientific depictions of the first decade of film, however, this remains a comic treatment of technological change.

The alteration in the depiction of scientists in early cinema begins around 1910. Perhaps fuelled by the industrial demand for longer dramatic film narratives, influenced by the growing mechanization of society (a result of improvements in science and industry), or the growing global uncertainty that led to the First World War, the decade changed the previously comic depiction of scientists. Films begin to refine the idea of the scientist, from hapless and humorous to misguided or evil. Fritz Lang's *Dr Mabuse, The Gambler* (1922) is a more fully formed example of the megalomaniac scientific figure attempting to take over the world but that work is preceded by a series of short and feature-length films where the scientific lack of control (previously a comic element) positions scientists as increasingly untrustworthy or unreliable. Scientific inventions or discoveries take on sinister overtones. *The Elixir of Life* (1911) features an immortality serum that abolishes death, with the (soon overcrowded) world population turning on the scientist. In *Love and Science*, a young inventor is driven mad by the romantic betrayal he thinks he sees using his video telephone creation. In *Lola*, a scientist brings his daughter back to life, but she is soulless, a callous figure that only looks like the girl she once was. In all three instances, the scientists are punished or killed because of their invention or creation. While some comic or misguided scientists exist into the 1920s, the dominant cinematic view of the scientist was moving back to the literary roots of Dr Frankenstein, creating a new uncertainty around scientific endeavour in films.

Another literary doctor encouraged this cultural and cinematic shift in portrayals of medical or scientific experiments. The popularity of Robert Louis Stevenson's *Strange Case of Dr Jekyll and Mr Hyde* (1886) had led to various theatrical productions since its release and then, in 1907, became the source material for numerous film adaptations. This narrative of divided personalities has been seen in the years since as an allegory for repressed sexuality (hetero- and homo-), drug addiction, Freudian psychology, or a study of the Scottish national character (Campbell 2008, 19). The book has a status as a horror classic, yet like *Frankenstein*, this story of a medical doctor who runs scientific experiments contains elements that also link it to nascent ideas around what would be called science fiction. As discussed above, transformation was a central attraction in films like *The Over-Incubated Baby* (1901), but *The Elixir of Strength* (1907) and *Doctor Jekyll and Mister Hyde* (1908, based on a stage version) offer cinema's initial attempts at Stevenson's original narrative. Between 1908 and 1920 there were a further five direct adaptations of Stevenson's novel, and three that developed the theme of potion-based duality. The division in Stevenson's Jekyll and Hyde, between saint and sinner, good and evil, offers a convenient metaphor for cinema's changing interest in doctors and scientists during these years. Given the time period also saw three adaptations of *Frankenstein* (1910, 1916, 1917), a version of H. G. Wells' *The Island of Dr Moreau* (filmed as *Ile D'Epouvante* in 1913), and Edgar Allen Poe's *The Murders in the Rue Morgue* (1914), the change in cinematic scientists from comic to mad was also accomplished through a visual transformation, from novel to screen.

Figure 4.1 The mad scientist's laboratory, a ubiquitous element in many genre films from the 1920s through the 1940s, seen here in *Frankenstein vs The Wolfman* (1943) (Universal Pictures/Photofest)

The narrative interest in transformation, reanimation, and creation is not linked solely to science fiction or horror but demonstrates the hybridity of proto-generic elements in early film. *The Secret Room* (1915), *The Lion's Breath* (1916) and *The Love Doctor* (1917) all featured transformations based around body swapping or brain transplants; *Go and Get It* (1920) implanted a convict's brain into a gorilla's body; while *The Hands of Orloc* (1925) and *Mad Love* (1935) saw a murderer's hands grafted on to an injured concert pianist. Creation or reanimation was often utilized by crime dramas or thrillers, with wrongly executed men being brought back to life to avenge themselves on the real killer (examples include *The Return of Maurice Donnelly*, 1915; *Legally Dead*, 1923; *Six Hours to Live*, 1932; *The Man They Could Not Hang*, 1939). While their connection to science fiction may only be slight, these films do act as part of the larger cultural shift towards depicting the scientist figure in a negative light, towards the 'mad' scientist associated with both horror and science fiction films. They also contribute to a wider generic iconography that would grow up around the scientist, particularly the technologically advanced laboratory (Figure 4.1): 'bubbling test tubes, complicated electrical instruments and other scientific paraphernalia' (*Monthly Film Bulletin* 1936, 28) describes the lab in *The Invisible Ray* (1936), but it also stands for the dominant idea of the scientific laboratory that developed through this time period. Such places, often shot in shadows and illuminated by sparks of electric light, became the generic realm of these dubious doctors. This all contributed to the growing uncertainty over scientists, and scientific inventions, an uncertainty that would culminate in post-World War Two tension around the creation of the atomic bomb.

One development of the popularity of these hybrid science-thriller themes was around invisibility, which again linked the scientific development of new processes and potions with a subsequent descent into madness. H. G. Wells' *The Invisible Man* (1899) provided a potent narrative for films between 1900 and 1950, although many took only the basic premise of an invisibility ray or serum created by science. The early trick film revelled in its ability to make people vanish, with either magic or science the source of invisibility powders or potions: *The Acrobatic Tramps* (1902) featured hobo figures who could appear, disappear and reverse their actions at will, while *Les Invisibles (An Invisible Thief*, 1905), *The Invisible Fluid* (1908) and *Invisibility* (1909) played invisibility for laughs, with invisible characters (normally men) performing practical jokes, undressing people, and causing objects to float in mid-air. The 1933 adaptation of *The Invisible Man* offered a balance of comedy and drama, returning the scientific genius to the centre of invisibility narratives, a combined creator and victim of his invention. The film also displayed a series of advanced special effects techniques to create the illusion of invisibility. Most notable was the use of the new optical printer, which could combine different layers of film to create famous scenes such as scientist Jack Griffin (Claude Rains) removing his bandages to reveal nothing underneath.[1] While later treatments of invisibility (for example, *Hollow Man*) would return to Wells' initial notion that invisibility would drive a man insane, most of the direct sequels before 1950 returned to earlier hybrid notions of science, comedy, thriller, and romance, pitting invisible men and women against crooks, foreign spies and Nazis.

The most potent example of the scientist's use of power in these films lies in what they create: the creatures, monsters, and robotic figures that would become culturally linked with the science fiction genre of the 1950s. Most of the early films treat machines as sources of humour and comedy, mirroring the treatment of their inventors or creators (Telotte 2009). Comic mechanical men are first seen in *The Clown and the Automaton*, establishing a trend for the first two decades of cinema. These artificial figures would often cause trouble for their operators or innocent bystanders by malfunctioning and setting up slapstick routines or chase narratives. Mechanization was not simply limited to robotic automatons. In *Mechanical Legs* (1908), a pair of artificial legs allows a legless man to participate in a chase; while *The Electric Hotel* (1908) presented the 'hotel of the future' where all services are available at the touch of a button, but where 'the ransom of progress' involved suffering comical electrical problems (*Bioscope* 1908, 14). Yet even in these different cases, mechanical men, replacements limbs and hotels are presented as a source of comedy, not danger. The destruction wrought is comic, not dramatic.

The main artificial automatons in these films are robotic rather than biological creations, offering a potent link with growing cultural concerns over the mechanization (or dehumanization) of society. Writers and novelists were questioning what impact humanity's increased reliance on mechanization could have, with E. M. Forster's *The Machine Stops* (1909) a typical example of anti-mechanization narratives. This growing uncertainty can be seen in cinematic treatments of robots, particularly whether machines were reliable servants, or suitable replacements for human labour. Comedic robotic servitude appeared in *The Motor Valet* (1906), *The Electric Servant* (1909) and *Dr Smith's Automaton* (1910), suggesting motorized servants were as untrustworthy as the scientists who created them. This scepticism over machinery and mechanical creations can be read as a reaction against the industrialization of factory assembly lines and the false promise of mechanization: from labour saving device to the automated war machinery of tanks and machine guns (Telotte 1999, 3). Industrial machines would keep going, never tire and never need replacing, thus representing the opposite of human labour, which needed rest, sleep and had a limited work life. The indomitable (and potentially indestructible) automaton recurs in several short films of this period. In the trick-comic film *The Rubber Man* (1909), a mechanical creation runs amok through town and village before being short-circuited by dousing in water; while *An Extraordinary Duel* (1909) features two men (one black, one white) who fight an endless battle where they are blown to pieces, hammered out flat, with limbs mangled and destroyed. Each time, their bodies are reanimated and rebuilt to continue the fight. Described as 'a clever and very amusing trick film' (*Bioscope* 1909a, 25) it displays an interest in the indomitable automaton, and the possibilities of mechanization. While both films are designed to display camera tricks and the comic effect of chase- or fight-based chaos, they speak to a larger interest in indestructible machine-like figures that informs later science fiction productions.

Indestructible and powerful. Soulless and servile. The automaton gained wider cultural capital with Karel Capek's play *R.U.R.*, which premiered in Prague in 1921, with a New York production in 1922. Following Mary Shelley's lead, Capek's robots become self-aware, with the desire to evolve and create their own life. Capek's play was regularly cited as a direct influence on *Metropolis*, the film that did most to popularize the robot in this time period. Taking previously comic qualities (indestructibility, servile nature, the potential for malfunction), *Metropolis* repositioned the automaton as a dramatic figure at the centre of a narrative around themes of futuristic spectacle, labour relations and the dangers of mechanization. These three themes converge on the figure of the robot, built by the scientist Rotwang (Rudolph Klein-Rogge), and transformed into a simulacrum of Maria (Brigitte Helm), a virginal religious figurehead for Metropolis' working-class population. The robot ('bad', or 'False') Maria (also Helm) is ordered to incite rebellion among the workers, by undermining and debasing the character of the real Maria. The robot performs as an exotic dancer, in a scene that offers the half-naked (robot) woman as a sexually dominant figure. The robotic female is thus presented as a fantastic spectacle (she is an automaton, exotic, dressed in diaphanous costumes), she exists as an inciting figure in both class-defined spaces (calling the workers to arms and distracting and deluding the male elite), and she represents the futuristic possibilities of mechanization (both negative and positive).

It would be inaccurate, however, to represent the robot Maria as a malfunctioning automaton. Despite causing the destruction of the city's lower levels, the deaths of workers and workers' children, and distracting the male elite from other pursuits, she is actually fulfilling her programming. The problem of futuristic machines in *Metropolis* is not their propensity for malfunction but the people who control such an advanced mechanized society. The leader of Metropolis, Joh Frederson (Alfred Abel), and the scientist Rotwang, are the ultimate arbiters of technology in *Metropolis*. It is they who force the workers to perform mechanical labour and wrestle with industrial technology, they who program robot Maria to incite a riot. The mad scientist is punished at the end of the film (thrown from the roof of a cathedral) but the robot survives. The indestructible nature of cinema automatons continues here: although the human skin of the robot Maria fades away when she is burned at the stake, the statuesque robotic figure remains complete amongst the flames, her 'inner structure intact' (Dadoun 1993, 147), her fate within the film remains open.

Perhaps the most compelling (and controversial) change that *Metropolis* brought to the cinematic automaton is the notion of robots built for pleasure, a theme that would become central to later genre treatment of automatons (see, for example, *Blade Runner*, *Cherry 2000* or *Weird Science*, 1986). In *Metropolis*, the robot becomes a sexual figure as well as an antagonist. Few films had positioned the robot as a sexual being before: while *Mechanical Husband* had suggested that women might prefer a robotic spouse, the topic was comic and the husband in question was not presented as a sexual figure (or sex object). The earliest mechanical female, *The Mechanical Mary Ann* is a servant, who malfunctions and destroys a house: hardly a sexually charged figure. The link between sexuality and artificial automaton created in *Metropolis* is stressed in later science fiction, most notably from the 1960s on, but in this pre-1950s period, one of few considerations of the theme comes in the British comedy *The Perfect Woman* (Figure 4.2), where Stanley Holloway's scientist creates a robot double of his niece (Patricia Roc). Here, the comedy again arises from a doubling of a female figure, and the confusion that such doubling creates. Both films engage with a limited notion of female sexuality, from *Metropolis*' virgin/whore distinction, and *The Perfect Woman* commenting on the proper behaviour of a British woman in society, but they continue to demonstrate the inability of (male-dominated) science to control their mechanical creations, or understand natural (female) creation.

Metropolis, although inspired by *R.U.R.*, largely stands alone in its treatment of robotic figures in this time period. The Soviet film *Gibel sensatsii* (*Loss of Feeling*,

Figure 4.2 Eccentric British professor Ramshead (Stanley Holloway) and his robotic creation (played by Patricia Roc), in *The Perfect Woman* (1949) (J. Arthur Rank/Photofest)

1935) is a partial retelling of Capek's play, although there is a noticeable narrative shift towards human labour being more prized than mechanization, likely a veiled propagandistic nod towards the USSR's mobilization of its mass population and Five Years plans for economic and agricultural growth. Along with *Metropolis*, this represents the strongest example of automatons used in a dramatic fashion, rather than a source of comedy. While *Frankenstein*, *Bride of Frankenstein* and *The Tin Man* (1935) revisited the more horrific options of artificial creation, neither film offered any new developments of the cinematic robots that had already appeared on screen. If anything, the slapstick of *The Tin Man* returned automatons to the more comic mode of the early 1900s rather than the more dramatic use of them in *Metropolis* and *R.U.R.* The absence of the automaton through the 1930s and 1940s may lie with the cultural shift towards a wartime footing, where scientific figures turned to military technology, or the influence of the Universal horror genre, which repositioned the mad scientist in relation to biological or medical experimentation. Apart from brief robotic cameos in the *Flash Gordon* and *Buck Rogers* serials, the artificial automaton would not be seen on screen until the 1950s, a decade that saw them become avatars of alien and fantastic technology rather than the creation of human scientists.

By the end of the 1940s, the automaton was absent from cinema screens and the scientific figures that created them were more commonly presented in terms of the misuse of atomic power. The mad scientist was now a stock character that could be used in a variety of genres, most notably horror and thriller films. Comic scientists were not totally absent (Stanley Holloway's eccentric professor in *The Perfect Woman*, for example) but the comedy scientist of the early years of cinema had largely been replaced by scientists inflected by Mary Shelley and Robert Louis Stevenson's driven and diabolical doctors. As the century progressed, the presence and uncertainty of real world science would increase the number of such figures in science fiction, further developing mad (and heroic) notions of the generic scientist.

Invasion

Invading aliens from another planet have been regarded as a staple narrative of the science fiction genre since the 1950s. The blueprint for such stories remains *The War of the Worlds* (1895), but H.G. Wells' novel was part of a wider cultural interest in both invasion and alien visitation in literature and society. An invasion of Britain had been threatened during the reign of Napoleon, and was mooted in the propagandistic novel *The Battle of Dorking* (1871). Visitors from outer space appeared in *Under Other Conditions* (1892), in recurring reports about Martians appearing in rural America, multiple sightings of 'cigar-shaped' UFOs in 1896 and 1897, plays about messengers from Mars, and psychics claiming to have visited the Red Planet (Dean 1998). In the period of film production covered in this chapter, however, alien invasion narratives are notable by their absence. Despite the popularity of adapting Wells' other novels for film there was no direct adaptation of this particular 'scientific romance' narrative until 1938, with Orson Welles' infamous radio broadcast scare. Invasion narratives need not be alien in origin: giant insects invaded the cinema screen in *Un Bon Lit* (*A Midnight Episode*, 1899) and *Un Nuit Terrible* (1897), while a huge mosquito invaded America in *A Jersey Skeeter* (1901). Such mutated visitations were infrequent in this period however, and with few alien invasions, the preference was for human-based wars of the world.

Restaged or fictional events from real wars had proven popular in early cinema, particularly filmed scenes from the Boer and Spanish-American Wars. *A Sneaky Boer* (1897), for instance, dramatized a cowardly attack on stalwart British soldiers, demonstrating both the power of propaganda and the fictional possibilities of representing distant warfare. The creation of fictional future warfare was influenced by H. G. Wells, most notably his novel *The War in the Air* (1908), where a zeppelin-led German invasion of America starts a global air war for supremacy of the sky. With an interest in futuristic warfare, new technologies and a description of the aerial bombardment of New York and other capital cities, *The War in the Air* was the template for a series of British and American films that continued through the 1910s and into the 1930s. Walter Booth's *The Airship Destroyer* (1909) was directly inspired by Wells' story, although this shorter tale played with contemporary fears of airborne bombing raids from invading airships and zeppelins. Although defeated in this film by radio-controlled flying torpedoes, the belief in some form of air warfare can be seen in the similar narratives of *Aerial Warfare, The Battle in the Clouds*, and *Won in the Clouds* (1914), or Booth's own continuation of the theme in *Aerial Submarine* (1910) and *Aerial Torpedo* (1910), where pirates torpedo a ship from the air, then dive into the ocean to retrieve its cargo. While such themes continue in later films such as *Am Rande Der Velt* (*At the Edge of the World*, 1927), *Things to Come* (where air supremacy is seen as the key to world peace), and *Midnight Menace* (1937), World War One and the rise in world tension during the 1930s meant that aerial bombardment and the threat of invasion had become science fact not fiction.

Destruction was also a key element of other invasion fears, particularly around non-human invaders, such as comets or meteors. The 1910 reappearance of Halley's Comet sparked fears of weather disturbances caused by its passing, concerns that were represented in a variety of short films. Cinematic treatments of celestial visitations combined apocalyptic notions with comedy in *The Comet/Frightened By the Comet* (1910), *How Scroggins Found the Comet* (1910), and *The Comet's Comeback* (1916), which offer humorous variations on the theme of imminent destruction: a scientist denounced for fear-mongering, an amateur astronomer fooled by a fake comet, and a comet that emitted a gas that caused people and events to move in slow motion. More dramatic portents around comets surfaced in *Verldens Undergang* (*The End of the World*, 1916) and *La Fin du Monde* (1930), both offering visions of society falling apart due to the imminent collision of comet and Earth. As such, they represent a strain of post-apocalyptic drama that was common in the late 1920s and through the 1930s as global tensions increased, and offer an early example of coalescing interest around space-borne destruction.

Not all invaders or visitors were unfriendly or bent on conquest, but fell into more traditional romantic or mentor roles. H. G. Wells' stories have often been described as 'scientific romances' and many early alien visitations combined similar elements in their inter-galactic love stories. *When the Man in the Moon Seeks a Wife* (1908) featured a humanoid Man in the Moon who visits London in order to find a mate. A comic fantasy, the film seems unconcerned about the invasion aspect of the moon man's visit, or the return of the chosen girl to the moon. The visitor is a fantasy, a source of wonder, not horror. Further afield in space, Mars was a popular cultural obsession at the turn of the twentieth century. Astronomer Percival Lowell published two books on his observations of Mars in *Mars and Its Canals* (1906) and *Mars as an Abode of Life* (1908), while American newspaper contests asked readers to come up with ways to get to Mars, or to write songs about men on Mars (Dean 1988). These more positive views of potential life on Mars can be seen in a late nineteenth-century stage play, which was adapted twice for film. In both versions of *A Message From Mars* (1913, 1921), the Martian visitor is not here to take over but to guide one human towards an understanding of the problems of the world. More of a guardian angel (not unlike Clarence, the otherworldly visitor from *It's a Wonderful Life*, 1946), this morality tale casts the alien invader as a beneficent visitor, the source of heavenly knowledge and wisdom not advanced technology or destructive power.

Unlike artificial creation, robots or space travel, invasion narratives before 1950 feature few of the generic traits associated with the alien invaders of *The War of the Worlds* or later derivations of it. Perhaps because of the presence of wars, both local and global, in the time period, interest remained on the future possibilities of human invasions of countries rather than alien invasions from space. The rise of alien invasion narratives in the 1950s arose from a wider interest in both space exploration and flying saucers in that decade: elements that were simply not present and culturally influential before World War Two. Yet despite the lack of discourse around aliens invading the earth, there was a more active interest around humanity leaving the planet, exploring (and potentially colonizing) other worlds, and investigating unknown areas of their own planet.

Exploration

Travelling from the Earth to the moon, to Mars, to the sun, or to other fantastic planets in the solar system and beyond, has long been a stalwart of science fiction literature and filmmaking. Equally, the surface (and interior) of the Earth remains unexplored territory, spawning a range of narratives that delve into the lost worlds of the planet, from undersea kingdoms to isolated islands (*20,000 Leagues Under the Sea*) and plateaus where huge monsters roam (*The Lost World, King Kong*). In the forty-eight years that separate Méliès' and George Pal's fictional moon journeys, other narratives of fantastic exploration relied heavily on the contemporary notion that enlightened European countries (and a newly expansive US) had the right to colonize, control and civilize new countries and peoples that had not developed (socially, culturally, technologically and militarily) to the same level as they had. Some of these stories of exploration can be read as satires, or comments, on that colonialism (following a tradition that included Swift's *Gullivers Travels* and Wells' *War of the Worlds*), while others relish in the spectacle of the lost world, rather than any particular allegory of conquest. From Méliès' space-faring professors and deep-sea explorers to Fritz Lang's industrial astronauts in *Frau im Mond*, these proto-generic films begin to define the conventions of fantastic exploration.

The prime text in discussions of proto-science fiction films remains Georges Méliès' *Le Voyage dans la lune* and its spectacular depiction of a human trip to the moon. Aside from its unique blend of fantasy, wonder and special effects, it also represents the first example of a scientific exploration of another world. Its deceptively simple narrative line – a band of scientists decide to build a rocket and visit the Moon – disguises Méliès' grasp of the exploration narrative. Like future fictional explorations of other planets, lost worlds and unknown kingdoms, the film details planning, construction, launch, discovery, interaction with locals (often violent, as here) and a triumphant return home. The influence of a nineteenth-century colonial mindset is clear – the native Selenites are devilish, fierce, uncivilized, whereas the stalwart white explorers are brave and resourceful – and there is no consideration of the fact that the explorers are invading the Moon as much as H. G. Wells' Martians invaded Earth.

Méliès' film was reliant on existing literature, including recent work by Jules Verne and H. G. Wells, particularly their novels *From the Earth to the Moon* (1865), *Round the Moon* (1870) and *The First Men on the Moon* (1901). Yet the film also contains links to examples of cultural discourse, from the fascination with Mars mentioned earlier to the popular interest with the Moon in the late nineteenth and early twentieth century. The late nineteenth century saw an expansion of astronomy as both a leisure and professional pursuit; observatories were able to rely on more powerful telescopes, and the introduction of photographic plates allowed images of the Moon's surface to be reproduced and studied. Alongside what the Moon looked like, popular culture remained fascinated with what a journey into space would be like: particularly at a time when great leaps in transport were being regularly achieved: from balloons to steam trains, aeroplanes to motor cars, scientific invention was constantly revising how people would, and could, travel in the future. As discussed in Chapter 3, tens of thousands of visitors to the 1901 Pan-American Exposition were able to take their own 'Trip to the Moon', which simulated a trip into space and through the Selenite-inhabited caverns of the Moon.

One of the most popular attractions at the 1901 Exposition, the Moon trip represents a major cultural investment in the notion of humans exploring space and travelling to the stars. Méliès' films provided cinematic stimulation for such cultural fascination with outer space voyaging, returning to space exploration in the years after *Le Voyage dans la lune*, most notably in *Voyage à travers l'impossible* (*An Impossible Voyage*, 1904), which depicts a trip to the sun. The film suggests a more casual sightseeing tour of the sun, with a cross-section of passengers (including women, a change from the all-male exploration of the Moon) climbing on board a train rather than into a bullet-shaped rocket. The choice of a train for fantastic travel mirrors the nineteenth-century fascination with the train, and its apparent ability to distort human perspectives of space and time by crossing vast distances at unheard of speeds. (Kirby 1997) Méliès' interest arguably focused on spectacle over narrative: not only the variety of sets and trick effects that could be shown (the train flies into the sun's mouth, passengers are 'frozen' in a refrigerated compartment) but with hand-coloured sequences of the yellow sun, and the red smoke that comes out of its mouth. Elements of this early work, from the iconography of spaceship and fantastic landscapes, thematic interests in explorers, to the reliance on special effects spectacle, would fuel later definitions of science fiction.

Other filmmakers imitated Méliès' work: Charles Raymond produced *The Cabby's Dream* (1906) with a cabman embarking on a fantastic journey with a magician; Gaston Velle's *Voyage autor d'une étoile* (*Voyage Around a Star*, 1906) has an astronomer sailing through space in a giant soap bubble; *New Trip to the Moon* (1909) demonstrated Segunodo de Chomon's expertise in visual effects; while Walter Booth and R. W. Paul's *The ? Motorist* launched a motorcar into space. This latter film combined a chase narrative with special effects, sending a couple on a wild ride, up a building, across the sky and into space. After driving round Saturn's rings, the car plummets back to Earth. The film draws together many of the elements from existing fantasy and trick films: the interest in speed, new technology (the train is replaced here by a motor car), special effects (transformations and model work of the car travelling through space) and exploration.

The bulk of space exploration features were produced after 1918, with narratives that deal with various teams of explorers voyaging to Mars and the Moon. After the events of the 1910s, most notably the destruction of World War One and the 1917 Russian Revolution, journeying to other planets offered neutral territory or an allegorical location to deal with such contemporary events. The Danish film *Himmelskibet* challenged expectations that Mars would be barbaric or warlike: an international crew from Earth arrive and meet a righteous and noble race, which is more advanced and peaceful than those from a post-First World War Earth. The Martians, echoing *A Message From Mars*, are able to offer advice to the returning astronauts. *Aelita* presented a futuristic and architecturally elaborate Mars, an ostentatious world ruled by a corrupt monarchy, including the duplicitous Aelita. A visiting Russian cosmonaut saves the 'red' planet from this societal structure by inciting a worker's revolt, fighting alongside the proletariat, and exposing Aelita's plans to rule the world (although, in keeping with earlier science fictions, the Martian episodes are ultimately the product of the Russian man's fevered imagination). *Just Imagine*, meanwhile, presents Mars as a quasi-barbaric location, with set design that emphasizes jungles and rock-built palaces, where native Martians are all twins, split into good and evil versions of themselves. This science fiction musical, the main representation of Mars by American film companies in the time period, differs from the Danish and Russian examples by not treating Mars as an allegory or a representation of Earth's problems, but as simply another exotic location where the main characters can indulge in slapstick fights, misunderstand the natives, and then escape in the nick of time. The reason for going to Mars is not the journey, or the desire to explore: rather, the pilot needs the societal distinction so he can marry the girl of his dreams and fulfil Hollywood's desire for romantic narrative closure.

Generic exploration narratives of this time period, whether they head into space, or into uncharted regions of the Earth, all follow the basic outline set up by Méliès' *Le Voyage dans la lune*. A small group of explorers (mostly men, though increasingly joined by at least one woman – normally reduced to the love interest) plan a trip, hire or build the necessary transportation, make the journey, encounter a strange civilization (and potentially, a fantastic monster), and return to Earth (or a civilized capital city) with their tale. Yet despite the dominance of such a structure, by the mid-1930s, the dominant view of space travel was not the realistic rocket launch of *Frau im Mond*, or the allegorical worlds of *Aelita* or *Himmelskibet*, but the vision of space travel found in the popular (and influential) comic strip adaptations of *Flash Gordon* and *Buck Rogers*. In these serials, the legacy of American pulp magazines such as *Astounding Science Fiction* and *Amazing Stories* (where the term 'science fiction' first gained prominence) reached the film screen. Commercially successful tales of lantern-jawed space heroism, these thirteen part serials featured all-American heroes fighting off alien invaders, zipping across the universe in rockets, firing ray guns and protecting the Earth. Flash and Buck weren't stuffy scientific figures or fascinated explorers but, perhaps more than any pre-existing novel or film about space travel, they popularized a particular notion of what space travel could be and what the nascent science fiction genre might offer. This exciting vision of space travel and exploring the stars would dominate cultural opinion around science fiction films for decades to come.

The Future

Many of the films discussed so far could be said to be cinematic predictions of the future: from future warfare and advanced automatons to trips to the moon and visitors from another planet. Yet most of these narratives (or the film's *mise en scène* more generally) suggested that events were taking place in an undefined present, the result of a recent technological breakthrough. This initial absence of futurity can also be found in much of the literature from which these early film narratives were drawing inspiration: *Frankenstein, Twenty Thousand Leagues under the Sea, The First Men in the Moon, The War of the Worlds,* and *The Invisible Man* were all based in present day (nineteenth century) settings. Only H. G. Wells' *The Time Machine* offered a vision of the future, and there were no immediate attempts to adapt that for film (although references to Wells' book, and the machine, did feature in several newspaper columns and reviews at the time). While people in the late nineteenth and early twentieth century were fascinated by what might be next, seen most clearly in the display of current and future technology at the popular World's Fairs and Expositions, there are few cinematic treatment of what such future worlds might look like until the production of *Les Progress de la Science en l'an 2000* (*Life in the Next Century*, 1909). *Bioscope* noted that this 'most amusing film' depicts the year 2010, a world where bread is automatically toasted, buttered and brought to the bedside, and where 'Pressing another button will bring the modern man's clothes to him ... He has by this time set aside all such fatiguing notions as walking, and will be propelled short distances by motor-feet.' The vague unease about mechanization in society is still present, as the film's protagonist rejects this mechanized utopia, casting 'all his electrical appliances to the winds with an air of boredom and disgust'

(*Bioscope* 1910a, 55). Like many visions of the future, this offered a more direct and damning indictment of present concerns around mechanization and growing consumerism.

A similar American film the following year (*Looking Forward*, 1910) expanded on the basic principle of the hundred-year jump but based it around the concept that the world of 2010 would be run by women. This worry about the growing power of women represents a societal change that had begun in the nineteenth century, where women began to demand more equality in all walks of life. From the opening of department stores that targeted the new female consumers, to changes in marriage and divorce laws, to developments in fashion, female suffrage was an increasingly political and cultural issue. Films often dramatized this change through the narrative prism of the future (another precursor of science fiction genre conventions to come). *In the Year 2000* (1912), *In the Year 2014* (1914), *Percy Pumpernickle, Soubrette* (1914) and *The Last Man on Earth* (1924) all present future matriarchal societies, where men are second-class citizens. Yet such futurism traditionally retreats to dominant contemporary gender roles, allowing men to 'regain' control of society, often by demonstrating the folly of a world run by women. *One Hundred Years After* (1911) follows this path, with scientist Tom Editt having his life suspended and waking up in 2011. Women are in charge, men are secondary (most films sustain this direct opposition: the suggestion of an equal society appears to have been equally fantastic and unlikely); women are 'tall, lithe maidens, attired in knickerbockers and wearing silk "toppers"' while men are 'undersized' and wear skirts (*Bioscope* 1911a, xxv). These visual discrepancies, the reversal of 1911 ideologies around gender, are soon put right by Editt, who returns future society to its 'correct' course by making love to the world's ruler and promoting male suffrage.[2] *The Last Man on Earth* takes a similar tack, suggesting that women are unable to fulfil male and female roles after an epidemic that wipes out men over fourteen.

Female power is central to other famous visions of the future from this period. *Metropolis* is a dual city: above, the city of the upper class sons, whose hedonistic lifestyle includes being entertained by exotically dressed courtesans; below, the city of the male workers who struggle to keep the machinery running on time. Working-class women are seen (they take part in the riots) but appear to largely function as mothers: only Maria and Robot Maria move between the upper and working-class worlds, and even there it is only the Robot Maria who appears to wield any power, through her (automated) sexuality. Despite the recent successful suffrage movement in America and Britain, many films opted to present sexual equality by stressing the changes in fashion that future women would have to look forward to (thus presuming that 1930s women would only be interested in such things): *High Treason* presents women in masculine clothing and 'plus fours', jodhpurs and fencing uniforms; *Just Imagine* offers reversible dresses and revealing lingerie whereas *Things to Come* has utilitarian togas for men and women (Figure 4.3). While the majority of films offered limited opportunities for female performance beyond the romantic role of

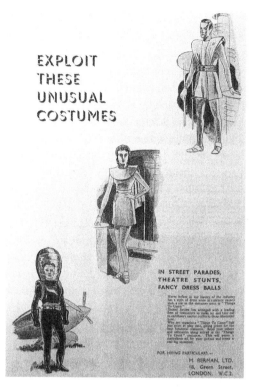

EXPLOIT
THESE
UNUSUAL
COSTUMES

IN STREET PARADES,
THEATRE STUNTS,
FANCY DRESS BALLS

FOR HIRING PARTICULARS —
M. BERMAN, LTD.
18, Green Street,
LONDON. W.C.2.

Figure 4.3 Speculative future societies are often created through distinctive costumes and clothes (*Things to Come* press book, 1936) (London Films)

the girlfriend or lover, there remains a suggestion of futuristic feminine power in the female rulers of *Aelita, Just Imagine* and *Siren of Atlantis* (1947).

Depicting these futuristic cities often relegates humanity to a secondary attraction, behind the spectacle of miniatures, models and optical work that conveys the visual splendour and majesty of future society. *Metropolis, High Treason, Just Imagine* and *Things to Come* are all high-budget attempts to convey futurism, and each relies on state-of-the art miniature models and set design to accomplish their visions of the future. Depicting the future through such technology became more complicated with the advent of sound in the late 1920s: what should the future sound like? The press book for *High Treason*, an early British sound film, notes a concern with aural representations of the future: 'sound recording ... is particularly good in the graphic realism of the aeroplane raids, the explosion in the Channel Tunnel and the women's triumphal singing of the Peace Song.' The emphasis here is on what sound can add to existing visual spectacle: explosions and air raids. Futuristic films in the early sound era realized that the future must also sound different to match the variations on reality offered by visual effects. Early generic sound conventions would include the crackle of electricity in scientific labs from *Frankenstein* to *The Invisible Ray*, the roar of rockets and high explosives in *Frau im Mond* and *Destination Moon*, and the whine and spark of ray guns in *Buck Rogers* and *Flash Gordon*. *Just Imagine*, the first science fiction musical, might be expected to display its generic credentials both visually and aurally: miniatures and painted backdrops are used to convey its vision of a futuristic New York dominated by skyscrapers and personal aeroplanes, and a trip to Mars. Yet while sound is essential for a reanimation sequence (with bubbling liquids, electric crackles, and the whine of generators), the dialogue is prosaic and the musical elements are steadfastly rooted in the late 1920s, not a possible 1980.

The vision (and sound) of the future being offered in these films is one based around the spectacle of possible advances in human architecture and creation. After the spate of anxious 'women-in-control' future fantasies of the 1910s, futuristic visions are enacted on a large scale. As such, there are few examples of this kind of high-budget filmmaking, with the four that dominate (*Metropolis, High Treason, Just Imagine, Things to Come*) having distinct similarities in their obsession with skyscrapers, lanes of flying machines, and the hint of fascistic (or at least, overly controlling) governments. Even the less fantastic (and therefore lower budget) serial adventures of *Flash Gordon* and *Buck Rogers* present future cities that have fantastic technology but are constantly under attack, or need saving from internal threats. That all of these disparate visions of the future have been so influential lies precisely in the suggestion of utopian and dystopian features that such advanced cities contain. None of the impressively constructed cities is perfect, and many reveal previously hidden layers of discontent: that contradiction would remain at the heart of visions of the future in the decades to come.

Conclusion: World War Two and After

Between 1895 and 1940, the film industries of various countries produced different and diverse films that contained elements that, in later films, would be identified as science fiction. Relying on existing conventions from literature and the explosion of cultural curiosity in nineteenth-century science and technology (most notably around transport and vision), early filmmakers took figures such as scientists and automatons, used thematic devices like spaceships, invisibility potions and futuristic visions and crafted film narratives around fantastic possibilities, events and happenings. It is possible to read these films as commentary on social and cultural concerns around mechanization, the failure of science to create peace, or the growth of distrust in technology more generally. What is clear is that this group of films, many using the most advanced special effects of the age, some relying on narrative power, began to establish a series of conventions for what would, eventually, become known as the science-fiction film. This was not the natural, or straightforward, journey depicted in many genre histories. Many films represented dead ends, in aesthetic or narrative terms; many others were forgotten, while some have since been canonized as genre classics. Yet as this chapter has demonstrated, it remains possible to tease apart recurring interests in science and creation, fantastic exploration, fear of invasion, uncertainty over technology, and concerns over the future (and, often, women). None of these are science fiction films, at least not in the sense of what that term would come to represent in the 1950s but they contain influential traces of things to come.

The heyday of this period of early experimentation largely runs until the mid-1930s. During the late 1930s and through the 1940s, it remains possible to find films with familiar narrative premises (for example, *The Invisible Man Returns*, 1940; or the time-travel comedy *It Happened Tomorrow*) but depictions of science and technology largely became tied to contemporary wartime issues. Scientists were involved in experiments with radiation and the bomb but appeared more frequently in thrillers or war films; there were few automatons being created (although the Frankenstein monster was seen in several sequels, most notably appearing alongside Dracula, the Wolfman, Abbott and Costello); and images of the future were noticeably absent. Fears of human-led invasion were no longer science fiction and the main alien invasion of the time period was the appearance (in serials) of Superman, an alien presence but one that chose to live as a human and protect the planet from evil. In fact, the serial market was one of the few places where genre products continued to thrive, with countless mad scientists, atomic bombs, unusual compounds, jet packs and ray guns (Benson 1985). The association of such character and narrative tropes with the children's market of serial adventures would colour cultural acceptance of the film genre in the 1950s.

The 1940s are, however, important to the continued health and development of the early science-fiction film, because they fostered the rise and expansion of special effects departments in the major studios. The Hollywood industry had used spectacle across multiple genres during the 1930s and now demanded authentic footage for a series of war films. Effects departments expanded and technologies were improved as technicians produced process shots, stop-motion animation and model work for studio productions. These components, essential elements in the expansion of science fiction film in the 1950s, were also important in stressing a realistic component within genre production. George Pal's *Destination Moon*, traditionally seen as the first science-fiction film of the 1950s, is more closely tied to this period of Hollywood production and the films explored through this chapter. With its interest in rocket science (a major element of American military might in the late 1940s), the film presents a narrative of space exploration more akin to *Frau im Mond* than the fantasy of *Forbidden Planet*. Pal expressed a desire to return spaceflight to reality, away from the space opera of *Flash Gordon* (Hickman 1977, 36) but his desire for realism means the film is best seen as a bridge from the realism of wartime film production to the more fantastic visions of science fiction for which the 1950s would become famous.

–5–

1950–70: Defining a Genre

> Hollywood's science-fiction output in the 1950s reflected the tensions, conflicts, and debates playing out in the broader American political landscape … accurately assessing the fears and desires of Cold War America.
>
> Brian Vizzini, 'Cold War Fears, Cold War Passions: Conservatives and Liberals Square Off in 1950s Science Fiction'

Academic work on the 1950s American science fiction film has tended to follow the broad parameters of this argument.[1] There has been a focus on narratives that deal with alien invasion, a fascination about what the monstrous figure of the alien represented, and an assumption that science fiction films dramatized fears about the Cold War 'Red Menace' of the Soviet Union. America in the 1950s is commonly portrayed as a conservative country, where right-wing political power was dominant, a more interventionist foreign policy was implemented, and alleged domestic subversion by communists was high on the political agenda (most commonly linked to Senator Joseph McCarthy's House UnAmerican Activities Committee (HUAC) investigations into left-wing organizations, including the Hollywood labour unions). Science fiction's appearance and popularity in this decade has been retrospectively linked to its apparent ability to deal with these larger political issues in allegorical form. This remains a problematic approach: it first reduces the narrative and thematic complexity of an entire decade of science fiction films to one perspective; it then assumes that those films (a small canon of what was actually produced and released) simply 'reflected' the whole of American society; and then rarely looks beyond America's borders to compare generic details with films produced outside of Hollywood. Science fiction films (and American societal fears) were fuelled by more than Cold War tropes and tension around foreign powers: the decade saw a continual increase in UFO sightings, the refinement of and uncertainty over atomic weapons, the beginnings of an aerospace-centred space race, as well as the 'suburbanization' of American society and the supposed loss of individuality that contemporary commentators feared came with that move (Jancovich 1996; Geraghty 2009). Science-fiction films of the 1950s and 1960s dealt with those and other themes while developing tropes from previous decades.

Discussion of the science-fiction films produced across both decades must necessarily engage with more than simply political or social influences. From 1950 on, film industries in Hollywood and elsewhere were being threatened by falling audience numbers, rising production costs, the impact of television and the growth of the teenage audience. The sudden success of science-fiction film production in the early part of the decade was challenged on all four fronts. Films such as *When Worlds Collide* (1951) and *War of the Worlds* were popular successes but by 1955 Hollywood studios claimed the audience for science fiction films was falling off – a particular problem given the increased special effects budgets that high-profile productions such as *Forbidden Planet* and *Conquest of Space* required. Without a significant return on investment, many studios cut back on costly genre projects and closed effects departments. More televised science fiction became available (much of it produced by the same studios) challenging the primacy of science fiction on the big screen. The growing teenage audience (a central demographic for the big Hollywood studios) offered another option for science fiction film aside from the blockbusters of George Pal and prestige films such as *On the Beach*. The low-budget success and saturation booking strategies of *Invasion of the Body Snatchers, Them* and non-studio productions such as *The Last Woman on Earth* (1960) and *The Wasp Woman* (1960) may have returned science fiction to sensationalist narratives and more basic effects work but the focus on a new audience and inventive distribution strategies prevented the genre from disappearing entirely from cinema screens by the end of the 1950s. Plus, while American science fiction productions may have dipped in number towards the end of the 1950s and through the 1960s, low-budget independent and prestige studio genre films were bolstered and influenced by international contributions to the genre, most noticeably from Britain, France, the USSR and Japan. This chapter will engage with this global concept of the science fiction film across these two decades, arguing that understanding genre in this time period must explore a wider scope of social and cultural influence than is commonly considered, and address a broad palette of films, from the (perceived) juvenilia of *Daleks: Invasion Earth 2150 AD* (1966) to the adult themes of *2001: A Space Odyssey*.

1950–1959: 'Genrification'

> Presenting Reds as ants or aliens served to establish their Otherness … Possession by pods – mind stealing, brain eating, and body snatching – had the added advantage of being an overt metaphor for Communist brainwashing. (Biskind 1983, 132–40)

The threat of alien invasion is a key narrative thread from the 1950s, and it is one that has garnered much academic attention. A range of films including *Invaders from Mars* (1953) and *Earth vs the Flying Saucers* visualized such attacks and explored humanity's response to alien assaults, whether through physical fighting or 'bodysnatching'. The dominant reading of 1950s alien invasion has been to situate it in relation to fear of the USSR, and its potential attack on (and subversion of) the American way of life (Biskind 1983; Warren 1997; Vizzini, 2009). These films were produced in a time period when communist forces in China and Russia were seen as one of the greatest threats to American security. Anti-communist rhetoric was at its strongest in the US, where HUAC held regular hearings on left-wing (read: communist) infiltration of American society (including Hollywood screenwriters, directors and actors). Such historical events fuel the belief that Cold War-inspired paranoia had a direct influence on film production. The science fiction premise of future atomic war in America fuelled *Five* (1951) and *Invasion USA* (1952), with the latter using war footage to depict visually an invasion by an unnamed foreign army that was Soviet in all but name. Most genre productions featured invasion narratives of less human devising. In critical readings that link aliens with the USSR, any form of 'Other' that invades America (or American territory) represents a potential Soviet invasion or infiltration of the West. Thus, *The Thing from Another World* becomes a Soviet sleeper agent, inactive until 'awakened' by curious American military men and scientists; the destructive Martians of *War of the Worlds* are a technologically superior 'Red Menace'; while the *Invaders From Mars* and the *Invasion of the Body Snatchers* dramatize concerns over soulless, communist drones replacing American individualism and freedoms.

Invasion of the Body Snatchers has become a pivot for such claims. Director Don Siegel continually repudiated the notion that he had created an anti-communist film, stating instead that his intention was to mock the conformity of American society. 'To be a pod means you have no passion, no anger, the spark has left you … It happens to leave you in a very dull world, but that … is the world that most of us live in' (Siegel, quoted in Kaminsky 1976, 73). Anti-Communist and anti-conformity readings of the film take different perspectives on the same material. For the 'Cold War' reading, the alien pod people's rejection of emotion, religion and the traditional rules of 'invasion' are seen as Soviet attitudes, painting the USSR as a godless, logical, ruthless nation that aims to undermine America culturally as well as militarily. Yet for Siegel (and others who support the 'conformity' reading) the emotionless pod people represent a movement towards the unquestioning, 'dumbing down' of American society in the postwar, suburban era. Here, suburbia is a rejection of true American values such as rebellion, tradition and independence: replaced by blind acceptance and cultural brainwashing. Both approaches see a deeper political or cultural attitude underlying the film and both assume that all audiences will be able to understand and decode such messages.

Such traditional narrative-based readings of these genre films have the central, problematic, assumption that 1950s audiences would have read the films in exactly the same way and identified the same underlying elements. Vizzini, mirroring other academics, claims that one such film, *Invaders from Mars*, was 'a thinly veiled (and simplistic) allegory with which audiences in 1953 would have no difficulty identifying' (Vizzini 2009, 29). While this ignores the rich textual evidence of the film itself in favour of a broad narrative summary, it presumes a dominant encoding that 'all' audiences would take from the film, reading the same political or allegorical message regardless of age, class, gender or background. Such readings run the risk of denying the range of perspectives that audiences might take up. Revealing all of those positions might be lost to modern reception studies, but reviews from the 1950s do offer some sense of what other perspectives may have contributed to such a discourse. The *New York Times*, for example, refers to *Invaders From Mars* as a 'pictorial "funnybook." Full of impossible actions and childish imaginings.' With no mention of communist agitators or agents, the reviewer sees it more as a film designed 'to meet the demands of today's space-struck youngsters' (OAG 1953). These two positions run the gamut between a self-aware adult audience who can identify and translate a filmic allegory and a young audience weaned on comic books and space fantasy. There is no correct answer to what these films represented, what they may have meant to diverse audiences in America, or to audiences across the world. Arguably, the best way to understand these science fiction invasion films is to accept that their fantastic premises may contain traces of contemporary events and issues but to equally be aware that they were never a simple reflection of 1950s anxieties or concerns, drawing instead on multiple influences.

Additional evidence of the discourses that surrounded, and helped identify, these science fiction films, can be gleaned from other contemporary reviews. While it was not seen in previous decades, the term 'science fiction' is in regular usage in 1950s reviews, from *Variety*'s comment that *Rocketship X-M* is a 'piece of science fiction that can be ballyhooed to the hilt' (*Variety* 1950) to the *New York Times*' dismissal of *The Day the Earth Stood Still* as 'a tepid entertainment in what is anomalously labelled the science-fiction field' (Crowther 1951). Such references demonstrate that a generic identity had entered popular usage, and suggest a shorthand reference that could be used between reviewers and audiences. Other review headlines from the *New York Times* and *Variety* suggest how those popular publications were defining the genre. *Variety* identifies a 'cycle dealing with space visitors from another planet' in relation to *The Man From Planet X* (1951) but makes no reference to what this visitor might represent (*Variety* 1951a); while 'top honours' for the 'interplanetary fantasy' *When Worlds Collide* 'rest with the cameraman and special effects technician', an early connection between science-fiction blockbusters and spectacular visual effects (*Variety* 1951b). In the *New York Times*, two headlines ('Here Come Those Flying Saucers Again' and 'Look Out! The Space Boys Are Loose Again') also dispute the notion that science fiction films were seen at the time as engaging with the Cold War menace of the USSR (AW 1953). In the examples taken from these two publications alone, any contemporary notion of the science fiction film genre appears to draw on other cultural tropes such as UFO sightings, the growth of aerospace research and a general enthusiasm for space stories among young audiences. While *The New York Times* and *Variety* should not be seen as representative of all critical opinion on these films (*The Times*' treatment of many genre films of the period as being for children suggests a dismissal of the genre due to its popularity, pulp roots and alleged juvenilia) but the reviews do point to a wider and more varied collection of potential stimuli.

One undoubted cultural influence on science fiction films was the rise in sightings of unidentified flying objects (UFOs), and the permanent change it made to the generic iconography of the science fiction film. The recurring image of a saucer-shaped object hanging in the sky came from a series of 1947 reports, including one that stated 'nine disks flying like a saucer skipped over the water' (quoted in Dean 1998, 56). Media use of the phrase 'flying saucers' was intended to deride the initial reports, but popularized it instead. By the early 1950s, as reports of abductions and alien contact increased, the flying saucer ceased to be a potential Soviet threat and became more commonly associated with aliens.[2] By 1952, popular American news magazines such as *Life* could publish headlines such as 'There is a Case for Interplanetary Saucers' and articles exploring their impact (Darrach 1952). The visual idea of a flying saucer caused a shift in generic imagery, becoming central to many science-fiction films produced from 1950 on. Rocket ships, rocket cars, even Méliès' rocket trains, become sidelined in favour of this sleek, simple icon. From the moment that Klaatu's silver saucer speeds across the screen and lands in Washington D.C. in the opening minutes of *The Day the Earth Stood Still*, the genre had found a new generic symbol.

The increased presence of the flying saucer in this time period is part of a process of 'genrification', where the recurring use of particular symbols both in films and culture suggests core elements of generic identity. Yet Vivian Sobchack has rejected the notion that 'spaceships' are an essential component of the science fiction genre because there is 'no consistent cluster of meanings invoked by the image of a spaceship' (Sobchack 1988, 65). However, there is a dominant and consistent representation of the flying saucer in the films of the 1950s: a negative representation built around mystery and destructive power. Most film UFOs are the source of violent invasion and devastation: the saucers of *War of the Worlds*, *Earth vs the Flying Saucers*, *Invaders From Mars*, *Killers From Space* (1954) and *Teenagers From Outer Space* (1959) either devastate large swathes of America, or release inhabitants who kill and 'body snatch'.[3] Even the huge silver saucer of *The Day the Earth Stood Still* retains the potential for destruction. Klaatu may be on a mission of peace (or authoritarian dominance – see Jancovich and Johnston 2009, 74) but the saucer remains the source of the power that makes the Earth 'stand still' and houses the devastating potential of Gort. This negative connotation confirms Sobchack's contention that spaceships tend to be seen as positive (human built) or negative (alien), but it ignores the historical import of the flying saucers to the 1950s iteration of science fiction. To place the flying saucer in the same category as all 'spaceships' (a diverse category that includes Cavor's flying sphere from *First Men in the Moon*, *Star Wars'* Millennium Falcon and the yellow hot rod of *Earth Girls Are Easy*, 1988) ignores the cultural potency of their image on 1950s film screens. While not all flying saucers were precursors of invasion (1955s *This Island Earth* features Metalunan saucers that are examples of advanced travel technology; in *Forbidden Planet*, the saucer is a human construction, used for exploration), it remains an important iconographical element within early attempts to categorize the science-fiction film genre.

The diegetic appearance of these flying saucers and the aliens inside them is often linked to the recent discovery of atomic or nuclear fission. Klaatu's flying saucer comes to earth because of atomic experiments; human expertise in nuclear power attracts the alien experts in *This Island Earth,* while both the *Invaders from Mars* and the *Killers from Space* appear close to nuclear test sites. Cultural perceptions of the atom bomb, and later the hydrogen bomb, would change during the 1950s, but science fiction films were broadly anti-nuclear power from the word go. Aside from drawing the unwelcome attention of alien visitors, atomic tests were capable of mutating ants and spiders into giant monsters (*Them!*, *Earth vs. the Spider*, 1958), destroying the planet (*The Day the World Ended*, 1955; *On the Beach*) or altering the human body (*The Incredible Shrinking Man*, 1957; *The Amazing Transparent Man*, 1960). Using atomic power, or some form of atomic radiation, was not unique to the 1950s. Radioactive substances had been the realm of the mad scientist during the 1930s and 1940s: *Dr Cyclops* (1940) used a radium formula to shrink people to 14 inches tall; while crooks used a radium-powered ray in *Ghost Patrol* (1936) to shoot down planes. With the development of atomic bombs by America and the Soviet Union, however, many science-fiction films dramatized atomic uncertainty.

Along with interest in real-world science, genre films often responded to changing perceptions of scientists, particularly in the new nuclear age. Real scientists, from Robert Oppenheimer to Edward Teller, remained problematic figures. Such scientists had invented the A-bomb and its use in Hiroshima and Nagasaki was initially seen as a positive development, at least in America. It sealed the USA's new-found position of superiority in world affairs, depicting it as a powerful, technologically advanced nation. The 1949 USSR atomic bomb tests led to anxiety over what the Soviets would do with such power and then, in 1950, Albert Einstein publicly asked both atomic powers not to produce hydrogen bombs. Amid growing concerns over how nuclear missiles might be used, and the destruction they could bring, the figure of the scientist in science fiction oscillated between its traditional role of instigator and unhinged Frankensteinian figure (as seen in Chapter 4) and a newer option, as a more heroic protagonist. Peter Biskind argues that many of these 1950s genre films dramatized a conflict between science (and scientists) and the military, with *Them!* showing scientists at the centre of events, finding solutions, and *The Thing From Another World* offering a scientist (Carrington) who will betray his human colleagues in order to study and befriend the alien monster (Biskind 1983). Tempting though this reading is, the depiction of science and scientists across this decade is much more complex and contradictory than those two examples. Professor Quatermass (Brian Donlevy), for example, contains elements of both Biskind's positions: he is abrasive and commanding, he causes the problem and discovers a way to eradicate it.[4] Equally, Dr Marvin (Hugh Marlowe) in *Earth vs the Flying Saucers* accidentally lures aliens to Earth, disobeys military orders so as to speak directly to them, and then develops a defence against the marauding saucers that are decimating cities around the globe. Marvin can be seen as mad scientist, sympathizer and heroic protagonist, changing persona as the narrative requires.

A central example of the 1950s mad scientist is Dr Morbius (Walter Pidgeon) from *Forbidden Planet*, whose quest for knowledge seems to have blunted his moral and social abilities. Literally discovering a new source of power on the distant world of Altair Four, Morbius has no idea what he has unleashed, or how to truly control it (a suggestive echo with the scientists of the 1940s Manhattan Project). As with many of the science fiction doctors and professors listed above, his sin is one of arrogance: the assumption of intellectual superiority blinds Morbius to real-world problems. The advanced technology of a vanished alien civilization, the Krell, has helped Morbius shape Altair Four in his own image, but he cannot control his own subconscious when a rescue team from Earth arrive on the planet. Rude, dismissive of his guests, and protective of his daughter, Morbius is never an evil figure but is ultimately undone by an assumption that he can control this new technology. Realizing the extent of his hubris, he sacrifices himself and destroys the Krell machines. The only remnant of this advanced technology is the robot-cum-butler, Robby, who is press-ganged into service as the spaceship 'astrogator', flying the inhabitants back to Earth.

Forbidden Planet is a unique science-fiction film on many levels: it was in Technicolor at a time when most genre films were black and white (the films of George Pal are the obvious exception here); it was Metro-Goldwyn-Mayer's first entry into the genre; it created arguably the first robotic star (Robby the Robot would appear in his own spin-off, *The Invisible Boy*, and other television and film appearances)[5] and it consolidated narrative assumptions central to later genre films. Most notably, it assumed that humanity would expand out to the stars and colonize new worlds, that exploration would function on a military basis and that humanity would be arriving at new planets in hyper-drive-capable spaceships. Space exploration was not a dominant theme of 1950s science fiction, despite the early presence of *Destination Moon* and *Rocketship X-M*. The former film suggested a privately funded expedition to the moon but there were few signs, in the early 1950s, that man was able to reach the stars. The lack of space travel narratives could be explained away by a compelling real-world narrative, as America and Russia entered what was described as a space race: both producing and testing liquid-fuelled rockets, developing intercontinental ballistic missiles (ICBMs) and then Russia putting Sputnik, a manmade satellite, into Earth orbit in October 1957 (and a dog in space a month later). By 1959, multiple satellites were orbiting the Earth (the US launched their own, Jupiter C, in January 1958), Russia had sent probes to the Moon, and both countries were actively pursuing manned spaceflight. Despite claims that *Destination Moon* could lead to 'a new interplanetary film cycle' (*Variety* 1950), real and fictional human space travel were both scarce in the 1950s.

Unidentified flying objects, the bomb, rocket tests, and the potential to put a man into space were key elements of this period of 'genrification', but they all represent an interest in advanced technology that swept across America in the postwar period. Credit cards, automatic doors, automobiles, and jet travel were now part of average, middle-class American life. It is possible to see science-fiction films responding to the new affluence around consumerist technology by returning to narratives and concerns around the ultimate labour-saving device: the robot. Robots in 1950s science fiction came in different shapes and sizes: from the giant man-shaped silver hulk of Gort to the more comical domed-headed figure of Robby the Robot. Genre narratives around such automatons quickly returned to the existing tropes developed before 1950: Robby goes from butler-cum-seamstress to out-of-control menace; Gort becomes an unstoppable weapon; while the introduction of a super-computer in *The Invisible Boy* predates other, later power-hungry artificial intelligences. Cinema's robot lineage offered few positive role models: the 'Bad' Maria of *Metropolis* remained the dominant (and indomitable) example. Yet some influence from literature, notably Isaac Asimov's *I, Robot* (1950), may have begun to filter in to 1950s robot characters. While both Robby and Gort remain indestructible they can be overcome through human emotion and intervention. Like Asimov's robots, Robby has been programmed not to harm a human, while Gort's destructive rampage is halted by a simple command. Like the earlier robotic images discussed in chapter four, these figures remain balanced between useful technology and rampaging machine, betraying a continuing uncertainty with mechanization even in a time period beholden to its products.

Robots, spaceships and flying saucers were examples of future technology that were often seen as spectacular images in science fiction films. But the 1950s also saw more down-to-earth technology utilized to enhance the spectacle such genre films could offer, through the use of special effects, 3-D, widescreen and colour filmmaking. Special effects technologies continued to advance through the decade, with Ray Harryhausen's stop-motion work on *Earth vs the Flying Saucers* and *20 Million Miles to Earth* developing and improving on earlier techniques. Model work and optical printing technologies were also enhanced by studio effects departments, particularly the Paramount team working with George Pal on his series of science-fiction films: *Destination Moon, When Worlds Collide, War of the Worlds* and *Conquest of Space*. The dominance of special effects within these prestige productions (also filmed in Technicolor) led to effects being promoted as 'Hollywood's newest screen star image ... The stars of George Pal's pictures **are** special effects' (*War of the Worlds* press book 1953, 6). Even at this early stage, producers such as Pal were aware that 'sophisticated film audiences could easily spot poorly executed visual effects' (Hickman 1975, 67) and worked hard to create an effective combination of effects, locations and actors. Despite the impressive display of (award-winning) visual effects in such films, low-budget genre filmmakers were often working with much more basic technologies. Men in monster suits, simple optical effects (back projection, 'invisible' aliens) and narrative devices ('body snatching' meant no need for elaborate alien costumes) could keep budgets down, and still provide effective genre entertainment.

Despite the introduction of these new technologies, the first flush of larger budget American science-fiction films was over by the mid-1950s. In 1955, shortly before the release of *Conquest of Space*, Paramount Studios stated that the science fiction 'fad' was over, and that 'such productions don't fit with Paramount's economic scheme' (quoted in Hickman 1977, 99). The big Hollywood studios were in financial problems during the 1950s, a combination of the Paramount decree of 1948 that forced all studios to divest themselves of their exhibition arms, a fall in cinema attendance, the growth of television, and the movement of large parts of American society from urban to suburban living (and therefore away from the major cinema chains). Studios closed or downsized their (often expensive) special effects departments, and focused attention on to popular, financially successful genres such as thrillers, Biblical epics and musicals. Through the late 1950s and into the 1960s, some studios continued to fund science fiction projects based around pre-existing book titles, but these featured more hybrid generic elements from comedy, action or melodrama (*On the Beach*; H.G. Wells' *First Men in the Moon*, 1964; *The Time Machine*; Jules Verne's *Rocket to the Moon*, 1967). The bulk of genre production in America was found in lower budget productions, fuelled by smaller studios such as Universal, or companies like American International Pictures and Republic, who produced quick, cheap genre fare for the now lucrative teenage market who flocked to double bills and drive-in theatres. Yet these low-budget genre films, with saturation booking and mass market promotional campaigns, offer an early industrial experimentation with new release patterns that would inform the campaigns for blockbusters such as *Star Wars* and *Close Encounters of the Third Kind*.

Against the dominance of the 1950s, there is a tendency to overlook the American science fiction films of the 1960s. There is no dominant view of Hollywood films of the period, no easy Cold War metaphor to apply, and (despite the real-world race to the Moon) few obvious cultural totems to link analysis to. Yet the 1960s are equally a decade of contrasts, producing at least two science-fiction films that represented a more adult turn for the genre (*2001: A Space Odyssey* and *Planet of the Apes*, 1968) and which had far-reaching effects on industrial attitudes towards generic products. This movement coincided with, and is perhaps a response to, an expansion of science-fiction filmmaking across the globe but particularly in Europe. The depiction of European cinema as artistic and critically acclaimed (particularly in contrast to American commercialism) stems from postwar cinema movements such as Italian neorealism and the French New Wave: films produced by film critics and writers who wanted to challenge the dominant film culture in their own countries and the outside influence of America. With an emphasis on realism and less melodramatic stories, there initially appeared to be no place for the fictional and melodramatic form of science fiction, at least as practised in 1950s Hollywood. Yet the films of Stanley Kubrick, Jean Luc Godard, Chris Marker, Alain Resnais and Francois Truffaut suggested new routes for science fiction or returned to earlier conventions that had lain dormant for decades. At the same time, other international cinemas, most notably in Britain and Japan, were producing variations on genre conventions and narratives that popularized precisely the melodramatic spectacle-fuelled science fiction beloved of Hollywood. Rather than see the 1960s science fiction genre as a simplistic choice between adult and juvenile, mainstream and arthouse, or studio and independent, it is necessary to consider what international science-fiction films contributed to generic conventions during these decades, what developments or challenges they offered to existing structures, and whether they offered a new direction for science fiction as the 1960s drew to a close.

Foreign Invasions

While it has been perceived as the dominant producer of 1950s science fiction, Hollywood was not the only national film industry to create such outer space dramas. The narrative, iconographic and cultural threads that came together to form ideas around the term 'science fiction' were drawn from multiple countries and sources. Germany, Britain, France, and the USSR all produced films that contributed ideas or conventions that influenced generic development before 1950 and the following two decades were no different. This section will focus mainly on those science fiction narratives produced by Britain, Japan, France and the USSR, in order to explore the alternative cultural concerns and notions around atomic power, alien invasion and the figure of the scientist that these national cinemas address.

One of the most dominant influences on later science fiction is Japan's *Gojira* (*Godzilla*, 1954), not least because of the subsequent industrial and cultural exploitation of its generic star image, a 150-foot tall prehistoric sea monster. Awakened and made radioactive by Japanese atomic tests, the creature is drawn back to Japan, where it wreaks havoc. The mutative properties of atomic power are an obvious concern here, particularly potent in a country still learning the long-term effects of the atomic bombs dropped on Hiroshima and Nagasaki. At several points in the film, there are pointed references to evacuating Tokyo 'again', or concerns that the Oxygen Destroyer (the only thing that might kill Godzilla) will be just as bad as A- and H-bombs. However, *Gojira* differs from similar American films (such as *Them!* or *The Beast From 20,000 Fathoms*) by presenting Godzilla as a star image, and potentially a tragic figure. Godzilla, although at heart a man in a monster suit rampaging through a model Tokyo, is the central draw in the film, ahead of any human stars. Across a series of sequels in the late 1950s and through the 1960s, Godzilla's status also changed from a mindless, destructive force to

Japan's protector from a range of other mutated, prehistoric or outer space menaces (the likes of Gorgo, Mothra and Mechagodzilla). Godzilla's star status was fuelled by further sequels, spinoffs and appearances: cross cultural projects such as *King Kong vs Godzilla* (1962), the television cartoon series *Godzilla* (1978–80) and an eventual Hollywood blockbuster adaptation in 1998. As the first iteration of what would grow to become a science fiction industry, *Gojira* represented a challenge to the dominance of American science fiction that was continued in other Japanese genre films.

Godzilla's most serious rival during the 1960s was *Gamera*, first seen in *Daikaiju Gamera* (*Gamera the Invincible*, 1965) and then in numerous sequels that followed the Godzilla model of creating new opponents for the star figure. Gamera, a prehistoric fire-breathing turtle also made the journey from terrorizing Tokyo to protecting Japanese children, monstrous threat turned ally. Other science fiction threats to Japan in the 1950s and 1960s added to generic imagery: flying saucers, often seen as an American obsession, bring aliens to Japan in both *Uchûjin Tôkyô ni arawaru/Warning From Space* (1956) and *Chikyû Bôeigun/The Mysterians* (1957).[6] The former contains elements of *The Day the Earth Stood Still* and *When Worlds Collide* in its story of star-shaped creatures that come to Earth to warn of an impending planetary collision. Although the film contains the traditional concerns about atomic power, it is ultimately pro-nuclear. The film's central scientific figure claims that power is only evil when used destructively; and when the World Congress agrees that the only way to save the Earth is to fire all atom and hydrogen bombs at the rogue planet, the film shows children cheering in classrooms. Far from being dangerous, here nuclear power is a useful scientific solution. *The Mysterians* is more traditional, both in featuring a monster destroying Tokyo and having advanced alien technology that (initially at least) human armies struggle to defeat. Like *Gojira, Daikaiju Gamera* and *Uchûjin Tôkyô ni arawaru* (and unlike many American science fiction films) the ability to resist and defeat the invaders comes from a joint effort between Japanese and international scientists. Japan's isolationist approach to world affairs pre-World War Two was now altered, with these science fiction films offering a view of the world as reliant on cultural interchange and knowledge.

Unlike Japan, Soviet science fiction from this time period was less international in scope, and more concerned with promoting the USSR space programme. Depictions of space explorations and more realistic science took the place of fantastic tales of mutated spiders, alien invasions or body snatchers. Like America, the Soviet Union had real-world success with what were previously science fiction concepts, most notably the Sputnik satellite orbiting the Earth and the first man in space. With political and cultural change after the death of Joseph Stalin (and the appointment of Nikita Khrushchev), there was an indirect increase in Soviet science fiction, both filmed and written. With all Soviet filmmaking state funded, many science fiction films offer allegorical tales of competition: North and South power blocs in *Niebo Zowiet/The Heavens Call* (1959); capitalist and communist viewpoints in *Chelovek-Amfibiya/The Amphibian Man* (1962); or Soviet scientific prowess in reaching Mars, or Venus ahead of any other country (as in *Planeta Burg/Storm Planet*, 1962). Western audiences were exposed to the technical skills of these Soviet science fictions (particularly the impressive special effects work on space stations, rocketships and robots) but in heavily edited, dubbed versions that had been refashioned for US and UK audiences by independent producers. In the case of *Planeta Burg*, the film was released twice in the US, under the titles *Voyage to the Prehistoric Planet* (1965, with additional scenes featuring Basil Rathbone) and *Voyage to the Planet of the Prehistoric Women* (1967, with new scenes of bikini-clad alien women added by Peter Bogdanovich). While it is possible to see signs of the original narrative and special effects, the subsequent re-edits and dubbing largely obscure the metaphoric nature of these Soviet genre entries. Despite the growth of science-fiction film and literature in the USSR across this decade, Western appreciation of these genre contributions would not be fully realized until the work of directors such as Andrei Tarkovsky was popularized through the 1970s and beyond.

Russia's apparent 'space race' with America left other countries eager to catch up. Britain was particularly reluctant to be left behind militarily, experimenting with both rockets and nuclear launch systems from the late 1940s into the 1960s. Yet Britain, no longer the head of an international Empire and still recovering from World War Two, struggled to assert itself in the new postwar world. The 1950s brought further change to the UK: the abolition of rationing in 1954 spurred a more consumerist society. The country's international standing was punished by the failure of its military campaign against Egypt during the Suez Crisis and there were challenges to traditional culture from rock n' roll, teenagers, increased immigration, and postwar ideas of female independence. The British film industry was also in upheaval: from a successful wartime production model to the postwar challenge offered by television, technology and teenagers. These disparate sources can all be seen in the growth of British science-fiction film in this period, but its focus on invasion and body-snatching is distinct from how those generic conventions appear in American films.

Sex is a central element identified by scholars of British science fiction: displayed as concerns over postwar female sexuality and empowerment in *Devil Girl From Mars* (1954); the teenage *coitus interruptis* by a phallic rocket crash landing in *The Quatermass Xperiment* (1955); in the presence of an atomic-fuelled alien attracted by sexual potency in *X – The Unknown* (1956); or disguised behind a narrative about 'alien' procreation in *Village of the Damned* (1960) (Chibnall 1999; Hutchings 1999; Cornea 2007) . In the first of those films, the female Martian invader comes to Earth to acquire male breeding stock (Figure 5.1). Nyah (Patricia Laffan) represents conflicting viewpoints on female independence. She is always in command, domineering, sexually aggressive and strong, from a Mars where women have been emancipated for centuries. Yet she is also dressed in leather, with a short skirt, fishnet stockings and long black leather boots, 'straight from the pages

Figure 5.1 Martian 'devil girl' Nyah (Patricia Laffan) invades a small Scottish village on the hunt for men, not atomic power (British Lion Film Corporation/Photofest)

of a fifties fetish magazine' (Chibnall 1999, 63). Few science-fiction films offer as strong a female figure, yet she is the film's antagonist, in a narrative where audiences were presumably supposed to be rooting for the (largely bland) human characters. This striking, sexualized Martian 'devil girl' is also dismissive of the concerns of American science fiction: Mars women need Earthmen for sex, not because they have split the atom.

If Nyah represented fears over increased female sexual power, the invasion of *Village of the Damned* dramatized concerns over another form of human-alien procreation. Here, the alien monsters look like human children, they do not arrive in spaceships or with robot helpers, but through the mysterious impregnation of all the women in a small English village: an insidious invasion rather than an overt one. Based on John Wyndham's novel *The Midwich Cuckoos*, the film depicts a group of children who, once born, grow at an amazing rate, and are influenced and controlled by an alien (foreign) power, while British parents, doctors and other authority figures are helpless against them. Rather than metaphors for Cold War agents or the loss of American individualism, these children appear to stand for a loss of British nationality or cultural patriotism: they do not regard themselves as part of the village, or country, but are beyond that. This variety of subtle invasion, a hallmark of Wyndham's work, is present in other British science fiction films (*Quatermass*

2, 1957; *They Came From Beyond Space*, 1967) and appears to be as rooted in Britain's specific cultural status. These invasions have been read as commentary on the fear of 'alien' agents hiding in Britain during the Second World War but, given the late 1950s setting, is more likely a response to the perceived domination of alien cultures: American consumerism specifically but perhaps also the various immigrants arriving from former British colonies (Hutchings 1999, 35–6).

British science-fiction films, like the wider British film industry, can be seen as sitting between Europe and Hollywood, wanting to play in the same generic sandbox but also engaging with science fiction narratives drawn from respected literature sources. The development of this quality production can be seen in several genre films produced in Britain (most notably Stanley Kubrick's Cuban Missile crisis satire *Dr Strangelove, or How I Learned to Stop Worrying and Love the Bomb*, 1964; and *2001: A Space Odyssey*), as well as in science fiction from some of the most prominent members of the French New Wave. Francois Truffaut came to Britain to make *Fahrenheit 451* (1962), an adaptation of the Ray Bradbury novel that offers a grim dystopia where government censorship has outlawed reading and created 'firemen' whose job is to burn every remaining book. Truffaut offers a visually startling version of the future, creating a bleached, washed out world where the only splashes of colour are the red engines of the firemen and the flames that consume the books. The aesthetic and narrative fatalism that runs through *Fahrenheit 451* offers a compelling and stylistically distinct depiction of the future that, like other British science fiction, sits somewhere between European arthouse and American commercial cinema.

Truffaut's fellow French filmmaker, Jean Luc Godard, created his own vision of the future in *Alphaville, une étrange aventure de Lemmy Caution* (1965). Less concerned with creating a coherent genre narrative than to provide a commentary on pulp fiction, cinema and genre hybridity, *Alphaville* has been described as veering 'from satirically tongue-in-cheek futurism, to a parody of private-eye mannerisms, to a wildly romantic allegory depicting a computer controlled society at war with artists, thinkers and lovers' (Sarris 2008). Godard's film constantly challenges audiences' sense of what science fiction is (or could be). It is a film about the future that makes no attempt to construct an artificial *mise en scène* or use special effects techniques. Instead, it relies on canted angles and night-time views of modernist 1960s architecture in Paris. The film is an investigation of a distant world (in both space and time) yet characters make references to twentieth century events and people. There are science fiction tropes at work – the fascistic future society, the mad scientist, the super-computer – but the main character (Lemmy Caution, played by Eddie Constantine) is a noir-ish private detective 'borrowed' from contemporary pulp thrillers, and the mad scientist is known as Nosferatu and Von Braun, potent links to German Expressionism, the horror genre, real world rocket science, and the American push towards sending a man to the moon. The playful nature of *Alphaville* is part of its appeal, and the science fiction trappings are simply part of a larger commentary on cinema and genre. Despite this, its application of nouvelle vague sensibilities to the genre, and interest in generic hybridity, emphasized a more intellectual brand of science fiction that would be influential on the genre through the 1970s and 1980s.

Alongside Godard and Truffaut's work sits one of the key films of the French nouvelle vague, *L'Année dernière à Marienbad* (*Last Year at Marienbad*, 1961). The film is rarely talked about as science fiction, yet its complex and shifting notion of time links it to narratives around time travel, spatial uncertainty and unreliable memory. While it is counterproductive to attempt to reduce the film to its narrative elements, the recurring features of movement in time, the impossibility of recapturing a specific moment in space and time, and the graphic complexity of the world it creates, all recur in more mainstream considerations of time travel and temporal discontinuity (perhaps most clearly in other combinations of time travel, memory and romance such as *Somewhere in Time*, 1980; *Eternal Sunshine of the Spotless Mind*; and *The Time Traveller's Wife*). Resnais himself would produce a more explicit meditation on time travel in *Je t'aime, je t'aime* (1968), where the protagonist used a time machine to relive a previous (and tragic) love affair. Given the contemporary lack of time travel stories in the wider field of science fiction film (only George Pal's adaptation of Wells' *The Time Machine* had had any popular success), Resnais' films create an intellectual bridge between the machinery of cinema to record and edit time with uniquely cinematic narratives of memory and loss. Along with Chris Marker's *La Jetée* (1962), a compelling short film assembled through a montage of still photographs that features almost no moving images, these French films explore the circular fate of time travel narratives, their link to memory and their mechanistic ties to the machinery of cinema itself (a machine that records and projects past events, literally recreating time). While the future success of time travel narratives owes a debt to science fiction writers such as Wells and Ray Bradbury (particularly *A Sound of Thunder*), the look and complexity of later temporal stories is also beholden to these artistic experiments.

Like other science fictions from around the world, many of these European, Japanese and Russian films were either designed in opposition to, or to gain admission to, the Hollywood system. Their ability to present new variations on existing generic tropes, or to challenge existing narrative structures, can (in retrospect) be seen as part of an ongoing maturation of science fiction topics within international cinema. This process can be understood in relation to the new industrial rival of television, where science fiction programmes as diverse as *The Adventures of Superman* (1952–7), *A For Andromeda* (1961), *Doctor Who* (1963–), *The Twilight Zone* 1959–64) and *Star Trek* (1966–9) were now available weekly (and free) to television viewers. Like the rest of the film industry, many global science fiction films of this time period tried to compete by moving fully into colour (*The Day of the Triffids*, 1962; *The Mouse on the Moon*, 1963; *Robinson Crusoe on Mars*, 1964), or by offering more advanced special effects spectacles (*The Time Machine*; *Barbarella*, 1967). Some projects embraced the possibilities of adapting television success for the big screen: including Hammer's three Quatermass adaptations and two *Doctor Who* films of the mid-1960s (*Dr Who and the Daleks*, 1964; *Daleks: Invasion Earth 2150 AD*). Yet the real push for filmmakers appeared to be finding stories that would be too 'big' for the small screen, a more epic form of narrative that required a larger budget to produce the necessary spectacle:

> *2001: A Space Odyssey* is the dividing line. Before it, any trip beyond the Earth's atmosphere was more a vision of pure fantasy than hard fact; stars twinkled, planets seemed forged in a Hammond globe factory, spaceships zipped about as if they were mere trinkets yanked along on piano wire ... after *2001* such illusions died a rapid death. (Persons 1994, 32)

2001: A Space Odyssey offered a pure science fiction and special effects spectacle, and has rightly been highlighted as an important moment within science-fiction cinema, particularly its claims to have moved beyond the juvenile. The film created new (or adapted existing) visual effects techniques, from early motion control to front projection and slit-scan for the final Stargate sequence.[7] Yet the claims that *2001* changed everything, this notion of it representing a 'dividing line' are misleading. *2001* builds on previous iterations of generic conventions (space travel, advanced technology, the unreliability of machines and computers) and relies on genre knowledge from mainstream and arthouse films, as well as literature and real-world space missions. Where *Metropolis* and *Things to Come* looked to the future of Earth, *2001* returns to the science fact (or scientific realism) of *Frau im Mond* or *Destination Moon*, repositioning science fiction towards the stars: not as a source of invasion (as in *The Thing From Another World*'s ominous 'Look to the skies' warning of 1951) but as the next step for humanity. It is a philosophical piece of filmmaking, reliant on (but never overwhelmed by) its technology (diegetic and otherwise), drawing from the Soviet and French filmmaking discussed above, as well as the 'pure fantasy' of Hollywood's previous imagined space trips. Its dominance as visual spectacle in the late 1960s, as well as in discussions of genre classics in the year since, is predicated as much on its development of existing generic traits as its innovative and unique qualities.

For all its popularity, scale and importance, however, *2001: A Space Odyssey* had little immediate impact on other science fiction films. As a monument to a particular vision of space travel and futurity, it largely stands alone. It offered a route to special effects-dominated spectacle, but there was no industry infrastructure to expand these new technologies to other productions. George Lucas has noted that it 'was the big special effects movie, but it was so big and expensive and awesome that it really didn't open up a lot of other possibilities, other than to be an inspiration that effects could be done in a quality way.' (quoted in Vaz and Duignan 1996, 6) The idea that *2001* was designed as an experience rather than a conventional narrative (it was first released in 70mm Cinerama prints, to select theatres) was also a concern for studio executives whose overriding interest was to make money: a particular issue in a time period when Hollywood studios were being bought by larger conglomerates that saw decreasing returns from the kind of 'roadshow' distribution formats that had been used for earlier spectacle-based films such as *Oklahoma* (1957) and *The Sound of Music* (1965). Kubrick's film was a puzzle: expensive and groundbreaking, generic but unique, financially successful but difficult to copy or reiterate. As a maverick hit, *2001: A Space Odyssey* was feted, but as the blueprint for science-fiction moving forward into the 1970s, it presented a series of problems.

Hollywood studios are traditionally pictured as companies that prefer their science fiction to be based on generically recyclable material, projects that provided known pleasures, films that were more melodramatic and action-packed than philosophical and poetic. Towards the end of the 1960s, Twentieth Century Fox produced a film that combined the recyclable with the poetic, and merged known generic pleasures with the philosophical nature of recent genre successes. *Planet of the Apes* had a vision of space travel that was fast-paced, dangerous and dynamic, combining elements of *Flash Gordon* and *Forbidden Planet* in a tale of four astronauts catapulted across space (and time) to a planet where apes are the dominant species and humans are dumb, servile savages. Yet at the same time, the film's overt commentary on American race (and international) relations draws from the history of adult and allegorical science fiction studied in this last section. These adult themes are not solely present in the text, but were highlighted in the film's publicity, with the press book stating it was 'an allegory for our times … an unusual and important motion picture.' While the studio was keen to link the genre's adult themes to its status as an adaptation (a common theme in 1960s studio science fiction film publicity), a series of pre-release quotations from the press book reveals critics were less focused on allegory and more on traditional Hollywood conventions: 'the tingling realism of the camera work and action sequences' (Kathleen Carroll, *New York Daily Press*), or 'the ingenious kind of plotting that people love to talk about' (Pauline Kael, *The New Yorker*). In many senses, *Planet of the Apes* offered Hollywood studios a new generic case study, a commercial antidote to Kubrick's *2001: A Space Odyssey*. With its melodrama, open-ended narrative, possibility for sequels (including, eventually, a television series) and scope for merchandising, *Planet of the Apes* ended the 1960s with a vision of the future of science-fiction film.

Conclusion

By the end of the 1960s, although the science fiction genre had not returned to the heights of the early 1950s, it was capable of sustaining three distinct production trends: the occasional studio blockbuster adaptation of science fiction literature (from *The Time Machine* to *Planet of the Apes*), the perennially popular low budget/exploitation companies (which now distributed re-edited foreign genre films alongside American and British product) and art house cinema releases that combined more esoteric subject matter with original aesthetic approaches. While Europe, the USSR and Japan offered alternative science fiction filmmaking styles and practices, Hollywood remained the dominant source of filmed science-fiction entertainment (in cinemas and on television). The growing international contribution to the science fiction genre had added subtle alien invasions, fears about nuclear power, dystopian futures and obsessions with revisiting the past to more traditional conventions around space exploration, mechanization and science run amok. In 1969, mainstream Hollywood producers had two financially successful genre products to look at for future expansion and imitation; two films that represented distinct variations on classic generic narrative tropes. *Planet of the Apes* was an adventure film with action, special effects, star cast, occasional political undertones and a classic American astronaut hero in the mould of Buck Rogers or Flash Gordon. *2001: A Space Odyssey*, meanwhile, was a meditation on the future of humanity, with exceptional special effects and a dense collection of ideas on evolution, alien intervention and rebirth. Science fiction as a cinema of ideas or science fiction as a cinema of high-paced, populist action-adventure: as the film industry moved into the 1970s, it was difficult to know which vision of genre would dominate.

–6–

1970–90: Science Fiction and the Blockbuster

At the end of the 1960s, one narrative element of science fiction became fact. On 20 July 1969, the Apollo 11 astronauts landed on the Moon. The topic of countless stories in literature, film and television was now reality. How did this impact the science-fiction genre as it moved into the 1970s? Chapter 5 argued that input from international genre films had helped legitimize mature mainstream American science fiction film, culminating in the popular success of *2001: A Space Odyssey* and *Planet of the Apes*. Along with the moon landing, 1969 also saw the release of *Marooned*, a space-based disaster movie about the race to save astronauts trapped in orbit. A discussion of the morality of sending men into space, *Marooned* continued the trend towards adult, dramatic stories while extending the realist approach to science fiction seen since *Frau im Mond* and *Destination Moon*. If science fiction can be defined as a genre that 'opens us up to new perspectives and imagines what might happen if things we took for granted were destroyed ... or altered' (Jenkins 2010) then the two decades covered in this chapter represent a wealth of examples of the kind of altered perspective and fantastic imagination the genre is capable of. NASA may have put a man on the moon, but the science fiction film continued to push further into outer space, and offered more complex ideas about the possible futures for the planet.

American science fiction of the early 1970s explored this intellectual and allegorical side of science fiction in both the mainstream and low budget exploitation sectors. The existing racial and political metaphors of the *Planet of the Apes* series expanded to include a thinly veiled commentary on black militancy in *Conquest of the Planet of the Apes* (1972) but such studio-led efforts were easily matched by independent films such as *Gas-s-s! Or It Becomes Necessary to Destroy the World in Order to Save It* (1970), which linked its poison gas narrative to the US annihilation of Vietnamese village Ben Tre (Franklin 1990, 22). Such real-world concerns may explain the abundance of Earthbound narratives in the early part of the decade (though budgetary restrictions are equally likely) but the presence of real space travel, astronauts and outer space landscapes did appear to fuel filmmakers' desires to return to the more fantastic realms of science fiction. Existing genre conventions that defied contemporary events and science (time travel, alien invaders, fantastic explorations and visions of the future) were resurgent from the late 1970s and through the 1980s, driven by the success of *Star Wars* and *Close Encounters of the Third Kind*. George Lucas' film series remains a dominant phenomenon because of the narrative and aesthetic impact it had on both science fiction and larger cultural assumptions about the genre, yet both films pushed science fiction and the effects-led narrative towards the centre of blockbuster production. As worldwide film production moved into the 1980s and beyond, the combination of generic pleasure, family entertainment and high-concept storytelling found in *Star Wars* would continue to fuel mainstream genre successes and offer a new definition of science fiction entertainment, even as the film that fuelled it all was accused of bringing 'childishness' and 'infantilism' to the film industry (Wood 2003, 147).

This time period represents more than a simple move from adult to juvenile filmmaking, though, and it is necessary to move beyond the success of *Star Wars* and its industrial impact in order to understand the shifting nature of the science-fiction genre. In cinema, this was the period of *A Clockwork Orange*, *Videodrome* and *Brazil* as much as the industrial light and magic of George Lucas and Steven Spielberg: but filmed science fiction was only one branch of a shifting generic network, only one contributory factor to any larger cultural understanding or definition of 'science fiction'. Although science-fiction film is often regarded as lagging behind written science fiction, the same period saw an interest in more intellectual narratives, space fantasy hybrids and the birth of cyberpunk from established writers Arthur C. Clarke, Frank Herbert and Larry Niven, and new talents such as Iain M. Banks and William Gibson. Televised science fiction adopted more adult themes (*Doomwatch*, 1970–2; *Blake's 7*, 1977–81) yet also provided more familiar fantastic or comic book approaches (*Space 1999*, 1975–8; *Buck Rogers in the Twenty-Fifth Century*, 1979–81; *V*, 1984–5). While some televised science fiction attempted analogous representations of contemporary issues (episodes of 1970s *Doctor Who* have been read as a commentary on British politics, racial attitudes, and industrial problems – see Tulloch and Jenkins, 1999), American television of the period can also be seen as restorative, a reaction against the recent failure of Vietnam and the resignation of President Richard Nixon, a chance to reassert (if only fictionally) the country's strength and claims of world leadership (Wright [1975] 2009, 95).

This wider generic framework necessarily crosses over with the changing cultural and political landscape of the 1970s and 1980s. These two decades represent a series of potent forces that affected science-fiction filmmaking, not least the expansion of feminism and gay rights, the 1970s global economic problems, the influence of Ronald Reagan's presidency (particularly around the cultural construction of masculine values) and the shifting geopolitics that saw a thaw in the Cold War. Equally, industrial developments altered how science fiction films could look, with the motion control technology of *2001: A Space Odyssey* improved and computerized to radically change the fluidity and speed of special-effects shots. Dominant from the late 1970s on, the speed of technological change across these decades was such that even in the mid-1980s, the introduction of basic computer-generated imagery was a sign of things to come, an early (if often unsuccessful) suggestion of future transformations. Away from film production, technology was key to debates around new dissemination methods for genre texts. With television now an established part of genre production, home video releases provided a new distribution and exhibition circuit for lower budget genre films, eventually replacing the American drive-in/'exploitation' exhibition model by the late 1980s. While the early years of the home video were dogged with debates over content (the British 'video nasty' furore around horror films specifically) they represent a crucial bridge that allowed audiences to explore mainstream and alternative genre filmmaking.

To varying degrees, then, these elements of real life science, cultural and political events and technological change affected the science fiction genre between 1970 and 1990, particularly as it became enmeshed within the developing Hollywood studio cycle of blockbuster production. These films also further an increased genre hybridity within film production: family science fiction, science fiction comedy, or military/science fiction stories were relatively rare before this period but grew in dominance over the years being covered. As has been clear in previous chapters, the science fiction genre is never constant, never easily defined but continually adapting and shifting. While many films from these two decades recall (directly or indirectly) previous genre success, many international genre productions from this time period offer unique developments of traditional genre notions around scientific progress, the figure of the alien invader and visions of the future. In the following sections, these broader genre features will be considered in more depth, to explore their specific uses within this timeframe.

1970–7: Maturity and Early Themes

Between 1970 and 1977, adult science fiction themes appeared in international mainstream and arthouse genre films. These films cover alien infection (*The Andromeda Strain*, 1970), population overcrowding (*Z.P.G.*, 1972; *Soylent Green*), the rise of dictatorial societies (*Conquest of the Planet of the Apes*; *Sleeper*, 1972), surveillance technology (*THX 1138*), postapocalyptic survival (*The Omega Man*; *A Boy and His Dog*, 1974; *Beneath the Planet of the Apes*, 1970) and the psychological impact of first contact with a totally alien life form (*Solaris*, 1973). Reflectionist critics (see Chapter 2) have read American films of this time as a response to a decade of social upheaval around political assassination, global financial chaos, the impact of Vietnam and the revelations around President Nixon, Watergate and his resignation from office. H. Bruce Franklin encapsulates this approach by noting that 'visions of decay and doom had become the normal Anglo-American cinematic view of our possible future' (Franklin 1990, 17). Although such films may indeed be seen as attempts to construct a view of the present by positing a particular (dystopian) future, it remains important to think of them in relation to a wider generic field and upheavals within Hollywood itself, as well as simply representing societal issues.

The late 1960s and early 1970s is seen as a disruptive moment in Hollywood history, a time when the established idiosyncratic studio system became part of a larger corporate and conglomerate structure, losing many of the distinctive characteristics that made each studio a distinctive brand in its own right. Robin Wood describes the 'central theme of the American cinema' of this period (not simply those in the science fiction genre) as 'disintegration and breakdown' stating that many films became 'super-productions, producers' rather than directors' movies, studio-dominated with a minimal intervention of individual creativity' (Wood [1986] 2003, 24–5). While Wood draws the obvious reflectionist links with Vietnam, feminism, gay liberation and black militancy, it is this breakdown of the traditional Hollywood film industry that points up many of the contradictions of the time period.

The failures of the studio system in the 1960s and the rise of a supposedly more adult and auteurist studio-based filmmaking has been covered in detail elsewhere (see particularly, Biskind 1998), but such accounts tend to ignore the popular success and mainstream generic entertainment that attracted 1970s audiences. The success of films such as *Love Story, Airport* (both 1970), *Fiddler on the Roof, The French Connection* (both 1971), and *The Poseidon Adventure* (1972) point towards a continued audience interest in generic filmmaking rather than adult or director-led works: these are films that foreground generic issues around love, musical numbers and disaster scenarios. While the biggest grossing science fiction film of the early 1970s is *A Clockwork Orange*, with a strong presence based around both auteur and censorship debates, there are several films (the James Bond entries *Diamonds are Forever*, 1971; *Live and Let Die*, 1973; some of the larger scale disaster movies) that obviously borrow from generic concepts around advanced technology, megalomaniac scientists and visually destructive possible futures.[1] In the years immediately pre-*Star Wars*, one of the most popular science fiction films was a British genre hybrid that borrowed from many of the popular categories listed above. The third most successful film at the US box office in 1975 (figures quoted in Shone 2004, 43), *The Rocky Horror Picture Show* offered a potent combination of science fiction, horror, musical and parody but was, at its heart, a nostalgic film about pre-conglomerate Hollywood, 1950s exploitation releases, the 'double feature' cinema programme, and 'classic' science-fiction films from *The Day the Earth Stood Still* to *The Day of the Triffids*.

Such audience figures suggest that science fiction films were rarely blockbusters in the early 1970s. The continued presence of genre films, therefore, can be best explained through a combination of elements: the (alleged) new openness Biskind identifies within Hollywood studios (for example, Francis Ford Coppola being able to fund George Lucas' dystopic *THX 1138*), a reliance on the adaptation of existing literature (particularly presold popular novels such as those by Harry Harrison and Michael Crichton), or developing sequels (the *Planet of the Apes* series on film, television and in comic books). Despite the claims made for this period by writers such as Wood and Biskind, corporate mainstream Hollywood acted as the old studio system had, pursuing genre projects with built-in audience success (adaptations, sequels, remakes) or which were created partially in the generic image of what had gone before. The production and release of George Lucas's *Star Wars* can be seen in this light, particularly given Lucas's original desire to make *Flash Gordon*. Yet the success of the film he did make revitalized and limited the science-fiction genre for the next decade and beyond.

Star Wars and the Genre Blockbuster, 1977–90

Robin Wood has said that the success of George Lucas's *Star Wars* challenged any claim for American cinema's newfound maturity. Although not specifically talking about generic identity, this statement does fit with other claims of *Star Wars* as a force for both good and evil within the changing Hollywood film industry. Commonly seen as a turning point for the genre, *Star Wars* actually built on the lessons learnt from *Planet of the Apes*, as well as previous genre successes such as the 1930s *Flash Gordon* serials. With this 'radical amalgamation of genre conventions and … elaborate play of cinematic references' (Schatz 1993, 23). Lucas (and his film) have become enshrined as a key player in the 'New Hollywood' of linear plotting, kinetic action, one-dimensional (or archetypal) characters and special effects movies aimed at a younger audience. Since the film's release, Lucas has successfully positioned (and repositioned) it in relation to culturally legitimate debates around mythology and narrative structure (most notably, Joseph Campbell's *Man of a Thousand Myths*), as well as lower cultural forms such as comic books and more esoteric arthouse links to Japanese cinema. The film also impacted social and political rhetoric, with US president Ronald Reagan's description of the Soviet Union as the 'Evil Empire' and his favoured space-based weapon known as the 'Star Wars' project. The purpose of this section is, however, not to judge the merits of *Star Wars* as an individual film but to consider the impact it had on generic production and the cultural awareness of generic traits through the 1980s and beyond.

On an aesthetic level, the film's set and model design emphasizes a dirty, often ugly view of space travel: sleek white X-wing fighters are overshadowed by the ungainly grey *Millennium Falcon*; the spherical Death Star is, in close-up, actually a complex pocked and spiky surface; the film cuts from long, clean corridors to sand-swept dunes, from grey control rooms to messy trash compactors. This develops elements of the dystopian cityscape of *Soylent Green* and the desert habitat of *Planet of the Apes*, while lacking the clean lines and beauty of *2001* or *Things to Come*. The focus on the fantastic future (or this 'long, long ago' past) as an often unpleasant, lived-in, and overwhelmingly human place would recur in *Alien, Outland* and *Space Hunter: Adventures in the Forbidden Zone*. Yet as earlier genre films have shown, this view of the future was not unique: the underworld of *Metropolis* is not pleasant or clean lined, it is dirty and industrial; while sleek futuristic cities are often contentious and diegetically dangerous spaces, from *Things to Come* to *Logan's Run*

(1976). *Star Wars'* use of these spaces re-emphasized its nostalgic look back at other generic forms, particularly the desert landscape of Tatooine and the conventional dusty open plains of the Western.

In narrative terms, *Star Wars* redirected genre attention back to the stars and away from the Earthbound focus of the early 1970s. After *Star Wars*, the starfield, spaceship design and motion control-emulated star travel dominated international genre production, with films that either attempted a direct emulation (*Battle Beyond the Stars*; *Giochi erotici nella 3a galassia/Escape from Galaxy 3*, 1981; *The Last Starfighter*, 1984) or used that genre success (and popularity) as a springboard to explore other corners of the genre (*Alien*; *Outland*; *Aliens*; *Enemy Mine*). *Star Wars* is also the film that launched the technology company Industrial Light and Magic (ILM), now one of the most dominant special effects houses in Hollywood. Industrial Light and Magic created a new motion control system for *Star Wars* and revolutionized the role of special effects within filmmaking, with particular impact on the science fiction and fantasy genres (Shone 2004). Yet *Star Wars'* impact on technology goes beyond the realm of special effects. The release of *Star Wars* on VHS in the early 1980s was seen as one of the key releases that legitimized the new home video format. Before the main film was released for rental (originally seen as the main revenue route for video, as opposed to individual ownership of tapes) Lucasfilm also authorized the release of *The Making of Star Wars* (1980), which became one of the best selling straight-to-video releases. During the 1980s, and into the 1990s, numerous releases of *Star Wars* and its sequels on video would dominate the market, emphasizing the film's role in defining genre characteristics for a new audience. *Star Wars* videos also fuelled new technological developments: the launch of Fox Widescreen Video (and the concurrent push towards widescreen televisions) at the end of the 1980s was backed with the re-release of all three *Star Wars* films, a suggestion that widescreen pleasure and genre identity were intrinsically linked (Johnston 2009, 198). *Star Wars'* role in the financial success and popularization of the video format can be linked to the growing audience access to low-budget genre projects such as *Damnation Alley* (1977) and *L'umanoide/The Humanoid* (1979), which were more successful through video distribution than traditional cinema exhibition. At the same time, the home video business increased audience awareness of older science fiction films from the 1950s and before, many of which provided the generic building blocks that Lucas had constructed his universe around.

With the success of *Star Wars*, its ever-expanding merchandising empire, its video release and its sequels, the film became a franchise case study that emulated and expanded on Twentieth Century Fox's previous success *Planet of the Apes*. Both big- and low-budget filmmakers clearly saw it as a template for generic entertainment that they could follow, and deviate, from, while the studios were happy to have a financial model that worked. In terms of international genre production, the film could be borrowed from, challenged or subverted. Meanwhile, audiences appeared eager for similar summer blockbuster entertainment. As the 1970s ended, the role of science fiction within this 'new Hollywood' would be emphasized by the mainstream success of genre blockbusters *Close Encounters of the Third Kind*, *Superman* (1978) and *Moonraker* (1979). Yet, as these examples suggest, generic pleasure was not simply limited to outer space adventure. *Star Wars* may have been a highly influential model for fantastic science fiction narratives, but as the genre moved into the 1980s, the bulk of alien exploration occurred not out in the stars but back on planet Earth.

Invasion Earth

Given the focus on invasion threats in the 1950 and 1960s, the 1970s saw a drastic reduction in the number of genre narratives concerned about overt alien attack.[2] The cinema's focus in the first half of the decade on issues around the environment or dystopian futures meant that, from the lowest budget to the highest, physical invasion was limited to outer space microbes (*The Andromeda Strain*; *Invasion of the Body Snatchers*, 1978), viruses (*The Alpha Incident*, 1977), mind-reading alien planet forms (*Solaris*), alien-infected 'Zones' (*Stalker*, 1979) or (echoing the 1950s giant insect invasions) alien and mutated insects (*The Giant Spider Invasion*, 1975; *Empire of the Ants*, 1977). Physically threatening invaders were scarce: there were humanoid alien 'invaders' in *The Rocky Horror Picture Show*, *The Man Who Fell to Earth* (1976) and *Superman* but they were mostly concerned with helping mankind rather than subjugating the planet. The aliens of *Close Encounters* and *Star Trek: The Motion Picture* (1979) were rarely glimpsed, but appeared to be inquisitive explorers, not imperial conquerors. Only Japanese science fiction (*Chikyû kogeki meirei: Gojira tai Gaigan/War of the Monsters*, 1972) and the 1950s sequel *Beware! The Blob* (1972) represented physical alien threats. The return from a galaxy far, far away to Earth in the 1980s, however, was accompanied by a series of narratives that combined the adventure and special effects-led spectacle of *Star Wars* with a renewed focus on tales of Earth invasion.

Academic and popular critical work on the 1980s science fiction film has tended to canonize certain films above others. Those films, which would include *The Terminator*, *Blade Runner*, *The Thing* (1982), *Predator* and *The Abyss* (1989), all represent Earthbound narratives of invasion, whether that invader comes from the future, has been buried under the Arctic ice, is hunting victims in an unnamed rainforest, or has lain dormant beneath the oceans. While the 1980s saw continuing brinksmanship and hostility between the USA and the Soviet Union, these films (and less canonized options such as the British science fiction-horror hybrid *Lifeforce*; or science-fiction comedy *Morons from Outer Space*, 1985) have not been commonly read as renewed Cold War fears, or fears of the Soviet 'other' invading (unlike, say, *Red Dawn*, 1984). These 1980s alien invaders were harder to categorize, partly because of the different political and cultural climate but also because of the growing hybridization of the genre, most notably with the supposed new 'action' genre and the rise of masculinized star figures such as Sylvester Stallone and Arnold Schwarzenegger.

Two of the most famous alien invasion narratives of the 1980s, *The Thing* and *Predator*, are closely tied up with these complex issues around stardom, masculinity, and claims of right-wing 'Reaganite' entertainment that link the films to their hybrid status as science fiction-action cinema. Robin Wood and Andrew Britton have both dismissed action films in this time period as 'mechanical and external' (Britton 1986, 2); predictable, ideologically and narratively repetitive, and difficult to analyse 'seriously' (Wood 1986 [2003], 146). As with the discussion of *Star Wars* and blockbuster cinema above, however, it has been observed that such criticism is more concerned with the narrative, mood and tone of such films, often eliding the role of the audience in selecting and enjoying such generic entertainments (Tasker 1993, 59–60). Looking at such films as hybrid genres requires the awareness that they are 'polysemic, speaking or not speaking to different audiences in different ways' (Tasker 1993, 61). Both *The Thing* and *Predator* engage with long-running conventions of the science fiction film (shape-shifting, invisibility, remote locations, the suggestion of infiltration and the figure of the 'Other') while also balancing tropes from action cinema (an emphasis on masculinity, visual spectacle, physical effects-based set pieces). Yet both films, along with *Aliens, They Live* (1988) and *Masters of the Universe* also bring a more masculine, militaristic tone to science fiction-action films that seems unique to this moment in film history.

Britton's term 'Reaganite' entertainment is relevant here, because of the links he draws between a resurgent American right-wing political viewpoint (represented by Ronald Reagan's presidency) and the (alleged) turn Hollywood made towards a right-wing agenda in action cinema more generally. From this stance, *Predator*, a film about a black ops military unit sent into a jungle warzone can be read as a reflection of America's growing military might in the 1980s, or, given its jungle setting, a redressing of a national setback, with Arnold Schwarzenegger's Dutch finally 'winning' Vietnam against a seemingly invisible enemy.[3] While such readings can be criticized for being narratively reductive (and reflectionist) they also ignore a more interesting question about the role of the male action star and the debates this figure raises around masculinity and genre entertainment. Kurt Russell (*The Thing, Escape From New York*, 1981), Arnold Schwarzenegger (*The Terminator, Predator, The Running Man*, 1987), Dolph Lundgren (*Masters of the Universe, Dark Angel*, 1989), and Roddy Piper (*They Live*) all feature in popular science fiction-action movies of the 1980s that position masculine values in a specific way. The latter three (Schwarzenegger, Lundgren and Piper) are also famous for moving from body-building, karate and wrestling to acting, with an emphasis on their 'hard bodies' as one source of visual spectacle.

Science fiction of the 1980s, however, cannot be reduced to such a small selection of films, one political viewpoint, or one version of masculinity. A more rounded form of masculinity could be found in one of the genre's most successful franchises, the *Star Trek* series, particularly around Captain James T. Kirk (William Shatner). Culturally renowned (and often mocked) as an intergalactic lothario in the 1960s television series, Kirk's masculinity is interrogated and overhauled for the film series. The films revisit his chequered romantic past (in the shape of an ex-lover and a son), explore the homosocial relationship he enjoys with Mr Spock and Dr McCoy, and examine how other forms of masculinity (represented by genetically engineered superhuman, Khan Noonien Singh, played by Ricardo Montalban, or the omnipresent warrior race, the Klingons) are potentially outmoded in the *Star Trek* view of the future. Kirk is still a man of action, still has potential as a romantic lead (most noticeably in *Star Trek IV: The Voyage Home*, 1986), but the series' aging cast members introduced a noticeable shift that questioned the easy notions of masculine action that the 1960s series often took for granted. In many ways, the change seen in Kirk could be traced through action stars such as Schwarzenegger and Stallone as their careers moved into the 1990s, where both stars embraced broader roles that integrated them within family and comic roles.

Family Science Fiction Films

Despite their popularity and ability to protect the earth from alien invasion, Schwarzenegger, Stallone and Shatner still offer only a partial view of the masculine heroes found in 1980s science fiction. The most financially successful genre films of the 1980s are family-oriented science fiction, many of which focus on younger masculine heroes: the likes of Luke Skywalker (Mark Hamill), Marty McFly (Michael J. Fox), David Lightman (Matthew Broderick, *WarGames*, 1983) and Elliot (Henry Thomas, *E.T.: The Extra Terrestrial*). This version of the genre hero, fuelled again by the success of *Star Wars*, also demonstrates the increased presence of mainstream and family elements within science fiction film production.

   E.T. appears to continue the theme of alien invasion discussed above, featuring one of the most visually distinctive invaders to descend on Los Angeles in this time period. The film, in common with other films such as *Starman* (1984) and *The Man Who Fell to Earth*, does fulfil similar narrative conventions: initial communication problems, cultural misunderstandings, a military chase/hunt for the invader, and the alien embracing (and potentially becoming addicted to) human products. *E.T.*, however, is also rooted in a rich history of children's literature, given a late twentieth-century polish. The notion of a child who discovers a new friend, and the adventures they share, was as potent in 1982 as it was in the nineteenth century when Mark Twain used it in *The Adventures of Huckleberry Finn*. That is not to lessen the impact of *E.T.* but to link its success to forces beyond the science fiction genre. *E.T.*, apart from one alien spaceship at the beginning and very end, largely avoids the visual trappings of science fiction, having as much in common with Hollywood's long history of filmed family entertainment as it does with popular perceptions of the science fiction film.

E.T. was not the first film to recognize the inherent possibilities of targeting generic product specifically at children or family audiences. Historically, the 1930s and 1940s film serials, Warner Bros' short animation *Duck Dodgers in the 24½ Century* (1953), or Hanna Barbera's animated TV cartoon *The Jetsons* (1962–3) were designed as mass entertainment, although with an eye to younger audiences. Perhaps naturally, it was the Walt Disney Company that first developed feature length science fiction for children: but these films were live action, not the animated fantasy adventures the company was most famous for. The earliest Disney film that could be identified as science fiction is *20,000 Leagues Under the Sea* (1954), a colourful CinemaScope epic that takes its cue from previous genre films, relying on special effects, impressive set design and visual spectacle to adapt Jules Verne's original story. Despite the film's success (and the parallel suggestion of futuristic pleasures offered in Disneyland's enticingly named 'Tomorrowland'), the company did not return to the genre until the 1960s and 1970s. Then, with hybrid genre films about a Volkswagen Beetle coming to life (*The Love Bug*, 1968) or a young brother and sister discovering their burgeoning (and alien) psychic powers (*Escape to Witch Mountain*, 1975), Disney developed a winning formula of comedy, drama and visual effects. The science fiction in such films was a simple narrative concept: *Herbie* does not dwell on the process by which the car became self-aware; *Escape to Witch Mountain* has no exploration of the alien community the children eventually rejoin. These narratives (and others, including *The Absent Minded Professor*, 1961; *Son of Flubber*, 1963) allowed the studio to focus on children- or family-centric narratives, punctuated with effects that heightened comic elements over visual display: the generic elements were less important than the stories such details could provide.

Family adventure films such as the Disney examples relied upon two particular character types: either the childlike adult who engaged in the comedy action (Jerry Lewis in *The Nutty Professor*; Dean Jones in *The Love Bug*) or an actual child, on the brink of adolescence. This latter option, which would dominate much of 1970s and 1980s family science fiction, has an early generic example in David MacLean (Jimmy Hunt) from *Invaders From Mars*: the sole witness of an alien ship landing in an old sandpit, David is loyal, intelligent and dogged, intent on revealing the alien's body-snatching plot no matter what the cost to his family and friends. The young male heroes of *E.T.*, *Explorers* (1985), *Flight of the Navigator* (1986), and *D.A.R.Y.L.* are his generic successors. By the 1980s, Hollywood had embraced demographic audience research and studios were increasingly aware of the number of young male customers that were attracted to the new summer blockbusters (and their associated merchandise): this offers one explanation for the industry's noticeable narrative focus on young boys on the cusp of maturing into their teenage years. Luke Skywalker is the obvious prototype here (if at the later end of the teenage spectrum) but film companies were increasingly targeting teenage males. There are earlier examples of teenage heroes from 1950s science fiction (Paul Newman in *The Blob* (1958); the *Teenagers From Space*) and Japanese anime (*Hi no tori 2772: Ai no kosumozon/Space Firebird*, 1980) but this increased production emphasis within American film meant the 1980s masculine hero was defined less by the action star than by young male characters that relied on empathy, emotion and intelligence over aggression and violence. Luke Skywalker may train to be a physical warrior in *The Empire Strikes Back* (1980), but it is his emotions and spirituality that save him (and the galaxy) in *Return of the Jedi* (1983). These characters are rarely the most popular, or the most athletic (they often represent the relatively new phenomenon of the hero nerd, or science geek) but they rely on their wits and ingenuity to defeat rogue computers (*WarGames*) or to conquer time travel (*Back to the Future*).

Technology: Mechanization and Innovation

The young heroes of these family science-fiction films are *au fait* with technology in a way that their parents are not. They are techno-literate, able to operate earthbound home computers and video recorders as easily as they can interact with new ideas and alien equipment. In *Flight of the Navigator* and *Explorers*, the inherent ability of teenage boys to build and use alien machines is central to the plot; Marty McFly quickly adapts to time machines and hoverboards in the *Back to the Future* series; the future teenagers of *Akira* (1988) interact with laser guns, cryogenics and cyborgs; while even Bill and Ted grasp the basic concepts of temporal cause-and-effect in *Bill and Ted's Excellent Adventure* (1988). Despite this apparent acceptance of technology by this new breed of heroes, these decades are also the source of new ways to be afraid of automatons, artificial creation and mechanization. It may be too simplistic to note the existence of a generational gap around technology (the cultural cliché of the younger generation who could operate their parents' VCR) but the dominant view of technology was (as in previous decades) something out of control.

The 1970s and 1980s featured a new focus on the process of robotic or artificial creation, with technology remaining a key element of the science fiction narrative. Technologies are problematic, often lethal, machines that threaten humanity's future, demand the ability to reproduce and attempt to pass for 'human'. Many of these unique and futuristic machines were brought to the screen through equally innovative technological means: the growth of stop- and go-motion animation, advances in computerized motion control, improvements in puppet and animatronics and the introduction of a nascent software application (computer-generated imagery) that would revolutionize filmmaking in the 1990s. This dual purpose of technology (as provider and narrative antagonist) would continue to fuel science fiction narratives in these decades and beyond, as computers became smaller, personalized and part of the everyday routine of human life.

The potency of robots and artificial intelligence came from larger cultural uncertainties around the role of technology within daily routines and how much human activity would be replaced by electronic means. Through the 1970s and 1980s, computer technologies (designed to be labour saving) became more prevalent across the world: everything from automated teller machines (ATMs) to mobile telephones contained microprocessors, while more factories and industries converted to heavy robotic machinery that could replace human effort. Representations of such technology in science fiction developed tropes from previous decades (and other media), with particular concerns over what it meant to be human, and how to identify a 'real' human from a robotic or biological simulcra: guests are unable to tell android and human apart in *Westworld* (1973) and *Futureworld* (1976); the robotic Stepford wives are intended to be better than the real thing; officers Ash (*Alien*) and Bishop (*Aliens*) are indistinguishable from humans until they bleed (a seemingly biological act in itself that complicates their standing in relation to 'true' humanity); the escaped 'skinjobs' of *Blade Runner* who show more humanity than the people chasing them; and Arnold Schwarzenegger's cyborg T-800 in *The Terminator* series, a machine body encased in synthetic flesh, designed to infiltrate the human rebellion of a post-apocalyptic 2029. These are all dangerous, 'inhuman' creatures endangering 'true' humanity, a synthetic 'other' to rival the genre's alien invader figures.

Robots were not purely malevolent figures in this period, with some uses returning to the comic figures of the silent era. Woody Allen impersonated a robot servant in *Sleeper*, C3-PO and R2-D2 were comic sidekicks in *Star Wars*, Twiki in *Buck Rogers in the 25th Century* was a robotic servant, while *Short Circuit* and *Short Circuit 2* (1988) featured Johnny Five, a human-built robot who becomes sentient after being hit by a bolt of lightning. Yet even in these comic roles, the robot never completely escapes its association with tension and mistrust: the robots of *Star Wars* are argumentative and moody; Johnny Five is a military robot who, despite discovering he has a 'soul', is powered by an atomic motor and has a missile launcher strapped to his arm. This uncertainty over the role of technology was not new: it is tempting to see films such as *Short Circuit* or *The Terminator* as modern versions of *Murder by Television*, where another equally revolutionary technology was presented on films as dangerous, unstable or murderous. Yet the rise of computer technology in domestic and work settings did raise awareness that the country, and the world, was becoming increasingly networked. *The Terminator* presented that future connectivity as a threat to mankind; cyberpunk suggested humanity would have to evolve and merge with the machine: as the next chapter will demonstrate, the global reach of computing and participatory networks would have a long-reaching impact on both narrative and industrial applications of technology.

Conclusion

These decades have been seen as the start of a second golden age of science fiction (Cornea 2007). From the artistic success of *A Clockwork Orange* and *Solaris* to the popularity of *Star Wars* and *Aliens*, the science fiction film genre moved further towards the mainstream of Hollywood and international film production. The period saw developments in how the genre could portray aliens, space travel, time machines and future societies and continued the narrative interest in using such figures to represent cultural and social issues around racism, gender, the environment and politics. Yet the lasting legacy of this period lies less in what these films were saying and more in how they were being displayed. The 1970s and 1980s represent a movement away from cinema as the dominant exhibition medium and the rise of television and home video as potent sources of generic pleasure: whether re-releases of existing science fiction films, 'straight to video' releases, or new television programmes. The science-fiction genre flourished with these new dissemination technologies, allowing it to find new audiences and to expand awareness of older genre entries. Technology also dominated production, as new techniques around motion control, animatronics and computer generated imagery (seen in *Tron* and *Dune*) increased the genre's interest in visual display. Technology had always been central to the genre's production and dissemination; as it moved into the twenty-first century, that combination would become even more important.

–7–

1990–2010: Science Fiction and
the Mainstream

In the final twenty year period covered in this genre history, science-fiction narratives and filmmaking technologies had collided to the point that previous definitions of science fiction as grand displays of 'industrial light and magic' (Sobchack 1988, 282) concerned with (and containing) special effects, technology-based narratives, and science-led plots, were no longer an accurate assessment of genre boundaries (if, indeed, they ever were). Outside such shifting borders, films as diverse as *Titanic* (1998), *Pleasantville* (1998) and *Gladiator* were now regularly employing computer-generated imagery to create the kind of realistic and fantastic narrative spaces that had previously been associated with science fiction. This increased diversification of special effects and technology-centred narratives led inevitably to further complications around attempts by critics or academics to apply generic borders or limitations. *Junior* (1993), for example, was marketed as a comedy pairing Arnold Schwarzenegger and Danny DeVito, but it also contained a scientific-medical premise (male pregnancy) that borders on science fiction, and recalls earlier generic interest in artificial male creation; equally, the comedy-drama of *The Truman Show* might be read as a commentary on the modern surveillance society but the display of that society is predicated on futuristic science and advanced technology. The growing hybridity seen in science-fiction narratives through the 1970s and 1980s had moved beyond plot-based elements in these later decades, as visual spectacles around the combination of reality and fantasy became a commonplace part of international filmmaking.

Across these decades, the role of genre filmmaking in defining the generic identity of 'science fiction' was at once reduced and enhanced by new dissemination and networking technologies. The rise of videogames, the Internet and mobile media devices (which, in the 1950s and 1960s, would have been seen as science fiction themselves) may have expanded the range of generic inputs but many of them can be read as continuations of existing genre tropes. Games such as *Doom* and *Halo* became more financially successful (and, arguably, more culturally pervasive) than most film releases and stressed a particular aspect of the science fiction genre for twenty-first century audiences. Yet the core thematic idea at the centre of both games, of the science fiction-action-military hybrid, contains a strong link to films such as *Aliens*, *Predator* and *Starship Troopers* (1997), a potent re-emphasis of film's continued contribution to genre conventions (the record-breaking success of *Avatar*, which uses similar narrative and visual tropes, would suggest film still has a role to play in this area). Other technological developments, particularly around the Internet, gradually increased the prominence of the computer (and later the mobile media player) as an essential tool for promoting generic product through Web sites, online trailers and forums. Fandom, already an active force within the science fiction genre (often around pre-existing titles such as *Star Trek* and *Star Wars*), was empowered by such technology. Internet forums, Web sites, and social networking made it easier for fans to engage with each other and to produce their own unique generic contributions (even if such contributions were often frowned upon by the original producers: Jenkins 1992 and 2006). While most fan work was done in relation to known media brands and franchises, the increased access to camera-phones, video cameras, and desktop software packages meant the creation of small, independent genre films could now occur anywhere. Uruguayan director Federico Alvarez's viral Internet video (*Ataque de Pánico/Panic Attack!*, 2009) showcased his ability to create short narratives and special effects; Gareth Edwards' *Monsters* (2010) demonstrated the power of independent filmmakers to produce feature-length films that married state-of-the-art digital effects with established low-budget movie genres (specifically around the road movie and character-based narratives). Popularized and promoted through the Internet, such developments showed that cultural awareness, and use, of generic conventions was as active as ever.

These decades also saw aesthetic changes within international film production, which had a direct impact on the science-fiction genre. The rise of 'steadi-cam' action sequences within mainstream production, providing shots that followed protagonists through a sequence in one long take, or which were edited into a fast-paced image stream, became prevalent in action thrillers such as *The Bourne Supremacy* (2004) and *Casino Royale* (2006). This emphasis on pace and style, bolstered by claims that it constructed a heightened, or 'ferocious' realism (M.S. 2004), could be seen in high budget blockbusters adapted from comic books (*The Incredible Hulk*, 2008; *Spiderman*, 2002) as well as lower budget genre films. *Cloverfield*, for example, combined mock-video camera footage with occasional glimpses of special effects-created destruction, while *District 9* married advanced special effects techniques and apparent live action verisimilitude to place its alien species in a 'realistic' slum setting outside Johannesburg. The movement towards constructing an aesthetic around 'real' images (*Cloverfield*'s alleged 'found footage' or the recreation of low resolution video or camera phone images in *District 9* or *Panic Attack*) was a move away from the more polished blockbuster approach of the 1980s and 1990s, but continued the preference for special effects work that inserted fantastic creations into a realistic space (a desire that had dominated the genre since *The Lost World*, if not before).

The main stylistic change in the genre towards the end of the 1990s and through the first decade of the twenty-first century, however, came not from the combination of special effects sequences within a largely live action setting but the move away from live action towards a completely computer generated world and computer generated (or enhanced) actors. As noted through the earlier chapters, science fiction films had continually adopted a variety of animation techniques within effects work, but capturing the complexity of human movement in fully rendered computer animation became a central goal of twenty-first century filmmakers. One early attempt, *Final Fantasy: The Spirits Within* (2001) divided critics, with a typical reaction lauding the 'computer animators [who] have cleared the major hurdles in the way of creating wholly credible human characters' but criticizing 'the emoting done by the computer drawings created herein ... [the] "acting" ... is no worse than that found in the majority of sci-fi films' (McCarthy 2001). The issue of acting style and realism, particularly around human movement and emotional acting in terms of facial expressions (most notably the human eye) became a default reaction among critics of projects such as *The Polar Express* (2004), *Beowulf* (2007) and *A Christmas Carol* (2009). In genre terms, these would be considered more 'fantasy' based than science fiction but, like the *Lord of the Rings* series (2001–3), industry and popular discourse around 'motion capture' was propelled into the wider cultural awareness around animation and CG special effects. 'Motion capture' systems, performance recording processes that allowed computer animators to work from the physical movement of real actors, became key components in almost all computer generated effects work. By the end of 2009, the promotional campaign around *Avatar* engaged with the same debates around motion capture, realistic acting, and the visual spectacle offered by computer generated animation. Its prominence and overwhelming financial success (despite offering little that was generically revolutionary in terms of narrative, characterization or theme) suggested it could provide a model for large-scale genre blockbusters into the 2010s and beyond.

Avatar may have become the most financially successful feature film in Hollywood history (in 2010 money at least) but discussions of the film rarely touched on its status as an animated feature film. Yet its success represented the apex of over a decade of American animated film production that developed science fiction projects on a scale never seen before. While there is a rich history of short animated films on both American film and television (*A Trip to Mars*, 1924; *Duck Dodgers in the 24½th Century*; *The Jetsons*; *Superman*, 1996) examples of feature length animated science fiction had come largely from the European or Japanese industries (*La planète sauvage/Fantastic Planet*; *Akira*). Japanese anime productions continued to explore generic narratives with films such as *Metroporisu* (*Metropolis*, 2001) and *Appurshido* (*Appleseed*, 2004), but genre animation within the American production system tended to dominate.[1] As with many trends within animation, the Walt Disney Corporation was a prominent producer of science-fiction animated features, from *Jimmy Neutron: Boy Genius* (2001) and *Lilo and Stitch* (2001) to *Treasure Planet* (2002) and *Meet the Robinsons* (2007). With its distribution deal (and later merger) with computer-generated animation specialist Pixar (creators of generic offerings

The Incredibles, 2004; and *Wall-E*), Disney offered a wide range of genre animation that called in at familiar narrative and iconographic territory: alien invasion, space exploration, super powers, 'mad' scientists and inventors, and robotics. Despite many of these films looking to the future, there is an overwhelming air of nostalgia about them: the robotic Wall-E collects souvenirs of a lost Earth, most notably a video of *Hello Dolly* (1969); while Jimmy Neutron's small town setting visually called to mind the 1950s locations of *Invaders from Mars* and *Back to the Future*. This trend towards being nostalgic for an earlier period (particularly the alleged 'golden age' of science fiction, the 1950s) existed beyond Disney and Pixar animations. *The Iron Giant* (1999) placed its adaptation of Ted Hughes' original book in a Communist-fearing 1950s; *Planet 51* (2009) depicted an alien planet that was almost indistinguishable from popular cultural notions of 1950s Americana (down to white picket fences and spaceship designs that mimicked classic American hotrods); and character design for *Monsters vs Aliens* was overtly drawn from classic 1950s creatures.[2]

Such nostalgia for the past was prevalent beyond animation. The American film industry, never slow to spot popular trends and successes, was frequently criticized during this time period for recycling and remaking existing properties, including many that directly harked back to Hollywood's generic past. Dinosaurs in the modern world, flying saucers invading from another planet, nuclear-powered monsters rampaging through a major metropolitan location and giant meteors coming to destroy the Earth: the recycling of generic ideas from films such as *The Lost World, Earth vs The Flying Saucers, Gojira,* and *Meteor* (1979) offered a strong reminder that industrial conceptions of genre thrived on the recombination and reworking of existing generic staples. Alongside this, there was an increased focus on sequel-led genre entertainment, 'special editions', prequels and 're-imagined' genre classics.[3] The 1990s included remakes of *The Island of Dr Moreau* (1996), *Frankenstein* (adapted as *Frankenstein Unbound*, 1990; and as *Mary Shelley's Frankenstein*, 1996), and *Invasion of the Body Snatchers* (*Body Snatchers*, 1993); there were recreations of older science-fiction texts such as the 1960s TV shows *Lost in Space* (1965–8) and *The Wild Wild West* (1965–9), and the 1950s bubblegum cards of *Mars Attacks!*. Christine Cornea identifies the latter as part of a cycle of 'science fiction parodies' that revisit the 1950s but the other examples of that cycle (*Men in Black, Independence Day, Armageddon*) are not interested in parodying just the 1950s, as they are a fusion of elements from throughout genre history. *Men in Black* may recall design elements of the 1950s, but it is more fascinated with the 1960s (much of the film's climax takes place on the site of the 1964 New York World Fair) and the 1990s resurgence in conspiracy theories around Roswell and other UFO sightings (helped by the contemporary success of *The X-Files* television show (1993–2002). Equally, while images within *Independence Day* recall the destruction of *Earth vs the Flying Saucers*, the film also draws generic information from *The X-Files, Star Trek* and *V*. This increased intertextuality, and awareness of generic predecessors, can be read as a more self-reflexive mode of generic production, but it is more accurate to note that science fiction films have always fed off pre-existing texts, whether novels, magazines, television shows or other films. Often derided by film critics and postmodern commentators as the film industry feeding on itself, trapped in a temporal paradox of its own (an ever-decreasing circle of pastiche and repetition), it may be more accurate to see this as the most recent attempt by Hollywood to capitalize on its existing library and genre branding (Grainge 2008).

Throughout its history, the Hollywood industry had used specific products (stars, titles, genres, auteurs) to brand companies, individuals and the industry as a whole. However, the increased corporate conglomeration of the late twentieth century increased the importance of generic products beyond their initial cinema release. In a continuation and expansion of the corporatization of the studio system begun in the 1960s and 1970s, multinational media conglomerates controlled multiple outlets for communication, entertainment, publishing and broadcasting. Most of the famous studio names (Universal, Paramount, MGM, Twentieth Century Fox, Warner Bros, Columbia) were now part of much larger media structures interested in creating cross-platform brands and franchises. Financially, many of the big entertainment conglomerates saw the cinema release as a 'shop window' for other, previously ancillary, products: the DVD release, the videogame, the comic book, the PayTV release, the television broadcast. For the big media conglomerates, film remained 'the most prominent image and identification ... [but had become] progressively less significant to the economic profiles and financial health' of such institutions (Holt 2009). The production of science fiction films such as *Jurassic Park* or *Iron Man* were now predicated on the film's brand extension and merchandising opportunities: increasing the variety of sites at which audiences could interact with generic marketing and imagery. Launch campaigns included fast food tie-ins with multinational brands such as McDonalds and Burger King; comic book and novel adaptations; soundtrack releases (often multiple releases of score, featured songs and songs 'inspired by' the film) and theme park rides at American institutions Universal Studios, Disney World and Six Flags. With rides based on *Back to the Future, Terminator, Batman,* and *Jurassic Park,* this potent link between blockbuster film and rollercoaster ride was seen by some critics as a return to Tom Gunning's 'cinema of attractions', where films were designed around spectacle rather than coherent narrative.

The increased dependence on ancillary branded products, most notably video games and online sites, has only exacerbated such criticism, although some cultural critics have claimed that rather than reject this capitalist divergence of branded products, the twenty-first century might promote a 'convergence' where 'trans-media' narratives cross over between different media rather than remaining solely on the film screen (Jenkins 2006). This debate has particular ramifications for genre production, as science fiction films (and film franchises) represent many of the major experiments in transmedia (or cross-media) storytelling. While Chapter 10 will explore this in more detail, it is important to note that the growth of such projects within genre production represents an increased awareness of multiplatform opportunities in the new media landscape.

While branded sequels, franchise prequels and cross-platform universe building represented one option for the increased expansion of genre storytelling, there was a uniquely generic narrative conceit that allowed filmmakers to revisit, recycle and occasionally change the past: time travel. Following on from a wave of popular time travel narratives of the late 1970s and 1980s (*Somewhere in Time, Time After Time*, 1979, the *Back to the Future* series), the desire to alter time (or the consequences of such actions) became central to the science fiction genre and its hybrid expansion into other areas. The growth of such narratives may have been fuelled by 'real'-world science (including theoretical discussions around quantum mechanics, string and M-theory) but can also be considered part of the larger cultural nostalgia for a perceived 'golden age' that was discussed above. Hollywood literally revisited its own past with new versions of *The Time Machine* (2002) and time-travel inspired reboots of television franchises *Lost in Space* and *Star Trek* (2009) that (to borrow common industry terminology of the twenty-first century) recast, 'reinvented' and 'reimagined' the existing characters and conventions from these 1960s television shows. While the period saw more traditional paradox narratives in *A Sound of Thunder* (2005) or *Donnie Darko* (2004), time travel was another component of the expansion of genre hybridity: *The Lake House, The Time Traveller's Wife, The Butterfly Effect* (2004), *Next* (2007), and *Déjà Vu* (2006) combined science fiction conventions with those from the romance, teen-pic, action and thriller movie genres, while *Southland Tales* (2006) merged all of the above with comedy and musical traits, to create an (often unwieldy) generically uncertain concoction.

This level of genre mixing and self-referentiality may also explain the growth of science fiction comedy across these two decades. While the previous chapter showed how family science fiction films such as *Short Circuit* or **batteries not included* (1987) could blend comedy, action and science fiction elements into a hybrid format, more specific spoofs and parodies of science fiction conventions began to appear in the late 1980s and continued into the twenty-first century. Fuelled by Mel Brooks *Star Wars* satire, *Spaceballs*, these science fiction comedies highlighted the absurdist qualities of many generic conventions, but they rarely undermined the genre directly. Instead, films like *Bill and Ted's Excellent Adventure, Galaxy Quest* (1999) and *The Hitchhiker's Guide to the Galaxy* offered a loving recreation of generic traits, working to reinforce broad cultural conceptions of what the genre might represent, on both narrative and visual levels. *Coneheads* (1993) and *Men in Black*, for example, offer variations on a standard invasion plot, except the stranded alien visitors are used as comic props to explore more basic human activities: immigrant acclimatization and inclusion in the American dream, illegal immigration, and (suburban) conformity. Science-fiction tropes featured heavily in both films (advanced technology, unusually shaped aliens, spaceships) but they play equally well as parodic treatments of American society or conspiracy theorists. Away from Earth, science fiction comedies such as *Galaxy Quest* and *Mom and Dad Save the World* (1997) had particular genre examples to spoof (*Star Trek* and *Flash Gordon*, respectively), but like most of these comedy hybrids, appear so concerned with getting the textual and visual details correct that they exist as love letters to the genre rather than satirical deconstructions of it.

Genre hybridity was also present in a potent narrative conceit that appeared to have links to real-world events: the depiction of parallel, or multiple, universes. Inspired by scientific theories from the Victorian era through modern day, explored by novelists as diverse as John Wyndham, Michael Moorcock and Robert Harris, and a central tenet on television shows such as *Sliders* (1995–2000) and *Doctor Who*, parallel universes (like time travel) allowed filmmakers to explore potent alternatives to modern-day life. This branch of science fiction has obvious links to more fantastic media: much of C. S. Lewis' *The Chronicles of Narnia*, for example, functions in a parallel universe that runs alongside our own, but with time moving forward at a different rate. Unlike the fantasy offered by Narnia, however, science fiction alternative universes closely resemble our own world (or aspects thereof), with subtle (or less subtle) changes. The alternative futures of films such as *Back to the Future 2* (1988), *Terminator 2: Judgement Day* and *Meet the Robinsons* are dark, dystopian visions, literally encased in shadows and featuring industrial pollution, anarchic capitalism and nightmarish visions of 'normal' family life. While such family-oriented films suggested a simple solution to this alternative (the actions of a lone hero are enough to return history to its 'normal' course of events and normative ideology), films like *A Sound of Thunder* and *The Butterfly Effect* explored the dangers of trying to recreate a 'normal' timeline in a world of quantum mechanics and multiverse theory. Perhaps the most potent demonstration of time travel in this time period was not in cinemas, but on television, as the popular series *Lost* (2004–10) became enmeshed in a complex plot around time travel, paradoxes and alternate possibilities; a plot that subtly increased the show's reliance on genre conventions from science fiction and fantasy through its six-year timespan.

These disparate threads around revisiting a golden age, changing the past, or imagining an alternate present or future can be found in many science fiction films between 1990 and 2010. There is a temptation to link this increased interest in reshaping the past to one particular date in this period: 11 September 2001. As has been clear throughout the broad genre history of the last four chapters, events from culture, society and politics have played a role in shaping narrative and thematic elements of the science fiction genre. In the last decade, there has been a tendency to see that 2001 attack on America (and the subsequent 'war on terror' launched by President George W. Bush) as a pivot around which all cultural industries have moved. This is not to return to simple reflectionist critiques of films or filmmakers, but to state that the first decade of genre production in the twenty-first century was talked about, and criticized, in relation to this moment. 9/11 did, at first, appear to challenge the trend for large-scale generic destruction of American cities and landmarks (popularized by *Independence Day* and *Godzilla*, 1998), even while that same fictional destruction was a feature of discussions of the attacks.[4] Christine Cornea, echoing other cultural critics, describes the experience of watching the events unfolding in New York on television and imagining she was watching a previously unknown science-fiction blockbuster (Cornea 2007, 264–5). Popular discussions of genre films being released in late 2001 and through 2002 focused on the presence (or not) of the Twin Towers of the World Trade Centre: the towers were featured in *A.I.: Artificial Intelligence* (2001) (and its later DVD release), but removed from a *Spiderman* teaser trailer, the denouement of *Men in Black II* (2002) and a futuristic New York from *The Time Machine*. Yet, while no one would dispute the defining nature of that day within contemporary culture, it seems disingenuous to see it as the dominant incident that affected all genre production.

It remains too early to judge whether recent events such as 9/11 or the wars in Iraq and Afghanistan have had a lasting effect on the science-fiction film. If the last decade of the twentieth century saw a movement towards larger scale sci-fi fuelled blockbusters and a coalition of computer-generated spectacle and realism, the first decade of the twenty-first century appeared to move towards more traditional fantasy worlds (the *Harry Potter*, *Lord of the Rings* and *Twilight* franchises), the dominance of comic-book adaptations, and a partial resurgence of the kind of serious science fiction seen in the 1970s: from the time paradoxes of *Donnie Darko* and *The Jacket* (2005) to the time-spanning possibilities of *The Fountain*. Perhaps the most overt influence of 9/11 on genre production was the temporary absence and subsequent return of the alien invasion narrative. The alien invaders of *War of the Worlds* could be read as a metaphor for home-grown terrorism and contemporary uncertainty over who to trust: in this remake, the Martian war machines were hidden within America awaiting 'activation' (as the film's promotional materials promised, 'They're already here'). Yet the uncertainty over who to trust has been a perennial generic theme since the 1950s and, if easy comparisons are required, could equally be seen as commentary on the Oklahoma bombings or the February 1993 attack on the World Trade Center, rather than the specific 2001 attack.

The emphasis of *War of the Worlds* on a lack of trust (with aliens hidden within the planet itself) was a more compelling theme throughout the period but one that was not simply related to external threats. Through the last two decades, science fiction films emphasized the human body as the ultimate threat, with a lack of trust in internal biological change or external genetic manipulation. The body has been a source of anxiety throughout the history of the genre (*Videodrome*, *The Fly* (1986), *Akira*), but growth of 'real world' applications of DNA, genetic manipulation and cloning appears to have fuelled the interest of generic narratives through the 1990s and beyond. In some cases, this presented a fusion of body issues and traditional alien invasion narratives: *Species* and its sequels present a dual invasion, of Earth and of the human body (which is required for alien violence and procreation). But from the late 1990s and through the first decade of the 2000s, the body became more untrustworthy and alien, an 'Other' that was not extraterrestrial in origin: the body's reproductive role fails completely in *Children of Men*, a genetic abnormality that fuels the film's near-future dystopia; in *Hulk* (2003), *X-Men* and *The League of Extraordinary Gentlemen* (2003), bodies are mutated and twisted into new forms, transformations helped (and made spectacular) by CGI special effects; while the body becomes the site of battles and invasions by scientifically engineered viruses and bio-weapons (*28 Days Later*, 2002; *Planet Terror*, 2007; the series of *Resident Evil* video games and films). This latter move, although a fictional representation that draws on various media panics from throughout the period (the Ebola virus, SARS, H1N1), places the blame for such outbreaks on big corporations and pharmaceutical companies (a 'biological-industrial' complex that runs along the lines of the more familiar military version). Unlike earlier genre hybrids such as *Outbreak* (1995), where scientist-hero Dustin Hoffman prevented a catastrophic virus from spreading across the planet, these recent science fiction films offered little hope that government or science could put this particular genie back in its bottle.

In *Resident Evil* (2002) and *28 Days Later* (films that draw from multiple genres), all the characters can do is flee the chemically and biologically created undead: hope appears to lie in small isolated communities, not the urbanized, commercialized world that spawned the corporation. Most telling was that science (and scientists), previously the source of last-minute solutions as well as initial problems, appeared to have failed. There is little sense of the optimistic, or fantastic, view of the future that can be seen in the genre between the 1950s and the late 1980s: Robert Neville (Will Smith) in *I Am Legend* cannot create the necessary vaccine; the scientists succumb to the 'Rage' in *28 Days Later* and *28 Weeks Later* (2008); 'Jurassic Park' cannot be saved by its team of scientists; and scientific experimentation continues to fuel madness in creators such as Sebastian Caine (Kevin Bacon, *Hollow Man*). Science was culpable in these narratives, rarely the source of resolution or reassurance. A reflectionist argument might claim this as a result of films mirroring contemporary concerns over the place of science within education (for example, the American debates over creationism versus evolution), uncertainties around scientific discoveries (cloning, genetically modified food), and the inability of science to find solutions to larger world issues around global warming. Indeed, the scientist hero of *The Day After Tomorrow*, a science fiction-disaster movie, cannot save the planet. His warnings unheeded, and with extreme weather freezing most of the northern hemisphere, all he can do is save his own family (his own small, isolated community). However, returning to the remake of *War of the Worlds* (where the aliens are not defeated by human science but because of the presence of Earth's germs and bacteria) offers a useful reminder that generic uncertainty of science (and its narrative inability to cope with all disasters, man-made or otherwise) has been part of generic canon since the late 1890s, if not longer. Science has always been fallible, within the generic narrative and without, but it remains central to the storytelling possibilities of the genre, and the non-diegetic ability to visually display those stories.

Conclusion

> [P]erhaps the science fiction genre has become a victim of its own success ... if one of its functions over the last couple of decades was to introduce and acclimatise a viewing public to a newly digitized world, then having achieved this it now finds itself redundant ... [the genre] that has challenged and pushed at the limits of both filmic realism and the medium of celluloid for so long might now become obsolete, just as we enter a post-celluloid age. (Cornea 2007, 267)

Making any definitive conclusions about the future of the science fiction genre (or, indeed, the industrial reimagining of its own past) is fraught with problems. Christine Cornea's eulogy for the end of the second 'golden age' of science fiction filmmaking may have been eclipsed by the success of *Moon, District 9* and *Avatar* but its central concerns remain valid. After all, the success of those three different films must be seen against an industrial landscape of generic hybridity where science fiction is in danger of becoming lost among multiple hyphenates: romantic-comedy-action-adventure-science fiction-thriller. The dominance of 3D within genre production, and the success of *Avatar*, seems to point to a three-dimensional future for science fiction, but a writer in 1953, mulling over the future of the film industry might have looked at the success of 3D genre film *It Came From Outer Space* and voiced similar sentiments. Equally, in 1955, Paramount Pictures announced that the science fiction film cycle was dead, burned out, and that audiences were no longer interested. History has proven all of these attempts at prediction false in one, or more, of their assumptions.

At the end of this chapter, and of Part II as a whole, it should be clear that writing an overarching genre history is a necessarily partial process that cannot hope to cover every science fiction film produced in the period chosen. It is equally clear that the thematic and narrative elements identified in Chapter 4 (artificial creation, scientists, invasion, exploration, the future) are still present in many modern genre narratives, albeit affected by the social and cultural perspectives that are often brought to bear on genre production. As both the alpha and (current) omega of the science fiction film genre, *Le Voyage dans la lune* and *Avatar* depict alien planets, insensitive human exploration, and warrior-like natives; each displays unique visual aesthetics for their time period; each is interested in the spectacle inherent in state-of-the-art special effects; each created by a heralded director, an auteur figure with particular visual style and thematic interests; each would go on to influence numerous imitators and future generic discourses. Yet such an analysis ignores a series of underlying interests that work to separate the films: the environmental overtones of *Avatar*; the fascination with the moon in Méliès' film; magician-scientist explorers rather than military-industrial soldiers; the influence of Wells versus the influence of Edgar Burroughs or Larry Niven.

When Alan Williams claimed that genre studies needed to go back to film history, to study all films that were produced (regardless of canon or cultural hierarchy) and to think of their cultural and historical meaning, it was with the hope that genre histories would expand out, begin to question and explore existing theories, and not take for granted what had been claimed for a genre, or a film. Part II of this book was designed to begin that process, not conclude it: if it has suggested new films, new areas, new possibilities, or new methodologies, then it has succeeded in its task. A science-fiction film genre history should be as concerned about *Aelita* as *Aliens*, equally engrossed in the temporal paradoxes of *Toki o kakeru shôjo* (*The Girl Who Leapt Through Time*, 2006) and *Biggles* (1986), as fascinated by *Devil Girl From Mars* as *A Clockwork Orange*, and as excited to explore the future of *Just Imagine* as it is of *The Matrix*. That sense of exploration has fuelled these last four chapters, which combined textual information, cultural context, industrial history, and multi-platform knowledge into a partial narrative of the science fiction film genre. There remains much work to be done to open up smaller, more focused, areas of this history, particularly around the richness of international genre production that this section has partially demonstrated, but for now, the book will move on to consider three specific case studies that expand on this section's interest in extratextual materials such as critical reviews, promotional texts and other discursive networks, to look at how they help educate and inform audiences about genres.

Part III
Selling Science Fiction

−8−

'Adventure Dramas of the Future': Creating Genre

Hollywood has no interest ... in explicitly identifying a film with a single genre. On the contrary, the industry's publicity purposes are much better served by implying that a film offers 'Everything the Screen can give you' ...

Altman, *Film/Genre*

The indication and circulation of what the industry considers to be the generic framework ... of a film is therefore one of the most important functions performed by advertising copy, and by posters, stills, and trailers.

Neale, *Genre and Hollywood*

Previous chapters have explored how existing work on the science fiction film has largely favoured the critical and academic categorization of genre. There has been a focus on how such films can be read, what larger socio-political debates they might be engaged in, how genre can be shaped by cultural influences from literature and 'real' science, and how genre production has developed and changed over time. Applying film history to genre studies has allowed an examination of particular historical moments, focusing on specific studios and their ability to respond to and exploit generic popularity; or to consider the impact of stars or directors who recur in genre productions. Yet throughout this work there has been little exploration of how science fiction films have been positioned and sold to audiences and what such generic texts may have meant to different viewers. This work moves genre away from the industrial and analytical roots of film studies and situates it in relation to work on reception and audience studies. The overview of the science fiction films in the previous chapters made passing reference to the cultural formation of genre through sources such as reviews, Web sites and film institutions such as the AFI. This chapter will continue that work by focusing on the early history of film advertising, specifically for films retrospectively identified as science fiction. Analysing posters and press books created to advertise these films reveals how such intertexts influence and affect generic identity and cultural awareness of genre characteristics. This does not offer unmediated access to what audiences thought. Rather, it suggests how studios attempted to communicate generic information to contemporary audiences, and whether marketing techniques created a coherent sense of what science-fiction films represented.

All films are 'accompanied by a host of promotional and popular forms … bent on elaborating certain of its elements' (Klinger 1989, 7). These elements function as part of the larger industrial (and ideological) system of Hollywood but they function in relation to each other, informing and shaping audience knowledge of films ahead of any physical viewing. The promotional system begins during production, where particular elements of a film are selected to form its 'consumable identity', which is then positioned and placed into a wider inter-textual world[1] (Klinger 1989). Through this process, which has existed since the early days of Hollywood, studios attempt to control the potential meanings that circulate around their films. Understanding the need to differentiate each product they made, the early film companies and studios chose to emphasize certain features of the film: most notably, 'genre, stars, plots, spectacle, or realism' (Staiger 1990, 6).

Studies of genre need to be more aware of this intertextual identity, and how promotional departments aim to manipulate audience's generic expectations well before the release of a feature film. In the quotations that opened this chapter, Rick Altman suggested that hybrid genre messages were more common in the classical Hollywood publicity system in order to attract the widest audience possible; while Steve Neale argued that the pre-release circulation of a film's generic identity will be one of the most important aspects of a promotional campaign. While the history of the science fiction film genre has revealed numerous examples of hybrid narratives and themes, Altman's description of promotional hybridity is too broad a concept to apply to all of Hollywood's promotional practices of the 1920s and 1930s. This chapter will, therefore, use a case study of pre-generic films (as seen in Chapter 4) to explore whether marketing materials used by studios, distributors and exhibitors have been used to promote specific visual or thematic conventions to audiences, or if hybrid identities are more common. In order to mirror Altman's earlier work, the main sources will be a combination of posters and press books for films that have, in the decades since, been identified as science fiction, from *First Men in the Moon* and *Metropolis* to *Things to Come* and *Flash Gordon*. This wide selection will allow the chapter to investigate early attempts to create a consumable identity for these films, ascertain whether any generic markers can be identified, or if a more hybrid approach has been taken to sell these scientific fictions to a wider audience.

The Silent Era

Publicity and exploitation in the film industry … included differentiating each film, advertising through several media, stressing a particular series of competitive features (genres, stars, and so forth), and advertising indirectly. (Staiger 1990, 12)

Before the advent of nickelodeons or purpose-built cinemas, early film advertising first stressed the machinery itself (the viewing of moving images was an attraction in its own right), then the company or individual organizing the screening, then a list of films being shown. With the growth of distribution companies and exhibition chains after 1905, and the appearance of a star system around 1908, film advertising began to shift away from technology and towards the promotion of individual brands, genres and stars (techniques borrowed from pre-existing theatre advertising). Publicity materials increasingly stressed star and narrative content through the 1910s, but poster design and content was slow to change. In one typical example from 1914, the Essanay Film Manufacturing Company used a double-page spread to list current and forthcoming attractions. On the left page, under 'Now Booking', there is a list of film titles, 'class' (or genre), approximate length and the date of release: the list includes *The Little He and She* ('Comedy Drama … 984 ft … Mon., Sept. 21'), and *Night Hawks* ('Detective Drama … 1964 ft … Thurs., Oct 22). On the right (facing) page, in slightly bigger type, Essanay publicized six specific titles with small descriptive statements around length, genre, narrative or star. *In and Out* is a 'story of two comedy musicians who turned sailors to save their lives'; while *A Letter From Home* is a 'two-reel dramatic offering … in which Richard C. Travers and Gerda Holmes give an excellent interpretation of the leading roles' (*Bioscope* 1914, 213–14). Although this is a trade advertisement, designed to attract exhibitors rather than a paying audience, simple typeface advertising such as this remained dominant in the film industry in this period. Such advertisements also clearly illustrate how genre has already taken root as a sales message, with exhibitors expected to recognize genres such as 'Comedy Drama', 'Detective Drama' and 'Western.'

Early films with a science fiction/fantasy narrative were also advertised in this way from 1909, but they emphasized other generic elements rather than offer a description of the nascent elements of these scientific narratives. Lubin Films listed 'Rubber Man' as a 'Trick Comic' (*Bioscope* 1909b, 22); while Edison Films had a half-page film advertisement that listed *Frankenstein* as 'A dramatic of absorbing interest, being an adaptation of Mrs Shelley's famous story' (*Bioscope* 1910b, 22). Comedy and drama were known generic markers, borrowed from literature and theatre, and could be understood by a range of audiences. While H. G. Wells and Jules Verne were known for fantastic science narratives and futuristic stories, there was no agreed term for such stories: although 'scientific romances' and 'futurist romances' were terms applied to Wells' work (Wells 1967, 7) they do not appear to have been widely used beyond his and Verne's writing.

Drawings and photographs that suggested the visual characteristics of different genres were soon included within film advertising, often allowing them to stand out from the longer list of titles: Vitagraph used a wagon trailer image to advertise *How States Were Made* (Bioscope 1912, xv), while Essanay used a silhouette of Charlie Chaplin's 'Tramp' character to promote a series of new Chaplin comedies

(*Bioscope* 1915, 24). The latter, of course, combined character, star image and genre, so cannot be taken as a pure example of genre advertising. Early examples of films with science fiction premises faced similar problems: how to visually display some central, widely recognizable element that could symbolize generic pleasure. The most frequent option, aside from star imagery, was to use unusual or fantastic visuals that portrayed the film as 'other,' different from normal dramas or thrillers. This can be clearly seen in an early example of photography in trade advertising for *A Message From Mars*, which combines visuals and star image in an attempt to convey spectacular or bizarre imagery (*Bioscope* 1913, xxi).

The two-page poster advertises a trade showing of the film with an emphasis on its star, actor Charles Hawtrey, who had played the same role on stage at the turn of the century. Hawtrey's name is emblazoned across the poster (three times), and is flanked by two images of the actor: one a posed portrait, the other a character image, in black clothes, clock, gloves and enclosing headgear. With his arms raised above his body, as though making a great proclamation, and with makeup that creates an angularity around his features, this is the image that dominates the poster. While the film title is listed (also three times), and there are details on the trade showing and the production company, United Kingdom Films, the composition of the poster focuses attention on to Hawtrey. While this might confirm a degree of star status, the emphasis on him in character, rather than the traditional portrait, is more oblique. There is a possible link back to the original theatrical production, but more than fourteen years had passed, so it appears unlikely that the costume and makeup would be that memorable. If star and theatrical links are rejected, however, it is possible that this image was designed to suggest generic or narrative qualities from the film. Hawtrey's character is a Martian sent to Earth (like a guardian angel), and this image plays up those alien qualities, with the pose, clothing and make-up. While it may be at one remove from the use of icons such as the flying saucer, the robot, or the rocket, Hawtrey's alien may have been one of the first science fiction visuals used within film advertising.

A Message From Mars demonstrates the gradual move within film publicity from a list of films (some with generic tags) towards a system that mirrored the industrial move towards feature length narratives and a star system. By the end of the 1910s, many posters showcased central actors, with painted or photographic images that attempted to encapsulate narrative events, stars or generic information. The poster for *Dr Jekyll and Mr Hyde* (1920), for example, is dominated by John Barrymore's central characters. Jekyll, in Victorian evening dress, dominates the right of the poster, with Hyde a leering phantom lurking over his shoulder. The left of the poster is taken up with the producer, title and credits (including Robert Louis Stevenson), and a crowd of women and children, over whom the figure of Jekyll towers. The main narrative information comes in a sentence on the right: 'The Screen's Greatest Actor in a Tremendous Story of Man at His Best and Worst.' The focus in this poster is on star and narrative information, although the spectral presence of Hyde does suggest the uncanny or bizarre element of the story. There is little or no extraneous information, little in the way of generic or romantic conventions. While the Jekyll and Hyde story may be regarded as on the fringes of science fiction, in this poster, genre is not as important as the status of the film as a star vehicle and an adaptation (the reference to Stevenson and 'a Tremendous Story').

By 1920, however, Hollywood publicity departments had other avenues for promotion beyond the film poster. *Dr Jekyll and Mr Hyde* was also promoted via a film trailer, a press book and in newspaper articles. A feature from the *Saturday Evening Post* highlights several of the same elements as the main poster (Adolph Zukor, John Barrymore, Paramount) but this advertising uses screen images to present the romantic (and sexual) side of the film. Barrymore's Jekyll is pictured kissing the hand of Millicent Carew (Martha Mansfield), while two pictures of Hyde show him with two separate women. The aloof Jekyll and Hyde characters from the poster have been replaced by, alternately, loving and sexualized figures. The expected readership of the *Saturday Evening Post* may offer one reason for this change: the poster was designed to be eye-catching in a cinema foyer, while the article was placed within a female-oriented publication. Yet, even while this article defines the film in romantic terms, a proto-generic element is also featured. In between the photographs there is a drawn image of Dr Jekyll at work, in his laboratory, surrounded by scientific and medical equipment. The romantic element may dominate this second promotional image, but it also features a potent generic location that would recur in other genre advertising over the next decade.

To control the multiple sites now open to film promotion, from posters and newspaper reviews to magazine article and exploitation stunts, the Hollywood studios created the press book that was sent out to exhibitors. The press book is best understood as part of a movement within the studios to dominate all aspects of production, distribution and exhibition. Techniques such as block-booking, where exhibitors had to sign up to a programme of studio films in order to guarantee access to certain star vehicles, allowed the studios to retain more control over their product but exhibitors had controlled local publicity practices for almost two decades (Staiger 1990). The establishment of National Screen Service (NSS) in 1919 was part of the film promotional industry's attempt to become industrialized and more in tune with what the studios wanted. While this was done primarily to get the studios 'out of the nickel and dime business of selling trailers and posters and stills to individual theatres' (Paul N. Lazarus, quoted in Johnston 2009, 171) it demonstrates that star- and film-specific advertising was moving from individual theatre owners to studio control. NSS set up regional distribution centres that stored copies of all the posters, lobby cards, stills, slides, and trailers that studios wanted to make available to local exhibitors. The press book was central to these plans, created to publicize the range of products that were now available to those theatre owners, and bookable through NSS. These books contain detailed information on star, narrative and any generic statements the studio wanted to stress through advertising.

Press books came in many forms in the first decade of their existence. The British press book for *Broken Blossoms* (1919) contains four sheets of closely typed information on narrative, director and star.[2] The American press book for *Metropolis*, by contrast, contains multiple pages of possible newspaper features, taglines, exploitation stunts, posters, trailers, images and lobby display suggestions. The latter represents the more common template for Hollywood films from the late 1920s on, and was mimicked by other national film industries, most notably in Britain. These press books represent a crucial aspect of the consumable identity created for genre films: although aimed at the exhibitor, they contain all promotional materials that audiences would have been exposed. While they cannot confirm which posters were used where, or which taglines were most effective, the range of options provides a window into how studios wanted to sell their films, what they wanted audiences to know in advance and, the flipside of that, what messages they gave to audiences about star, narrative and genre.

An early press book, for the British film *The First Men in the Moon*, offers a nascent example of what such press books might contain. Across its thirty-two pages, the press book details the production company, cast, narrative, and the available promotional materials. Like *Dr Jekyll and Mr Hyde*, the book stresses its status as an adaptation (of H.G. Wells' novel), the 'difficult undertaking' that such a production entailed, and Gaumont's determination to 'present to the moving picture public a picture with an entirely new interest … The extraordinary trip of a sphere from the earth to the moon … will engage the attention of any audience.' (*The First Men in the Moon* press book 1919, 7) These three elements constitute the main sales message: Wells', the scale of production, and how spectacle could be used to attract audiences to this unusual film. Scale and spectacle are sold through photographs from the film, which punctuate a lengthy plot summary. Featuring small explanatory captions, the photographs capture the set design, costumes, characters and visual effects: the dishevelled scientist, Cavor; his spherical spacecraft; the metallic and instrument-laden interior of the sphere; the rocky surface of the Moon; the insectile costumes of the Selenites, with their thin legs, carapace and large bug-like eyes; and the bulbous multi-mouthed Mooncalf. The visualization of Wells' ideas are a key selling point throughout the press book, which states that the photographs are available 'on loan' for free to exhibitors. Echoing the *Message From Mars* poster, strong generic visuals are a key element of the sales message: there are photographs of the supporting characters and the suggestion of a betrayal, but it is the spaceship, the mad scientist, and the alien creatures that offer the strongest images.

Unfortunately, what the *First Men in the Moon* press book lacks is any suggestion of the posters that were available. The final page states that four posters were available ('one twelve-sheet, three six-sheet'), as well as 'two kinds of announcement slides' (glass slides that could be shown between films, a very basic form of trailer) but there were no samples of these advertising materials. It seems likely from the rest of the press book that they would have stressed the link to Wells ('Of all the writers of fiction who have ever lived, perhaps none have achieved the widespread popularity and renown achieved by Mr. H. G. Wells with his imaginative stories'), and probably featured those same recurring images of the Sphere, aliens, the landscape of the moon, or the mad scientist. The suggestion from this early example is that this imagery made up part of the consumable identity of the film, but even with the link to H. G. Wells, the press book features little generic language. There is reference to Wells' stories as 'far fetched' and 'imaginative' but no direct reference to words such as science or fantasy, or indeed any existing genre (drama, comedy, thriller). This 'extraordinary trip of a sphere from the earth to the moon and the interesting details of lunar life' was presented as an essentially genre-less film.

Almost a decade later, the Paramount press book for *Metropolis* reveals that genre marketing had become a much more industrialized process. Still reliant on key imagery, this was now applied across multiple tag lines, poster designs, newspaper articles, review features and photographs. The front page of the *Metropolis* press book contains a lengthy narrative synopsis, but it does not dominate. The synopsis is simply one element among many in a busy broadsheet format: there are 'Film Facts' about the director, author and photographer, and 'Exploitation' ideas that include tie-ins with local Germans and automobile dealers, as well as the more traditional posters, catch-lines and newspaper contests. This front page does contain two images – a drawing of Freder (Gustav Froelich) and a still of Maria (Brigitte Helm). Picturing the film's main actor and actress does little to advance any generic identification, although the Helm photo does show Maria with electronic apparatus attached to her head, a suggestion of the scientific elements of the film. A more specific reference to genre comes in the bottom right hand corner of the cover, in a short paragraph called 'Type of Film':

> 'Metropolis' pictures a city a thousand years from now. The rich people live on top of the earth while the workers homes are deep down in the bowels. The master mind of Metropolis has a soulless automaton made and tells it to preach contentment to the workers. Instead, it advises them to leave their machines and revolt.

Like *First Men in the Moon*, no specific genre is mentioned; but unlike the British film, this description contains several key phrases that could point to developing notions of a specific genre. The futuristic city of 'a thousand years from now' and 'soulless automaton' both tie in to previous films with similar fantastic premises, offering a nascent intertextual relationship with known properties such as Capek's play *R.U.R.*, *Machines That Think* (1922) or the rash of 'one hundred years later' films that were released in the 1910s and 1920s. The notion of futurity, visual spectacle and science fiction films was suggested in the *First Men in the Moon* press book, but is more explicit here. Suggested catch-lines include 'Movie Magic – Metropolis' and 'Fantastic – Fanciful – Futuristic – Metropolis'. The link to special effects and the idea of the 'fantastic' offers a connection to other 1920s films such as *The Lost World*.

The press book regularly returns to issues around the future, mechanization and the 'marvel' of the film, while drawing in other elements, specifically female sexuality. Posters and newspaper advertisements picture skyscrapers that tower over a mass of drowning people, next to which stand a well-built half-naked man and a manically grinning woman bursting out of a tight black dress (representations of Freder and Maria). The accompanying copy reads 'Where Do We Come From? Whither Do We Go? Is this your future or the gigantic fancy of a mechanical mind? Don't miss "Metropolis" the marvel movie of the age!' The future city and the reference to the mechanical are mirrored on other posters, and could be seen as nascent generic markers. Yet the placement of the robotic 'Bad' Maria on the poster appears to have more to do with sexual passion than futuristic mechanized cities. The wide manic grin on the woman's face and her general wild nature (as drawn), suggest the central melodramatic role that Maria (and her robot) play in the later stages of the film. Other materials, notably the colour lobby cards, are dominated with similar key sequences and images: Maria, the robot Maria, Maria and Freder, the underground masses, the giant machines and the towering skyscrapers. There is very little focus on Joh Frederson or Rotwang, while Freder is only ever pictured with Maria. Despite several images of this couple, the emphasis is not on love and romance. The sales campaign prefers the spectacular to the intimate. One catch line appears to link all of these elements: 'Erotic – Exotic – Erratic – Metropolis'.

This focus on skyscrapers, future spectacle and erotic female automatons does allow some form of early generic identification to form around *Metropolis*. The press book encapsulates many elements that might be regarded as belonging to a proto-science fiction genre, or at least a sales message that attempts to stress science fiction elements. There is a stress on the futuristic setting of the film, the advanced technology on display and the use of special effects to create spectacle and awe. The most interesting use of specific genre identification comes in the reviews section of the press book, where newspaper reviews are collected together and made available to exhibitors. Many of the reviews cite other, similar, works – H. G. Wells, Jules Verne and Edward Bellamy are cited as potential sources of inspiration, while there are more specific references to Mary Shelley's *Frankenstein* and Carol Kapek's *R.U.R.* in relation to the creation of an artificial robot/automaton with no soul. The reviews underline the spectacular elements of the sales message: 'stunning and imaginative' (*New York American*) 'Thrilling Spectacle … New Marvel Cinemiracle' (*New York Sun*) and 'one of the most extraordinary pictures ever produced' (*New York Daily Mirror*). Despite the absence of 'science fiction' as a known generic term, the *Metropolis* press book develops certain linguistic and iconographic approaches to futuristic films that would recur in later film promotion.

These examples of silent film advertising sketch out a series of potential generic pleasures, if not a coherent approach to identifying one central genre. The strongest, and most cohesive, genre statements that emerge from these press books and posters are rooted in visual spectacle and pre-existing cultural forms, most notably the fantastic literature of Wells and Verne. While the materials may not support the belief that 'filmmakers and audiences' understood an international development of science fiction 'icons, plot devices, and themes' (Telotte 2009, 45) they do point towards a growing intertextual generic network that promotional materials could draw upon. Visually compelling fantasies of lunar landscapes, lost worlds and advanced future cityscapes were featured at the centre of sales messages. Automatons, spaceships, dangerous machines and mad scientists were not as immediately prevalent, yet remain potential publicity ingredients. Altman's claim that studio publicity down-played genre credentials in favour of hybridity can be seen in certain examples, most notably the various poster depictions of *Metropolis'* central couple. Yet these elements never dominate. They represent secondary promotional messages, behind the emphasis on adaptation or effects-produced visual splendour. As the international film industry moved into the sound era, however, that tension between hybrid sales messages, visual spectacle, and the other nascent generic conventions, would shift again.

Genre in Early Sound Film Advertising

The Vampire Bat (1932) may sound like a horror film, yet it is about a scientist intent on using human blood transfusions to create life. Possibly fuelled by real scientific developments in Russia and America around storing and preservation of blood, the film could claim both nascent horror and science fiction conventions. Yet the press book insists it is a 'thriller,' a 'Murder Mystery Drama' and a 'shocker' that will make audiences 'shudder and gasp'. Appealing to such disparate generic groups suggests the wider hybrid form of advertising Altman has argued for, and there are other notable examples from the 1930s. *The Man They Couldn't Arrest* (1931) is a 'superb thriller' about a complicated machine that can listen to any conversation, with posters that stressed detective thriller elements through images of trench-coated figures in trilbies. The press book for *The Man Who Lived Twice* (1935) describes it as the 'Strangest Drama Since "Dr Jekyll and Mr Hyde" ... blood chilling ... a leap ahead of science', a combination of drama, horror and possibly science fiction. Even *Men Must Fight* (1933), about a future European war, was advertised as 'vivid film drama' and 'romance'. In each case, the potential science fiction elements of advanced technology, scientific developments or future civilization have been toned down, possibly to appeal to a wider audience.

Yet all these preceding examples are films that have only a tangential premise or identity as proto-generic narratives. As discussed in Chapter 4, many films of the 1930s and 1940s used a science-fiction plot device or character (notably a machine, or a mad scientist), but more closely resemble contemporary thrillers, detective stories or horror films. To understand how promotional materials were dealing with the different strands of what would become known as science fiction, it is more revealing to investigate how the 1930s equivalent of *First Men in the Moon* or *Metropolis* were being promoted.

The futuristic *High Treason* was the first all-dialogue film from Gaumont-British and its press book mimics the earlier tone of *First Men in the Moon* in stressing design elements and narrative (the visual look of the film) over more hybrid notions of drama or romance. Although the press book assumes there will be an interested female audience for the film, that interest is based around future fashions (a gender stereotype also seen in the press books for *Men Must Fight* and *Things to Come*):

> 'High Treason' has an essentially feminine interest in its forecasts of the fashions of 1940 ... whilst it is suggested that women will adopt an eminently practical garb in masculine plus fours for office work and men's overalls for factory work, she will choose divided skirts with knee breeches for evening wear, bizarre designs being favoured.

Underneath drawings of some of these fashions, and exhibitions of female fencing (which has replaced cabaret dancing in clubs), the text continues that the female office worker of the future will be able to shower and refresh at her 'thoroughly utilitarian' office, before stepping into 'her evening clothes which are immediately adjusted with one fastener.' This discussion of fashion should not distract from the emphasis the book is placing on futurity as a central appeal for the film. Its vision of the future may not be as far-flung as *Metropolis* but the press book equally relies on the appeal of future imagery and future technology to attract an audience.

Throughout the press book, visual content and design elements are stressed over romance. There is a brief mention of 'the producers' having 'wisely interwoven the world's greatest theme, the omnipotence of love in all ages' but the substance of the promotional material is visual. Like *First Men in the Moon*, the narrative is illustrated with captioned photographs. From a shot of New York gassed by aircraft, a showgirl standing up to the military, the bombing of the Peace League Headquarters, to a courtroom scene, the pictures focus on the futuristic drama and look of the film. While the *High Treason* press book does not follow the traditional Hollywood press book format of the era, the stress on how the film looks, its creation of futuristic architecture, fashion and society and its special effects (most notably the bombing of New York) offer strong generic ties between this promotional material and earlier silent and sound examples. The emphasis on strong effects imagery, for example, can be seen in the use of zeppelins in posters for *The Last Hour* (1930), or the emphasis on 'the Great British drama of futurity and bizarre backgrounds' in advertisements for *The Transatlantic Tunnel* (1935). The generic link between visual spectacle, futurity and mechanization remained a key element of these nascent science fiction films.

With the term 'science fiction' yet to become widely used (or defined) outside of magazines such as *Amazing Stories*, it is more common to see phrases such as 'The Next Wonder of the World' or 'Today's Drama of Tomorrow' (*The Transatlantic*

Figure 8.1 The cover image from the *Things to Come* press book, 1936 (London Films)

Tunnel press book, 1935). While the similarity to *Metropolis'* poster rhetoric around wonder, marvels and futurity is particularly telling, similar elements would feature in the press books for two contrasting visions of the future from 1936, *Things to Come* and *Flash Gordon*. While sharing interests in science, exploration and technology, this film and film serial foreground different pleasures to their assumed audiences.

The front covers of both press books offer a sense of what is to come inside. *Flash Gordon* features a dramatic image of Flash (Buster Crabbe), his shirt ripped open to the waist. *Things to Come* features a drawing of Oswald Cabal (Raymond Massey) in a futuristic wide-shouldered tunic, pointing dramatically into the night sky (Figure 8.1). The tone of both books appears set: *Flash Gordon* as melodramatic space opera (images from the cartoon strip also appear on the poster), *Things to Come* adopting a serious, perhaps more artistic pose. Authorship is important to promotion for both films: both Universal (as studio) and Alex Raymond (creator and copyright owner) are mentioned on *Flash Gordon*; while it is *H. G. Wells' Things to Come*, with smaller type recognition for London Film, William Cameron Menzies and Alexander Korda. This popular/quality distinction continues through both press books. *Things to Come* stresses Wells' stature as a prophetic writer, the magnificence of the film's achievement, and its status as a major landmark within British cinema. *Flash Gordon* offers journalistic hyperbole around potential star figures, the creation of the comic strip, a chapter-by-chapter description of the narrative, and striking photos of Flash, Dale Arden (Jean Rogers) and Ming the Merciless (Charles Middleton).

This tone of populist versus quality identified above is not consistent throughout the press books, with *Things to Come* offering a more commercialized promotional campaign than the Universal serial. There are exhibition suggestions around parades, rallies and theatre marquees, while tie-in books, records, haircuts, sportswear, costumes, and sandals are all available to the general public. The *Flash Gordon* press book, by comparison (possibly because of its status as a serial, not a feature film) strives to situate its commercial comic-strip roots in modern science. It suggests that the 'imaginings of today become the inventions of tomorrow', with reference to current rocket tests and their possible role in future transport. Citing the historic progression from balloons to the Wright Brothers, the press book concludes, 'can anyone say, with absolute certainty, that rocket ships are beyond all possibility?' In both cases, the press books work to broaden the 'consumable identity' of each film, offering different messages for alternative audiences. At the same time, this broader promotional array delineates genre characteristics: the link with real science, or with potential developments, has been the basis for science fiction films since its earliest years; while a greater notion of merchandising (although less developed in this period) becomes a key genre convention with the advent of *Forbidden Planet, Planet of the Apes* and *Star Wars*.

The importance of visual design in earlier promotional examples is matched in both press books. *Things to Come* is a 'spectacle unequalled in its magnitude' with its 'futuristic settings … the dominant note.' The overall tone is the 'importance of bigness' with lesser sales messages around women, romance and the human drama. *Flash Gordon* is equally spectacular, with the press book emphasizing many visual effect-based elements: 'Settings so fantastic that they startle the imagination … A city suspended in the sky … a rocket ship that shoots through space and rays that melt huge steel structures.' But not all such discussions are narrative based, with other articles stressing the production knowledge required to make these effects happen. 'Strange costumes and weird make-up' are mentioned in the *Flash Gordon* press book, but *Things to Come* contains the most overt reference to visual effects in its press releases. One article, 'The Men Who Work Miracles,' introduces London Films' special effects department and the 200 men who produce 'technical miracles … ranging from the disappearance of a man into thin air to the destruction of a city.' Revealing the use of models, and how they interact with real actors, the *Things to Come* press book offers a very modern concept of 'behind the scenes' knowledge to match its use of nascent genre-based merchandising.

High Treason, Things to Come and *Flash Gordon* may represent different narratives, production contexts and promotional techniques, but they are linked together through their attempts to suggest specific narrative and production pleasures to an audience. Following on from the press book of *Metropolis*, and its stress on future events and spectacular visuals, these sound films move imagery to the front of the sales message, underlining its importance in these early years of generic identification. Futuristic technology (from ray guns to new fashions) appears in articles and photographs; advanced travel options are pictured (the Space Gun of Wells' film, *Flash Gordon*'s spaceship); and there is a rhetorical stress on the real-world possibilities of the scientific fiction being displayed. Through the 1940s and into the 1950s, these elements would recur in advertising materials and become conventional aspects of science fiction promotion: while the emphasis on how fantastic special effects are created – and the assumption that such effects are a crucial element of these generic films – would become more dominant with the advent of television and the creation of 'behind-the-scenes' programmes that explored all genres of film production.

Conclusion: 'A Tale of Gadgets and Almost Indescribable Things'

These early examples of genre promotion challenge Altman's initial assertion that studios preferred hybrid advertising messages. The examples above prove that it was possible (and arguably more profitable) for studios to stress a particular generic identity rather than offering a more hybrid message around action and romance. Those elements are never absent from the campaigns examined through this chapter, but press books and poster work for films such as *The First Men in the Moon, Metropolis, High Treason, Things to Come* and *Flash Gordon* have revealed a potent foregrounding of proto-generic conventions. Awareness of the consumable identity that studios attempted to create around these disparate films has shown that certain characteristics recurred in posters and press books. *First Men in the Moon* offered an initial visual effects-based message with photographs of spacecraft, lunar landscapes and aliens; posters depicting *Metropolis'* futuristic city and fear of mechaniza-tion developed the scale of such visuals; while *Things to Come* and *Flash Gordon* emphasized special effects and the potential they had for spectacular images.

Things to Come and *Flash Gordon* arguably offer the most compelling list of potential generic elements, and it is from those conventions that later science fiction advertising would build: visual spectacle, advanced technology, futuristic arch-itecture (and fashion), rocket ships (and space travel), sinister aliens, laser guns, 'real' science, and special effects techniques. These are not the only iconographic or thematic elements that science fiction would feature from the 1950s on (the figure of the robot is lacking in these examples, for instance, though was more dominant in *Metropolis'* advertising) but they represent the dominant traits visible in these early examples of film promotion. As 'adventure dramas of the future' became more prevalent, these traits would be more commonly associated with the new generic identity of science fiction. However, this chapter opened with the assumption that a film's consumable identity can be traced through the range of promotional materials. While this analysis of posters and press books has begun to demonstrate the importance of generic messages within the consumable identity of science fiction films, the following chapter will expand that investigation by looking at the use of genre imagery and rhetoric in one of the film industry's most potent promotional tools.

–9–

Genre and Spectacle in Science Fiction Trailers

The film trailer is an innovative piece of screen advertising that has been at the forefront of film promotional techniques since the 1910s. A highly structured creation, the trailer has narrative and aesthetic qualities that separate it from other advertising materials and which make it a potent source of information on the historical development of stars, technology and genre (Haralovich and Klaprat 1982; Klinger 1994; Kernan 2004; Johnston 2009).[1] Its limited running time of two to three minutes has often been seen as a marker of overt salesmanship and spectacular imagery over subtlety or layered communication yet the structural elements of excerpted scenes (from the feature), editing (including wipes and dissolves), music, sound effects, dialogue, voiceover, inter-titles and graphic imagery offer a complex *mise en scène* that carries multiple levels of meaning and inference. Analysing these layers allows a deeper understanding of how the trailer creates meaning, cues viewers towards specific aspects of a forthcoming release, and uses visual imagery and rhetoric to highlight and develop generic pleasures.

Chapter 3 discussed the critical belief that the visual spectacle created by special effects techniques has been seen as a key generic convention, but there is little work on how such images are received by audiences, or how spectacle has been positioned within the genre's promotional materials. It has been claimed that modern blockbusters (many with a science-fiction premise) are sold 'on the basis of spectacular attraction. The scale and quality of spectacle is a major factor in the advertising, promotion and journalistic discourses surrounding their release' (King 2000, 4). If science-fiction film promotion does rely on spectacle, then the film trailer (the first audio-visual link viewers have with forthcoming features whether through a cinema, television or computer screen) would be expected to display and hype that spectacle, making it a central promotional message to attract future audiences. The trailer also raises issues around claims that science fiction spectacle allows audiences to 'sit back and revel in the spectacle of the special effects' (Banks 2002, 145). Given the direct address of trailers, and this apparent compression of visual spectacle within the trailer narrative, it would appear likely that spectacle would be more overt in trailers, perhaps even greater than in the narrative feature films they advertise.

This chapter will explore the claim that spectacle is a major factor in science fiction marketing by examining trailers from three distinct eras of the science-fiction genre: the 1950s (specifically *The Day the Earth Stood Still* and *War of the Worlds*); the 1970s and 80s (*Close Encounters of the Third Kind* and *The Empire Strikes Back*); and the 1990s (*Independence Day* and *The Matrix*). These trailers ultimately reveal historical changes in the use of spectacle within genre marketing, from early attempts to combine spectacle and narrative, to a lack of effects-based imagery, to a modern reliance on such images. Rather than a constant and continual use of spectacular imagery, trailer analysis reveals an ebb and flow of visual display. Each trailer (and time period) contains new developments in special effects technologies and a resurgent interest in the genre (both industrial and popular), making them prime case studies to examine genre marketing techniques and the place of generic visual spectacle, across the decades.

Trailer Spectacle before the 1950s

Trailers first appeared around 1912, first as 'series slides' that exhibitors projected between reels (Sargent 1915), 'coming next week' announcements at the end of serial instalments, and then as an 'advance strip of film' that offered a brief preview of a forthcoming photoplay (*Moving Picture World* 1916, 2094). The early popularity for trailer advertising is evident in the launch of National Screen Service in 1919, with a department devoted to trailer production and distribution. Through the 1920s and 1930s, alongside posters and press books, the trailer became Hollywood's primary sales technique, at the forefront of studio attempts to control the promotion of stars, narratives, technology and genres (Kernan 2004; Johnston 2007). By the 1950s, and the popular expansion of the science fiction genre, trailers were the key element of a successful publicity campaign, and intrinsic to any attempts by studios to define and market generic attributes.

The place of spectacular imagery in trailer structure was originally set during the 1920s, when NSS trailers combined animation, graphics, title work and feature-based imagery into a coherent narrative structure: the trailer for *Madame Pompadour* (1927) uses these devices to focus attention on to the film's star, Dorothy Gish, the visually sumptuous settings of eighteenth-century France, and the early generic markers of the historical drama (ornate costumes, set design). As the trailer for *Noah's Ark* (1929) demonstrates, the introduction of sound did not detract from the display of visual spectacle. None of the film's stars are mentioned in the film's trailer, which places the emphasis on spectacular effects-driven imagery and promotional language. The bulk of the two minute trailer contains long shots of water sweeping across the landscape, blasting into walls, churning into harbours and knocking over cities. The scale is epic, with people largely reduced to distant figures being drowned or sacrificed to the flood. Spectacle here is visually arresting, linked to the popularity of Biblical epics such as *Ben Hur* (1925) and related ideas around scale and increased vision: the trailer voiceover comments that audiences will 'SEE the rise of the Tower of Babel … SEE the ritual of human sacrifice. SEE the construction of the great Ark … SEE the flood that destroyed the world.' For the *Noah's Ark* trailer, spectacle and genre are the key elements to the trailer's attempt to lure in an audience.

With few archival trailer prints available for films such as *Metropolis, High Treason* or *Things to Come*, the best proto-generic example of visual spectacle is the trailer for *The Lost World*. Despite opening with a title ('Mighty prehistoric monsters clashing with modern lovers') that suggests a hybrid narrative, the visuals of this trailer are built around adventure and stop-motion spectacle over romance. The trailer focus is almost entirely on the animated dinosaurs, with close-up scenes of the tyrannosaurus' head or the fight between it and a brachiosaur. The trailer also stresses the link to extended vision, claiming that audiences would 'see it … see wonders never shown before.' Special effects – and the related generic spectacle – are described as expanding vision, offering something more than traditional fare. This call to vision extends to clips where the special effects 'star', the tyrannosaurus rex, is integrated with live action humans, or with known London settings. The placement of these monstrous creations continues the press book emphasis (seen in Chapter 8) on the special effects spectacle as a key promotional attraction in this early period of genre creation. By emphasizing spectacle, the enhanced reality created by special effects ('this strange and sensational story lives before you') and offering a sense of behind-the-scenes production knowledge ('Seven years to bring it to you – seven years of hard work'), *The Lost World* trailer establishes some basic generic markers. Although not unique to the science fiction genre, these early conventions offer a basic structure that can be applied when looking at examples from later decades.

'New and Startling Powers from Another Planet': Genre Trailers in the 1950s

The dinosaurs of *The Lost World* were presented as spectacle, but that spectacle was fictional (the concept of such monsters appearing in 'real' locations and people) and non-fictional (a fantastic display of stop-motion technology). In the 1950s science fiction trailer, the notion of a special effects 'star' and its relation to reality was infused with the contemporary context of space travel and UFO sightings. With special effects engaged in a discourse around realism and realistic locations and often defined in relation to new (and alien) technology, this new approach to generic marketing positioned spectacle as something that could be alternately feared and desired.

One of the earliest science fiction trailers of the 1950s, *The Day the Earth Stood Still*, roots any potential spectacle-based trailer narrative in realistic terms. The trailer opens with an abrupt cut from the 20th Century Fox logo and fanfare to a brisk announcement about interrupting the programme for a report on a large object heading for the East coast of the United States. In an attempt to maintain the illusion of a real news broadcast, the trailer cuts to a television studio and newsreader commentary. The potential for spectacle is being teased here, the revelation being held back. Even when the pictures cut to Washington, the images are of soldiers and watching crowds, not the spaceship itself. About forty seconds into the trailer, an attention-grabbing wipe (wipes were a common technique to focus vision on particular areas of the screen) positions a helmeted, humanoid figure walking out of a hatch on a flying saucer. Accompanied by dramatic music, and panicked reaction shots of soldiers and onlookers, this introduction can be read as spectacular. The addition of declamatory intertitles ('They came 250 million miles out of space to hold the world SPELLBOUND with new and startling powers from another planet!') gives further emphasis to the image, yet the sequence differs from *The Lost World* in featuring no special effects to underpin this visual spectacle.

The trailer continues in a similar vein, balancing potential spectacle with narrative elements: images of Klaatu (Michael Rennie) on the saucer confronting soldiers, giving a speech about Earth being burned 'to a crisp' if they do not heed his warning. The main potential for spectacle rests in the robotic figure of Gort, who features as strongly as Klaatu in the trailer narrative. He is shown stalking around the saucer, threatening Patricia Neal, and carrying Klaatu's body back into the saucer. Despite the best efforts of the trailer's rhetoric and visuals to present the robot as a threatening figure ('The screen has never conceived a creature like this', Klaatu's warning that Gort 'could destroy the earth') there is a reduced sense of spectacle, at least in part because Gort is that most basic of special effects, a man in a suit. The trailer has little special effects-based imagery, bar a brief laser blast from Gort's eyes. The flying saucer remains in the background of many shots, but it is never emphasized: without showing audiences the 'new and startling powers' of these alien invaders, the core of the trailer lacks an effects spectacle to mirror the early genre experiments of *The Lost World* trailer.

In generic terms, however, *The Day the Earth Stood Still* trailer offers strong identification with existing and developing science fiction conventions. The flying saucer is visible throughout the trailer, the robotic Gort is the closest the trailer has to a star image, and the trailer title and dialogue make reference to outer space and other planets. Yet the most telling link to the growing presence of science fiction in this time period is a direct statement of generic identity. At the end of the trailer, after the cast and director intertitles, the whole image changes. The background is an edition of *Look* magazine (one of the major picture magazines of the period), with the trailer's final title over it: '*Look* Magazine calls it: "The Best of the Science Fiction Movies!"' Images of flying saucers and robots had already suggested a generic identity for *The Day the Earth Stood Still*, but this final trailer title names the genre, and relates those images to a wider cultural understanding of the term 'science fiction.'

In the two years following *The Day the Earth Stood Still*, science fiction became a more established genre within Hollywood, with the release of films such as *The Thing From Another World, It Came From Outer Space* and *When Worlds Collide*. Despite featuring different science fiction premises, trailers for all three films continued to balance narrative information with visual spectacle. *The Thing* trailer stressed the unknown origins of its creature ('is it human or inhuman') but gave only brief glimpses of a shadowy creature. Spectacle was more central to the 3-D trailer for *It Came From Outer Space*, linking the three-dimensional process with generic conventions. With 3-D titles over a distant starfield and planet, a ray-gun blast 'into' camera, an alien point-of-view shot and the interior of the crashed spaceship, 3-D and genre-based spectacle offer a compelling combination (Johnston 2008b). A 'flatter' version of generic spectacle can also be found in the *When Worlds Collide* trailer: planets hanging in space, the building of a huge rocket ship, and destructive special effects that depict tidal waves and volcanic eruptions. Here, a dual narrative structure recalls *The Lost World*: excerpted images and trailer voiceover describe the basic plot of the film, the threat 'from another world,' and the scientific efforts to build a space Ark. Alongside this runs a narrative of production detail and behind-the-scenes information: how Paramount are the source of 'the most shattering experience the screen has ever given you' and that these are 'the most amazing awe-inspiring scenes ever put on film.' The trailer builds to its special effects climax, with a title exclaiming '*This* may not happen for a million years *but now* you'll see what could happen.' The reference to vision, and the apparent reality of special effects, ties the *When Worlds Collide* trailer to the earlier conventions from the 1920s.

Yet looking across these, and other, 1950s trailers reveals a disparate approach to the placement of special effects spectacle. *The Day the Earth Stood Still* trailer may have used the term 'science fiction' but this direct generic claim is unique in these trailers. The *War of the Worlds* trailer avoids direct reference to 'science fiction' in titles or voiceover, even while creating generic spectacle around the concepts of alien invasion and destruction. The trailer opens on a starfield with Earth at the centre. The use of a star filled sky or galaxy had fast become a recurring image in 1950s science fiction (as seen with the trailers for *It Came From Outer Space* and *When Worlds Collide*, above). The trailer quickly reiterates other generic conventions: a meteor falling to earth in a remote landscape, a wedge-shaped flying machine ploughing into a field, explosions and newspaper headlines that exclaim 'Invasion' and 'Men From Mars'. There may be no direct statement but the trailer's opening images make an overt connection to contemporaneous science fiction films. Yet while these opening examples are spectacular, and are presaged by declamatory intertitles that state the film (and trailer) are 'filling the screen with a Mighty Panorama of Earth-Shaking Fury' this level of special effects-created spectacle is not carried through the bulk of the trailer. Around the forty-five second mark, there is a key special effects image, as the bulbous green 'head,' thin metallic neck and glowing body of an alien ship lifts slowly out of a crater. This is the fulcrum of the trailer, its most potent and visually striking image. Unlike the *When Worlds Collide* trailer, which builds up to a display of destructive special effects, the *War of the Worlds* trailer attracts attention with an early array of effects. After this moment, special effects and generic imagery fade from the sales message, which moves to scenes and imagery more in keeping with war movies than science fiction. From alien invaders to human protagonists: generals poring over maps of America, soldiers firing guns, hiding in trenches, people evacuating the cities in lorries. The move from fantastic opening images to human panic and hysterics may tie in to earlier ideas around diegetic and non-diegetic sales messages. Over the images of alien ships and destruction, a voiceover ties contemporary events into narrative detail, declaring that 'the much ridiculed flying saucers ... [were] the flaming vanguard of the invasion from Mars!' Later, scenes of humanity fighting and fleeing conclude with an intertitle that returns to behind-the-scenes information, stating 'Now, After Two Years in the Making! H. G. Wells' Famous and Fantastic Story Comes to the Screen.' The absence of visual effects at the end of the trailer and its return to production terminology redefines the scale of the project in terms of adaptation and genre, not spectacle.

These trailers, for *The Day the Earth Stood Still* and *War of the Worlds*, represent two canonical science fiction films. Yet the evidence suggests that, even during a concerted period of genre production, studio marketing was still unsure of what elements to focus on. These are not the hybrid sales messages Rick Altman describes (Altman 1999, 57–9) but early attempts to frame and define 'science fiction' in both visual and rhetorical terms. Unlike the dominance of special effects spectacle in *The Lost World*, the balance of spectacle to narrative was shifting from trailer to trailer in the 1950s, with spectacular imagery rarely dominating the consumable identity being created. Certain generic elements do recur: flying saucers feature prominently (even in the trailer voiceover for *War of the Worlds*, a film that does not feature 'true' saucers at all); the robotic figure of Gort is mirrored in trailers for *Robot Monster* and *Forbidden Planet*; and laser guns or laser beams remain popular (harking back to the days of *Flash Gordon*). Overall, however, the 1950s science fiction trailers represent a tension between effects spectacle, narrative and a realistic integration of effects and live action. Because of the financial problems faced by Hollywood studios, and their fading interest in science fiction, the potential for special effects to become visual spectacle was not fully realized in the 1950s. Two decades later, science fiction trailers would adapt again, focusing on new special effects technology and a renewed interest in generic spectacle.

1970s Trailers

Effects departments were a casualty of this corporate downsizing. Artists scattered to the four winds or retired; cameras and optical printers and other finely built instruments were consigned to scrap heaps, put in storage or sold off cheap. Without a creative structure in which retiring craftsmen could pass on their specialized knowledge to students of the magical arts, it was hard to imagine how special effects, and the sense of wonder they brought to the movies, could survive. (Vaz and Duignan 1995, 5)

While Paramount's 1955 decision to drop science fiction films from their production slate and close their special effects department was mirrored in other studios. The above quotation paints an overly bleak picture of the supposedly lean years of the science-fiction film genre. Studio science fiction was still produced, from George Pal's *The Time Machine* and *The Mouse on the Moon* to *Planet of the Apes* and *2001: A Space Odyssey* (Figure 9.1). Each film (and trailer) struck a different balance between narrative, 'realistic' effects and the more spectacular opportunities of special effects. *2001,* as Chapter 5 demonstrated, continued to remain an exception to mainstream science fiction filmmaking: its Cinerama trailer contains no narrative or dialogue, offering instead a display of spectacular model work and special effects. Compelling though this trailer is, the rebirth of special effects technology is more traditionally placed around 1977, and the release of *Star Wars* and *Close Encounters of the Third Kind.* It is also a potent moment to consider whether new visual effects techniques were being used within promotional campaigns to heighten the presentation of generic spectacle. As with the 1950s examples, however, examination of trailers from this time period challenges the idea that more visual effects spectacle equates to more spectacle-based trailer narratives. With issues surrounding the production of the necessary special-effects techniques, and the limited availability of finished footage, the display of spectacular images in trailers was reduced in this period.

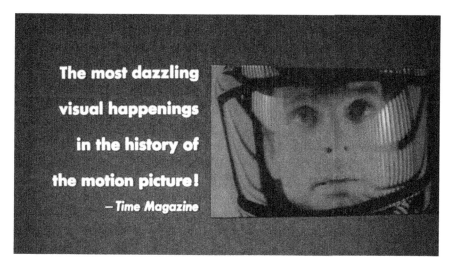

Figure 9.1 The Cinerama trailer for *2001: A Space Odyssey* (1968) emphasizes the film's visual spectacle (MGM/Cinerama)

The trailer for *Close Encounters of the Third Kind* balances several competing narrative strands, offering plot information, star personas and generic conventions. There is little special effects work on offer but the trailer appears to be withholding its ultimate visual spectacle of alien spaceships, using that lack as an audience lure in its own right. In the place of spectacular imagery, the trailer functions as a short behind-the-scenes featurette: production knowledge is offered in place of stunning visuals. The note of building suspense is initiated by the first image: a deserted road at night, heading for distant hills, behind which a white glow appears. As the voiceover explains the definition of close encounters of the first, second, and third kinds ('sighting of an unidentified flying object … physical evidence of a UFO … actual contact'), this white light continues to pulse, until it flares out to fill the screen. From this, the trailer shows photographs of Steven Spielberg, Julia and Michael Phillips, Douglas Trumbull, John Williams, Dr J. Allen Heimler, Richard Dreyfuss and Francois Truffaut, with accompanying hyperbole around their accomplishments. The emphasis on the production personnel appears to acknowledge the growing cultural awareness of these figures, particularly in genre fan audiences (this can be seen in the launch and popularity of science fiction film magazines *Starlog* in 1976 and *Cinefex* in 1980). Yet the use of such credentials serves to dilute generic identification and the potential for spectacle.

The trailer voiceover heralds those being pictured in relation to previous success (a familiar trailer technique with stars: see Johnston 2007): Steven Spielberg is the director of *Jaws*, the Phillips' are the producers of *Taxi Driver*, Richard Dreyfuss is the star of *American Graffiti*. The accompanying photographs are journalistic, not revelatory: Spielberg directing, John Williams conducting. The only suggestion of generic identity is Douglas Trumbull, who 'goes far beyond his achievements in *2001*' (he is shown with model images), while Dr Heimler is 'the world's foremost authority on unidentified flying objects.' This emphasis on production knowledge (and personnel) goes far beyond similar moments in *The Lost World* or *When Worlds Collide* trailers, which made reference to the length of film production. These sequences book-end two excerpted scene montages (focusing on the mysterious orange and white lights that cause toys to come alive, characters bathed in a similar light) but the trailer is more interested in personnel than visual effects or spectacle. Although the trailer promises that 'what you will see has never been seen before' (a common claim in generic trailers, as shown above), the trailer gives very few glimpses of what those visuals might be.

This attempt to lure audiences in by suggestion rather than displaying spectacular images is almost as old as the trailer itself: the 1925 trailer for *The Phantom of the Opera* kept its central character (and the make-up of Lon Chaney) out of trailer footage; while the *Bride of Frankenstein* trailer showed audiences a bandaged female figure with the inter-title 'What will she Look like?' However, the *Close Encounters* trailer relies on audience knowledge of film industry personnel and stars over generic imagery, an unusual technique in this, and other, time periods.

The larger issue concerns what underlying reason might account for this lack of spectacle. In 1980, when the *Close Encounters of the Kind Special Edition* trailer was released, the spectacular imagery of the alien mothership and the appearance of the small grey aliens were key factors in the sales message. This trailer narrative had a different purpose – to attract an audience back to see something they had largely seen already – and used additional visual spectacle to hint at new footage that was new and unseen. The lack of such spectacle in the 1977 trailer comes from a common issue around special effects. Namely, that many special effects images were not physically completed when trailers were produced. The lack of spectacle in trailer messages must be understood as a partial consequence of film production schedules, where special effects images were traditionally produced towards the end of filming. The knock-on impact of this policy to potential special effects spectacle in 1970s trailers is clearly displayed in many genre trailers from *Alien* to *E.T.: The Extra Terrestrial*.

Even trailers for those films most closely linked to the late 1970s explosion of special effects and science fiction suffer from this lack of spectacle. The 1979 teaser trailer for the *Star Wars* sequel *The Empire Strike Back*, for example, uses production drawings by Ralph McQuarrie and photographs of the main cast, but no moving images (bar the camera flying through a starfield); while the main trailer features only one motion control image of space dog fighting (something that exemplified many of *Star Wars*' original special effects sequences). Both teaser and trailer suffered from production schedules: the teaser was produced in late 1979 in time for a Christmas release; the main trailer was produced around January 1980, well ahead of finished effects shots, and forcing the reliance on set design, makeup and physical costumes. There was no opportunity to promote this blockbuster using visual spectacle, so trailers focused on character and known pleasures instead. Generic images gain more focus: the robotic characters of C3-PO and R2-D2; spaceships and lightsaber battles are emphasized in the drawings and there are numerous alien costumes throughout. However, for a film series that provided groundbreaking and spectacular generic imagery, the trailers struggled to offer a free sample of that spectacle.

The evidence of these trailers does not dispute that this was a resurgent time for science fiction films, or that those films used spectacular visual effects within their narratives. However, the trailers do reveal that such films had to be sold to audiences without many of the central sequences that would become famous. This was not something unique to the *Star Wars* series or trailers. The *Alien* and *E.T.* trailers kept special effects imagery at a minimum, for similar reasons around the availability of completed effects work (although, both may have had other reasons for restricting access to their central alien character). Some science fiction trailers featured practical over visual effects: the *Blade Runner* trailer created a narrative around its action sequences and characters, with occasional glimpses of police hover cars, or the distant ziggurats. In all cases, however, the lack of spectacle was a direct result of effects work being scheduled towards the end of the production cycle. Perhaps the most compelling example of effects-created spectacle from this period was the trailer for *Tron*, and its display of animated and computer-generated images. Although they are placed within a strong narrative that featured many of the film's live action scenes, the shots of light cycles, tanks, and a vast spaceship that runs on a line of light are visually arresting and spectacular. It is perhaps a sign of things to come that it was computer-generated spectacle and not model or optical work that created the most compelling spectacle in trailers from this time period. The desire to display such spectacle, and the prominence of science fiction elements in mainstream cinema, would lead to science fiction trailers changing how film production schedules were created.

1990s Trailers

In 2007, blockbuster film producer Avi Arad (Marvel Studios) described selecting 'five to ten trailer moments' from mainstream film productions such as *Spiderman 3* (2007) and planning those scenes early in the production schedule to allow them to be used throughout trailers and other marketing materials (quoted in Silverman 2007). This change in production practices was a direct response to the problems of displaying spectacle in early 1980s trailers seen above but it was not an immediate change. The main pivot for such a sea change came from the new effects technology of CGI, experimented with during the 1980s (and briefly visible in trailers and films such as *Star Trek II: The Wrath of Khan,* 1982; *Dune* and *The Abyss*) but only broadly applied towards the mid-1990s. Analysis of trailers from the latter years of that decade pulls together many of the issues raised through this chapter: whether special effects spectacle dominates modern blockbuster advertising, how trailers resolve issues around realism and special effects, and what other generic imagery and production rhetoric is used to suggest known genre pleasures. This is also a period when computer-generated effects transferred into other films and genres, from *Forrest Gump* (1994) to *The Perfect Storm* (1999). Both the expansion of effects work, and the reworking of production schedules for trailers, necessarily affects how visual spectacle was being positioned across the various promotional materials being created: from posters and television features to Web sites and behind-the-scenes videos. Trailers may have been the catalyst for this change but they were not the only genre marketing technique to be affected.

Computer-generated visual effects were partially on display in the main trailers for *Terminator 2: Judgement Day* (the 'liquid metal' Terminator) and *Jurassic Park* (the CGI dinosaurs) but these films were not the catalyst for reorganizing of Hollywood's production schedules. The film that did feature prominently in discussions of spectacle, science fiction and the modern blockbuster film was *Independence Day*. This modern version of *War of the Worlds* rewrote traditional filmmaking schedules in order that key visual effects scenes – most notably the destruction of the White House and the Empire State building – could be included in the teaser and main trailer (Shone 2004, 233). Analysis of the teaser reveals conventions from an earlier genre trailer, for *When Worlds Collide*: both feature a mystery-based narrative, building to an effects-based climax, and then a montage of destructive effects-created spectacle. In the case of *Independence Day*, that spectacle coalesces around a 'star' image: a blue-green shaft of light stabs out of the sky and into the White House, detonating the building in all directions, spraying fire and debris towards camera. This image, combining model work, explosives and CGI, is obviously intended as a spectacular final image, a lure that audiences would not be able to resist. It is perhaps the first modern equivalent of the 'special effects star' that George Pal promoted in marketing materials for *War of the Worlds* fifty years before: a visual effect that combined fantasy, reality, generic imagery and pure spectacle.

The use of this shot in the *Independence Day* teaser and main trailer could be used to describe these previews as pure spectacle: but that would miss the larger issue surrounding such imagery. The spectacle of the White House exploding is the climax to a specific narrative development, not a disconnected scene that has no relation to the rest of the trailer. The idea that this moment might be seen as pure spectacle is, however, related to the act of moving special effects shots early in production so they would be available for inclusion in the trailer. Such shots quickly became the recurring image that was repeated in other forms of advertising, from posters through to short television spots. Further iterations of the image (whether in ten-second television trailers or in press kits) isolate it from narrative context and emphasize the spectacular aspects of the sequence: it becomes a central element of the film's 'consumable identity'. The teaser and main trailer for *Independence Day* do make such effects shots more prominent than most other trailers of the time period but they function in relation to the narrative. It was the extraction of those images, and the subsequent publicity they received, that built up the expectation of CGI spectacle within visual marketing materials. By the end of the 1990s, with further developments in CGI, special effects spectacle was more prevalent in trailer messages than at any other point in trailer history.

The repetition of central effects images set up by the *Independence Day* advertising echoed through other summer blockbuster trailers of the 1990s. Compelling effects images dominate trailers for *Men in Black*, *Starship Troopers* and *Star Wars Episode 1: The Phantom Menace* (1999): images that were reiterated through a broader visual marketing campaign that now included television spots, behind-the-scenes features (on television and video), and Web sites. Taken out of context, the special effects star image did appear to be a purely spectacular computer generated visual. Within trailers, however, such imagery was traditionally still located within a narrative, even if some trailers featured slimmer narratives than previously. As with the earlier discussion of 1950s trailers, it would be false to claim that 'all' genre trailers followed this pattern. Computer-generated images may feature in blockbuster trailer advertising but different trailers feature fluctuating levels of such spectacles. The trailer for *Alien Resurrection* (1997) keeps most of its creature effects hidden in shadows, or shown in brief glimpses; while the *Men in Black* teaser opens with a huge flying saucer crashing to Earth and ploughing through a park. The breadth of genre narratives in the time period necessarily introduced a variety of trailer structural techniques, not all dominated by effects spectacles.

The Matrix trailer best illustrates this balance between trailer narrative and an effects-based spectacle. Since its release, the film has been renowned as a groundbreaking development and application of computer graphics, particularly for a technique known as 'bullet time' where cameras swoop and move round a slow-motion action sequence. As with *Independence Day*, however, there is an attempt to narrativize the trailer appearance of 'bullet time'. It occurs within a larger explanatory structure that introduces the main characters of Neo (Keanu Reeves), Trinity (Carrie-Anne Moss) and Morpheus (Lawrence Fishbourne), the notion that the 'real' world is a dream, and the question of what 'the Matrix' truly is. Initially, special effects appear in snatches: Trinity jumping between buildings, Neo's hand and arm being covered in some black morphing fluid, Neo and Morpheus 'floating' above a cityscape. The main generic tropes are a dystopian future landscape and a brief glimpse of futuristic machinery: but these are overshadowed by the dominance of action-based imagery that has no strict generic identity. Spectacle begins to encroach on narrative in the final third of the trailer, which is based around a frenetic montage sequence of action and generic imagery. The effects-based movement of an agent 'dodging' bullets, Trinity floating up in the air and kicking an attacker (while the camera drifts around the action), and slow-motion fight scenes in a subway speed past, suggesting a potent mix of action and science fiction elements. This combination of generic elements overwhelms the narrative here: these elements have no distinct purpose to trailer narrative beyond the display of effects and action. The trailer then ends with a final spectacular image: Neo dodging bullets in a 'bullet time' sequence that slows the motion down to show bullet trails streaking past his twisting figure. The final words of the trailer – 'you have to see it for yourself' – are taken from the narrative (Morpheus' warning about the Matrix) but they appear to function here in relation to the spectacle that the final third of the trailer has displayed for audiences.

The trailers for *Independence Day* and *The Matrix* demonstrate the changing nature of blockbuster marketing through the 1990s. Trailer structure itself did not change drastically, although there was a growing tendency towards the frenetic montage sequences seen in *The Matrix* by the end of the decade. Spectacle, now largely created by CGI effects, was a more important element of trailer structure than in previous decades. Yet narrative remained the dominant element of trailer production, introducing the concepts behind the film and the main characters and largely containing spectacle in specific sequences or images. Unlike *Independence Day*, *The Matrix* trailer featured multiple effects images rather than one key moment, so was not discussed as effects spectacle in the same way as the 'White House' shot, and its repetition across multiple marketing materials. The impact of that one moment and the change in production schedules, is still being felt in genre (and non-genre) productions but it reconfirms the importance of the trailer within film-industry marketing (and production) terms. As these analyses have shown, a complete understanding of how genre and spectacle are positioned for audiences necessarily begins with these coming attractions.

Conclusion

The trailer has been the key audio-visual promotional material for almost a hundred years. Even now, in the twenty-first century, the trailer moves freely across media, debuting on film, television, video games, DVDs and the Internet. The preview is still one of the prime locations for displaying advance 'free samples' of future film productions, and the likeliest venue for luring a wide audience with a montage of spectacular images. As the three time periods analysed throughout this chapter prove, however, the placement and display of such spectacle is not a straightforward process and is closely linked to issues of genre popularity and special effects development. What these trailers have revealed is a spectrum of trailer structures that focus on narrative, character and generic elements, with displays of spectacle limited or enhanced by underlying special effects production practices. This demonstrates that genre trailers cannot be reduced simply to visual spectacle. Instead, that spectacle must be related to other structural elements and generic features of the trailer.

The balance of trailer narrative and spectacular imagery has been a facet of trailer structure since 1925, if not before, and over the decades those spectacular images have suggested and created compelling generic imagery: from the flying saucers that visited Earth in *The Day the Earth Stood Still* or *Independence Day* to the dystopian visions of the future in *Blade Runner* and *The Matrix*. Such imagery represents studio assumptions around what they believe audiences will respond to: assumptions that include spectacle but are not limited to it. Effects-based images are one element of a generic sales message alongside other genre conventions around narrative, stars and themes. The use of such imagery may have started in trailers but is now increasingly used across a wider range of audio-visual screens. With imagery being produced earlier in the filmmaking process, marketing for films such as *Cloverfield* and *Transformers: Revenge of the Fallen* (2009) can use those in trailers but also make scenes and sequences available through Web sites or on television entertainment shows. The important difference here is the lack of narrative context, which can increase the idea that such images are only about spectacle, not about the balance of spectacle and narrative seen in trailers. The use of these sequences may confirm George Pal's conviction that special effects are the true stars of the genre but they challenge the primacy of the trailer to show such images. There is no sign of the trailer fading from genre marketing techniques – the release of new trailers is still an important event on film and fan Web sites – but the growth of fan and studio websites does challenge the potency of the format and suggests genre trailers may face an uncertain future. Investigating a range of such Web sites, the next chapter will explore how they engage with and develop generic marketing techniques, influence recent developments in multi-platform storytelling, as well as offering a more active role to fan communities who want to be involved with their favourite genre properties.

–10–

Science Fiction, Audiences and the Internet

In 1984, William Gibson's science-fiction novel *Neuromancer* imagined a network of 'interconnected computers and databanks, which users entered by directly connecting their consciousness to the network or matrix ... Once inside, users could pass along the network and access the databanks' (Bell 2009, 32). This vision of digital connectivity, dubbed 'cyberspace', has been highly influential in generic narratives since the 1980s (most notably in novels by the likes of Gibson, Bruce Sterling and Richard Morgan and in films such as *The Lawnmower Man* and *The Matrix*). While the real-world network of the Internet has not yet become a space where users connect their 'consciousness' or 'jack in', as Gibson described, it has affected the relationship between genre producer and audience, creating an (alleged) participatory space for interaction and contestation.

This chapter will explore that space in relation to two specific functions of this online relationship: marketing and fan participation. As in Chapters 8 and 9, this work will develop and complicate the claim that film marketing tends to avoid specific genre messages, by looking at how online promotional materials for science-fiction properties use generic information to target and attract fan audiences. These Web sites, therefore, are the latest 'interpretative frames' attempting to 'influence the public consumption of cultural artefacts' (Klinger 1994, xvi). Since the first basic text- and image-based sites of the late 1990s, the use of Web sites, video documentaries, trailers and alternative reality games (ARG) has grown exponentially in the first years of the twenty-first century: both *A.I: Artificial Intelligence* and *Cloverfield* made use of the Internet to create complex online challenges for genre fans to explore. Yet this extended marketing campaign is only one element of how online participation has complicated the producer-fan relationship. Fan audiences are described as the 'most active segment of the media audience' (Jenkins [2006] 2008, 135) and have rarely been passive in relation to genre properties (science fiction universes were expanded through fan interaction before the Internet: see, for example, Jenkins 1992, Penley 1991b, 1991d). The chapter will therefore move on from industrial use of the Internet to consider how the move online has made fan activity both more visible, and more contentious. Given the increased presence of science fiction fans producing 'fake' trailers, posters and fan films for existing genre films and television series, this level of participation with cultural texts often stands in opposition to the producers who would prefer to retain control over the extended narrative of their generic universe.

At the centre of these debates lies a series of theories and production tendencies best summed up by Henry Jenkins' phrase 'convergence culture', which describes a complex industrial and cultural process where producers and fans engage (Jenkins [2006] 2008). This process is rarely as one-sided or directed as many producers imagine and (as suggested above) can often represent a site of struggle around ownership, resistance to producer or studio policy and direct fan-based action. While the areas covered in this chapter do not cover the full range of online producer-fan interactions, they point out some of the genre-specific areas where such interaction and contestation has taken place.

Marketing Science Fiction Films Online

The idea of convergence culture is not restricted to the Internet, but it has become the most visible site where the relationships between fan and studio can coalesce. One perceptible form of this interaction was the transfer and development of existing studio publicity materials on to Web sites. The movement of genre marketing materials on to the Internet largely holds true to the idea that all modes of 'new' media borrow from existing 'old' media in order to establish themselves within culture (Pingree and Gitelman 2003). Early film-specific Web sites relied on text and photographs to display existing posters, news, interviews, star biographies and narrative information on a basic site. In many senses, these were online pressbooks, displaying relevant film information to all audiences (rather than the exhibitor focus of studio pressbooks). The Web site for *Star Wars* (www.starwars.com), developed by Lucasfilm, featured many of these elements in 1997–8, when it began to promote the production process of *Star Wars Episode 1: The Phantom Menace*. However, rather than simply display posters, news, and interviews, the site also made short video documentaries available that offered audiences a glimpse inside the making of the much-anticipated prequel.[1] Much heralded at the time, such videos are now a commonplace addition to genre and non-genre Web campaigns.

The addition of audio-visual sources such as documentaries, interviews and trailers expanded the scope of what Web sites could offer but they were largely repurposing information rather than creating anything medium-specific for genre fans. Producing trailer content specifically for the Internet raised the expectations of genre audiences, particularly when these trailers featured heightened fast-paced editing that required the trailer to be downloaded and rewatched: an activity that encouraged participation, with individual fans debating and discussing the content of such official trailers with the larger fan community (Johnston 2008a, 148). This work has direct links to earlier discussions of genre marketing, focusing attention on to established iconography within science fiction sequels, prequels, or adaptations: the teaser trailer for *Star Trek* (2009), for example, displayed the construction of the (new) Enterprise while the teaser for *Star Wars Episode 2: Attack of the Clones*

(2002) had a brief glimpse of a spaceship associated with fan favourite character, Boba Fett. Equally, dense trailers for video game adaptations *Doom* and *Resident Evil* contained brief snatches of recognizable weaponry or design elements with which existing fans would already have been familiar.

Designing more complex and dense advertising materials for known genre products is one way in which production companies hoped to encourage fan participation in online marketing. Web campaigns for *A.I.: Artificial Intelligence* and *Cloverfield* complicated this concept of fan engagement by designing Web campaigns that led committed genre fans on a hunt through various sites for clues or potential narrative spoilers. Following the lead of *The Blair Witch Project* (1999), a horror project that used online sites to build up a fictionalized back story around an urban legend, the first trailer for *A.I.: Artificial Intelligence* made reference to a 'Sentient Machine Therapist,' Jeanine Salla. Fans who searched for that name on Google found links to more Web pages which debated topics such as 'thinking robots, robot liberation and a murder mystery' (CNN 2001) while being exposed to a wider universe depicting the future of the twenty-second century through unique design features, magazines, family Web sites and political movements (Boswell 2001). Such genre elements as sentient robots, robot suicide and debates around robot rights echo back to earlier texts such as *R.U.R.* and *Cherry 2000*, but these elements were not being presented in the traditional form of a cause-and-effect narrative. Instead, these thematic and world-building elements were scattered across numerous Web sites, a marketing campaign that was dependent on the dedication of genre fans to construct (or reconstruct) the story themselves, share information and debate it online, in order to create an additional 'viral' element to the publicity campaign.

Although few Hollywood films deployed this level of marketing (the Web site for *Inception* (2010), for example, relied on traditional posters, videos, and narrative summaries), it remained central to some of the more visible genre successes of the early 2000s. *The Matrix* sequels (discussed further below) represented one of the major examples post-*A.I.*, and *Cloverfield* developed the earlier work on viral campaigns to, again, encourage fans to participate in the discovery of a complex backstory. The first *Cloverfield* teaser trailer, with its reference to www.1-08-08.com, began to seed clues about a character called Rob Hawkins (Michael Stahl-David), with photos of him and other characters, alongside links to his MySpace page. The use of social networking sites was particularly innovative, with several characters regularly updating in 'real time,' counting down to Rob's leaving party (on 8 January 2008, also the film's release date). Though this initial activity featured few genre elements (beyond the teaser's suggestion of a monster attacking New York: a genre staple), a comment that Rob was taking a job with the Tagruato Corporation began to introduce more familiar science-fiction tropes. As with *A.I.*, dedicated fans who searched for Tagruato found an official Web site and links to Slusho, a soft drink made from 'sea-bed nectar' that Tagruato produced. Further exploration (shared among the collective of fans, who now had their own Web sites on which to share information, such as www.cloverfieldclues.blogspot.com) revealed footage of an attack on Tagruato's Chuai Station, doctored photographs, and reports of something mysterious headed underwater towards New York.[2] The use of viral marketing campaigns allowed producers to target genre fans with suggestive imagery and themes (robots and futuristic design in *A.I.*, suggestion of mutations, monsters and conspiracy theories in *Cloverfield*). The combination of old and new media (trailers and Web sites) suggested a wider participation between studio and fan audience than before, with a particular focus on revealing a larger story world or generic universe.

Transmedia Storytelling in Science Fiction

The online campaigns for *A.I.* and *Cloverfield* (and a recent, more generically obtuse example, *The Dark Knight*, 2008) link up to larger debates within generic film and television production around narrative extension and fan audiences. Trans- or cross- media storytelling has been fuelled by corporate convergence and the ability of genre narratives to exist across multiple media platforms. It has become more common among genre television series in the U.S. and Britain, with *Heroes* (2007–10), *Lost*, *Flash Forward* (2009–10), and *Doctor Who* offering extended multi-platform narratives, but one of the strongest (and earliest) examples of this trend comes through *The Matrix* film trilogy. Henry Jenkins uses *The Matrix* franchise to demonstrate the narrative overlap (and reliance) on multiple platforms, with elements of a central story progressing from film to comic book to short animated film to videogame back to film and then to a multiplayer game set in an expanding online universe. The growth of such projects within genre production represented a renewed interest in fan communities by creators, producers and corporations, driven by a belief that invested fans (a category that, through the first decade of the twenty-first century, had become increasingly mainstream) were higher consumers of such cross-media texts, willing to follow this extended, canonical, narrative. The creation and maintenance of coherent story universes was already familiar in *Star Trek* and *Star Wars* (and fantasy worlds such as J. R. R. Tolkein's *The Lord of the Rings*), but genre creators and corporations were increasingly conscious of using cross-platform storytelling within genre production in film, television, videogames and beyond.

Transmedia storytelling fleshed out the larger narrative of *The Matrix* universe through the production of short animations (released on DVD as *The Animatrix*), a video game (*Enter the Matrix*), comic books (*The Matrix Comics*), and an online ARG (*The Matrix Online*). Creating a multimedia production was not a new event in Hollywood (novelizations, video games, merchandise, and theme park rides were all common brand extensions by the late 1990s), but Jenkins claims that *The Matrix* added a unique element by continuing its central narrative across all these media platforms: thus, characters who only appear briefly in *The Matrix Revolutions* are fleshed out in *Enter the Matrix*; narrative subplots that are quickly resolved in *The Matrix Revolutions* actually occur in more depth in *The Animatrix*. Watching the three films would give audiences access to a streamlined master narrative, but the full narrative experience was gained by moving across media. In a similar fashion to the viral marketing campaigns discussed above, *The Matrix* required this level of fan participation to make sense of its complex story-world:

> Fans raced, dazed and confused, from the theatres to plug into Internet discussion lists, where every detail would be dissected and every possible interpretation debated ... *The Matrix* is entertainment for the age of media convergence, integrating multiple texts to create a narrative so large that it cannot be contained within a single medium. (Jenkins [2006] 2008, 96)

Crucial within this theory is the concept that each medium adds something new and unique. Unlike merchandising, where there is rarely a narrative function to a T-shirt or an action figure, Jenkins argues that each new iteration of the genre universe, each new text, offers a new entry point to the narrative, making 'a distinctive and valuable contribution to the whole ... Reading across the media sustains a depth of experience that motivates more consumption' (Jenkins 2006 [2008], 98). The power of transmedia storytelling in these genre examples is driven by creator and economic justifications but it relies heavily on fan participation to an unprecedented degree. It remains unclear, however, whether a mainstream audience that does not engage with these narrative extensions can continue to comprehend the master narrative.

These twenty-first century examples of transmedia storytelling suggest that there is something about the introduction of the Internet that has motivated this increased assumption around fan interaction and participation. Yet within science-fiction film and broadcasting history there are equally strong examples that existed before the digital turn. The DC Comics superhero, *Superman*, has existed across a variety of media since the character first appeared in *Action Comics* in 1938. Created by Jerry Seigel and Joe Schuster, this science fiction story concerns an alien child that is sent to Earth in a rocket ship seconds before his own planet is destroyed. Discovered by an earth couple, the Kents, the child grows up, discovers he has superpowers, moves to a nearby big city, and lives a double life as a mild-mannered reporter and a superhero, while falling in love with the *Daily Planet*'s female reporter, Lois Lane. By the early 1940s this basic narrative was being added to by a newspaper strip, a radio serial and an animated film series. As with *The Matrix*, certain story points only made sense if audiences were aware of all the different iterations of the character. Superman's parents (Jor-El and Lara) and Superman's real name (Kal-El) first appeared in the newspaper strip; the radio show added Kryptonite and *Daily Planet* staffers Perry White and Jimmy Olsen to the *Superman* universe; while both the radio show and Fleischer Studios' animated series made Superman fly (he only leapt tall buildings in the comic book). It is possible to see *Superman* as a transmedia narrative, with the story existing across three distinct media: publishing (comics and newspapers), radio and film. In order to comprehend the story world of Superman completely, audiences would need to be familiar with all of these different media. This fulfils many of Jenkins' notions of transmedia storytelling, albeit 60 years removed from the digital turn and the Internet, which are so central to that concept.[3]

Yet the difference between *Superman* and *The Matrix* returns to ideas around fan participation and the density of the media with which they are interacting. Equally, all of the examples listed above were eventually worked into the comic series, meaning that it remained the main narrative that the others adapted or to which they added. With the expanded universes of *A.I.*, *Cloverfield* and *The Matrix*, producers were requiring fan audiences to expend more energy, to engage with a wider range of media texts and to work as a collective to piece together the range of clues and narrative pieces that had been strewn across media platforms. There remains an uncertainty over the balance between the narrative opportunities inherent in transmedia storytelling and the overarching industrial need to use such expansions to encourage audience consumption of branded products. However, tensions between fan audiences and the owners of genre franchises are not new and, as with the other examples of convergence culture discussed above, have been exacerbated and made visible by the introduction of the Internet.

Science Fiction Fans

Online marketing, studio and film-specific Web sites, viral marketing techniques and cross-media expansions of narrative universes could all be described as 'top-down' promotional techniques that try to target specific audience groups: in the case of *The Matrix* and *Cloverfield*, this included science fiction, horror and anime fan communities. Yet there is an equally strong grassroots (or 'bottom-up') movement among genre fans to claim elements of their favourite science fiction universes for themselves, to use them in ways that official producers are often uncomfortable with and take legal action to try and restrict. Science fiction fans have been adopting and adapting the content of their favourite generic texts for decades but the development of new desktop computer technology has led to a wider awareness of fan-produced works that draw upon (and enhance) existing generic conventions and tropes. These 'fake' trailers, posters, fan films and fictions demonstrate how genre fans have used the medium-specific opportunities of the Internet to gain some degree of control over the production of cultural texts and offer their own, unique, narrative extensions to corporate franchises.

While some fan use of digital technologies has been discussed in negative terms, notably around online piracy (for example, the illegal downloading of a work print of *X-Men Origins: Wolverine* in Spring 2009), most discussions are more positive in nature. At the same time as studios began to explore the possibilities of online marketing, a variety of fan Web sites began to appear. Some, in the form of *Ain't It Cool News* or *Coming Attractions*, existed to inform fans of news (or 'spoilers') about forthcoming films; while others were film- or franchise-specific fan sites that replicated many features of existing fanzines. Normally labours of love, individual sites could feature episode guides, screen images, fan fiction and artwork that were collected and collated offline and made available online. Science fiction texts were central to both varieties of Web site, alongside fantasy, horror and comic book adaptations. Again, the primacy of specific genre audiences in these debates suggests an additional reason why studio attempts around viral marketing and transmedia storytelling tend to target those demographics. Many of these sites feature an online extension of 'textual poaching' (Jenkins 1992) – an offline activity around fan fiction and artwork that has flourished in an online setting (often to the displeasure of those older fans who have been producing their own fan extensions for decades).

This 'poaching' can take many forms, though many mimic the officially sanctioned format of the object of affection: notably fake posters and trailers for projects fans would like to see. Several fan-produced trailers for *Star Wars Episode 2: Attack of the Clones* were incredibly competent compilations that could be read as a laundry list of elements die-hard fans were eager to see in the second prequel, or which responded to rumoured appearances of actors or characters (perhaps the most famous example of this is a fan trailer featuring images of Christopher Walken, multiple Boba Fetts, and a rampaging horde of Jedi warriors that, on closer inspection, were a kilted army borrowed from *Braveheart* with digitally added lightsabers). Alongside this trend, recent years have seen a spate of trailer 'mash-ups', fake advertisements that combine different films and genres for comic purposes. With several genre-specific entries (*300 Jedi, Star Wars: The Empire Brokeback, Brokeback to the Future,* or *The Terminator* and *The Matrix* recast as love stories), these mash-ups represent one of the more visible online 'poaching' activities. While both trailer-based activities rely on re-editing existing film footage (and soundtrack elements such as dialogue, music and sound effects), they are often more interested in the character dynamics and emotions as displaying spectacular special effects. With many fans interested in characterization and emotional connection and most studio online material designed around extended narratives and special effects, this fan reuse of copyrighted material in distinct and unlicensed ways points up one of the main areas of departure between these two online activities.

The trailer mash-ups are an online sphere where different readings of a film, a franchise, or a character, become most visible. Although many are designed to be comic perspectives that read 'against the grain' (using *Brokeback Mountain* to 'reveal' homosexual subtext in *Star Wars* or *Back to the Future*), this represents a move away from the established (copyrighted) universe: a move that production companies and corporations have tended to frown upon. Paramount tended not to pursue legal action against *Star Trek* fans in the 1980s who were writing 'slash fiction' (about a homosexual relationship a large group of female *Trek* fans saw between Captain Kirk and Spock), the rise of the Internet has (again) made such work more accessible. Rather than appearing in limited run fanzines, or exchanged among like-minded fans at conventions or small meetings, online slash fiction is only a hyperlink or Google search away. To look at one example, the Fandom Haven Story Archive (www.fhsarchive.com/autoarchive/categories.php) divides their archive of fan fiction into GEN (general), HET (heterosexual) and SLASH. With over 100 different categories of fan fiction, there are numerous genre entries. Some are familiar and popular (options for all *Star Trek* series and movies; *Star Wars*, *Babylon 5*) whereas others are more focused (*Battlestar Galactica*, both new and original; *Smallville*; both *Stargate SG-1* and *Atlantis*; *Blake's 7*). There is a tendency for television series to dominate: only *Lord of the Rings*, *Pirates of the Caribbean*, *Star Trek* (movies) and *Star Wars* appear on the list. There can be a playful quality to many such stories but the degree of sexual content concerns franchise owners, who believe that such stories break a tacit agreement between producer and fan, taking copyrighted characters into situations that were never intended by their creators.

Given that the growing use of multiplatform marketing techniques and transmedia narratives rely on fan participation, the use (or misuse) of copyrighted material is unlikely to cease. As demonstrated above, fan participation with fictional universes has a long history that predates the Internet by decades and will no doubt continue to fuel part of genre audience interaction with these science fiction texts and characters. Henry Jenkins believes that the industrial and fan models of the audience (broadly speaking, audience as willing consumer versus audience as individual creator) need to converge to allow the fan to gain investment in new and unfamiliar genre universes. Yet the growing power of conglomerates, and the multiplatform world that genre products now exist within, seems more invested in a standard model of leading and guiding audiences than empowering them to develop their own unique contributions to that universe.

Conclusion

This chapter has focused on the rise of Internet-based developments around fan and corporate production (the *Cloverfield* marketing campaign, *The Matrix* transmedia narrative, fan stories and videos) but genre texts have expanded on other technologies. Fuelled by the success of the Internet (and mirroring certain technological aspects) twenty-first century mobile phones have become more than portable audio communication devices. By 2010, most phones contained a camera, e-mail, music and video players, access to social networks and other Internet sites and a growing number of applications (apps) that could convert the phone into a map, measuring tape, compass or electronic book. The phone had become a real world equivalent of *The Hitchhiker's Guide to the Galaxy*, or a combination of *Star Trek*'s communicator and tri-corder.

This link to previously fictional technology is not accidental because it reasserts the interplay between the science fiction genre and the cultural awareness that has grown up around generic conventions and technologies. Yet the expansion of mobile phone apps offers its own impact on the chapter's discussion of fan audiences and technology-based genre extensions. At a basic level, science fiction texts are now available in a portable format: an Apple iPhone, for example, could contain the complete science fiction works of H. G. Wells; a collection of *Superman* comics; downloaded episodes of *Blake's 7*; trailers for *Inception* (2010) and *Never Let Me Go* (2010); fan trailers such as *Brokeback to the Future* or a recent genre feature such as *Hot Tube Time Machine* (2010). Given the propensity of genre fan audiences to be early adopters, the same corporations keen to target those groups with transmedia narratives or multiplatform marketing, are aware of the potential of these new devices.

One early example of where this might lead is the use of augmented reality within mobile phone apps. A term given to applications that combine virtual data with the 'real world', these use a phone's GPS, compass and camera to offer additional overlaid information: directions to the nearest underground station in London, the nearest Wi-Fi connection, the location of the nearest Twitter user or excerpts from a tourist guide (Parr 2009). These early examples offer little that is specific to the science-fiction film, or genre marketing, but additional apps developed for the iPhone included the ability to use your phone as a ray gun, with different weapons available that could be used to 'shoot' people captured using the phone's video or still camera (Elliot 2009). These gaming possibilities offered the most obvious development for genre marketing, seen clearly in the *Iron Man 2* (2010) augmented reality app released alongside the film on LG phones. Here, genre elements were combined with the basic tenets of the augmented reality app, offering users the chance to 'see the world as Tony Stark sees it' (Total Immersion 2010): using the phone's camera to get a picture of themselves, the app would form the helmet and armour of Iron Man over the owner, 'turning' them into the superhero. The phone then gave a 'heads-up' display of what the world would look like if seen through the computer display from inside the costume, and allowed the owner to use the phone to control the Iron Man figure in an AR game that utilized the phone's motion detection software.

The press release from Total Immersion, Paramount and Marvel highlighted concepts and terms familiar from earlier applications of new technology to genre products and genre audiences. This campaign was 'one of the most compelling extensions to a film franchise' that was 'engaging consumers across a range of brands' (Total Immersion 2010). As with the *A.I.*, *Matrix* and *Cloverfield* campaigns, this app is described as extending narrative, expanding the possibility of fan interaction with a known franchise and creating lucrative brand extensions for the conglomerates controlling those franchises. Rather than empowering and engaging fans, or offering the immersive experience that is suggested here, this new technological marketing device contained the same predetermined limits as a Web site or a press book: fan participation is contained and prescribed, rather than open.

This connection between genre marketing and new technology may not be unique to the science-fiction genre, but in the last decade it has been science-fiction properties that have explored these possibilities: *Star Wars Episode 1: The Phantom Menace* used its online video documentaries to popularize Apple's Quicktime software; *The Matrix* used DVD and the Internet to expand its narrative; the *Cloverfield* campaign popularized alternative reality games; *Star Wars Episode 3: Revenge of the Sith* (2005) launched a wide range of downloads for Orange mobile phones; and *Iron Man 2* has explored the potential of mobile media devices as a new genre marketing tool or platform for transmedia extensions. As this chapter has demonstrated, these corporate-led approaches to increasing audience participation with science fiction universes represented one approach to fan interaction. The other approach, where fans control and release their own contributions, is more contentious in the industry (where such use of audio-visual footage is often seen as copyright infringement) but is equally being encouraged by technological development. Desktop editing software, file sharing on the Internet, social networking sites, and the increased capacity of video cameras on mobile phones has made it easier for fans to self-produce and disseminate their ideas. There is no sign of Henry Jenkins' hoped-for rapprochement between these two approaches but it is clear that these contentious (and now highly visible) interactions will continue to fuel the relationship between genre producer and genre audience.

Conclusion

The introduction to this book noted that it was not concerned with a concrete, unyielding definition of the science fiction film genre because the best way to approach this (and arguably other) genres was to appreciate its flexibility and hybridity. As the preceding ten chapters have demonstrated, the science-fiction genre has never been easy to define: the disparate threads of the pre-1950s films offer scattered elements that suggest later generic definitions and the hybrid possibilities of the science-fiction format; the 1950s, the first period to have a firmer genre identity, is more complex and multiple than the traditional alien invasion/Cold War menace metaphor allows – and since that first 'golden age', international film industries have tended to use American science fiction as a model to emulate, develop or directly challenge.

During the writing of this book, Hollywood films such as *Avatar* and *Inception* have reconfirmed the blockbuster status of certain science-fiction projects, the international contributions *District 9* and *Moon* have combined genre credentials with lower budget 'arthouse' success and the rediscovery of lost footage in Argentina has propelled the German proto-genre classic *Metropolis* back into cinemas and public consciousness. These are five distinct films, each with different perspectives on the genre, each containing unique conventions that make it hard to offer a strict definition of what it is about all five that makes them 'science fiction'. It may be their use of technology, their interest in the relationship between human and science, their depiction of the 'Other' (whether that figure is human or alien), or their visions of the past, present and future. In many cases, the director, producer or studio may have marketed the film as science fiction, the critic may have used that term in describing it, audience members may have chosen it based on known generic pleasures and academics may have chosen to include those films in a book on the genre. Each of these groups plays a role in the larger definition and policing of the borders of genre and, although this book never intended to declare any such generic position right or wrong, this investigation has hopefully opened up those different perspectives on genre creation and expansion.

In these closing pages, then, it is worth restating what the book did intend to do and that is to broaden the discussion of genre. It is becoming more commonplace to hear students of film genre talk about Jason Mittell, Mark Jancovich and even, sometimes, Andrew Tudor, and to see them understand that a combination of cultural, industrial and textual information is a necessary shift within genre studies. This book hopes to have made its own contribution to that debate by opening up different periods, presenting new perspectives or introducing new film titles to this ongoing process of exploration and investigation. There remains much to be uncovered and revealed about the history of the science fiction film genre: the pre-1950 period is under-researched, even given the smaller number of films that have survived and are available to view; the focus of 1950s science-fiction film promotional materials and critical reviews may offer a challenge to reflectionist readings of the period; while the changes in science fiction film production in other countries from the 1960s onward contain potent challenges to definitions of the genre drawn purely from American examples. And those are simply film-based projects. The book has occasionally strayed into other media but there are significant links between film, television, video games and the Internet that lie outside of this current study but which present equally fertile ground for how genre is created and exists across multiple media formats.

So, as *Science Fiction: A Critical Introduction* concludes, it is important to stress the final word of that title. This book has aimed to introduce the major debates and critical positions available within current science-fiction genre studies, as well as point towards the vast range of competing approaches, methodologies and potential titles that could be included within any future study. The rest is now up to you, the reader, to develop, to apply, and to challenge. The future of science fiction genre studies is still unwritten, still open to interpretation and unique research, still out there.

Like so many of the science fictions studied herein, this is not the end – simply the beginning.

Notes

Introduction

1. This book will use the full term 'science fiction,' but may use the shorter 'sci-fi' or 'SF' as required: and thus does not see these terms as distinct entities, rather as abbreviations.

Chapter 1

1. Robert Maltby argues that early genre choice was driven by male critics, who focused on male genres (the Western, gangster and *film noir*) that dramatized masculine stories. Chapter 2 will explore this theme in relation to the science-fiction film.
2. The Sam clones are also differentiated through costume design. They are given different clothing styles to suggest their different ages (they are three years apart), attitudes and taste. The 'new' Sam is much more regimented and military, while the 'old' Sam is more slovenly.
3. The absence of the musical, the horror film or the war film, despite all three being dominant in different periods of American film production, represents a particularly curious lack.
4. The selection process included 1,500 members, who voted on a pre-selected list of 500 films (50 per genre), with the ultimate aim to drive 'audiences to discover and rediscover the classics of American film' (AFI 2008b, 2).
5. The AFI ballot additionally noted that 'By presenting dreamlike realms where fairies flourish, witches scheme and pigs fly, fantasy demands that audiences believe in magic and hope for wishes to come true' (AFI 2008c, 16). Notions of 'magic' are seen as absent from science fiction, although as Arthur C. Clarke once observed, any sufficiently advanced technology can seem like magic to those who do not understand it.
6. The only genre not covered would be science-fiction-courtroom drama. Although there are no science fiction films that borrow from this 'genre', there are numerous examples from science fiction television, including the *Star Trek: The Next Generation* episode 'The Measure of a Man', *Star Trek: Deep Space Nine*'s 'Tribunal' and *Doctor Who*'s 'The Trial of a Timelord'.

Chapter 2

1. This assumption is fuelled by media portrayals of such characters: from *The Simpsons'* Comic Book Guy and Neo in *The Matrix* to Harry Knowles, the creator of Aint-It-Cool-News, who present a particular masculinized version of the 'geek'. Of course, the reality is that most science-fiction fandom probably follows the *Star Trek* example, with a more equal split between men and women.

2. Recent examples of reflective analysis would include the reaction to characters in *Star Wars Episode 1: The Phantom Menace* and *Transformers: Revenge of the Fallen*. Both films came under attack for stereotypical characterizations: in *Phantom Menace* the villainous Neimodians and the slapstick CGI creation Jar Jar Binks were seen as, respectively, Asian and Jamaican stereotypes; while critics of *Transformers: Revenge of the Fallen* derided the film for blatant racist caricatures.

3. Of course, it could be argued that this supports a broader normative system: Lambda chooses heterosexual love rather than the moon's (potentially homosexual) society.

4. This colonialism is given additional visual emphasis when the Grungees, who have been speaking their own language throughout, learn English in order to write a goodbye sign for their capitalist buddy George Jetson.

5. That is not to say that this approach privileges individual thought, given that a key work in the field, Laura Mulvey's 'Visual Pleasure and Narrative Cinema,' limited the spectatorial positions available to an audience.

6. Some fan cultures (or members of specific fan cultures) are not 'active' in the ways discussed here, and might express their fandom in equally valid but largely unobserved or unquantifiable ways (see Geraghty 2006 on less visible aspects of fandom).

7. Booker's specific examples are *Star Wars*, *Alien* and *Blade Runner* versus *Close Encounters*, *Jaws*, and *Saturday Night Fever*: the comparison of genre texts with non-genre may skew the effectiveness of the argument, but its larger points about how different audiences engage with different genre texts can be applied to a wide range of science fiction, from *Star Trek* to *Serenity*.

8. Although female writers and producers for science fiction film and television are becoming more prevalent, the genre still lacks well-known and popular female screenwriters, directors or television show runners. The most notable female genre creators include Kathryn Bigelow (*Strange Days*) and Jane Espenson (*Buffy the Vampire Slayer*, 1997–2003; *Dollhouse*, 2009–10; *Battlestar Galactica*, 2004–9; *Warehouse 13*, 2009; *Caprica*, 2010–).

9. *The Simpsons* (1989–), *South Park* (1997–), *Futurama* (1999–) and *Family Guy* (1999–) are only the most visible examples of televised animated comedy that pushes self-referential and postmodern conceits to their limits.

Chapter 3

1. Dioramas added extra three-dimensional elements to their scenes, to convince their audience of an increased sense of realism.
2. As Scott Bukatman observes, however, this immersion in the apparently 'real' is unlikely to have been complete: the audience were willing spectators, having paid a fee to enter (Bukatman 1999, 249).

Chapter 4

1. Although reliant on similar techniques to earlier invisibility films, the 1933 effects did expand the possibilities of trick photography and were promoted as groundbreaking in a cover story for *Scientific American*. 'Now You See Him: The Invisible Man Revealed', *The Invisible Man: The Legacy Collection* DVD (Universal, 2004)
2. The notion that this narrative denouement could be seen as a promotion of female suffrage, given the film's reversal of other 1911 traits, is presumably not the intention of the film which, like many others, is about men regaining power, not women gaining it.

Chapter 5

1. Jancovich (1996) and Geraghty (2009) offer two of the strongest exceptions, and rebuttals, to this approach yet Vizzini (2009) suggests that earlier interpretations still have power and influence.
2. This move from Soviet threat to alien craft was encouraged by two books published in 1950: Donald Keyhoe's *Flying Saucers Are Real* and Frank Scully's *Behind the Flying Saucers*.
3. The Martian war machines of Wells' *War of the Worlds* were updated due to contemporary influences. According to director Byron Haskin, the original description of them 'didn't fit in with … the flying saucer scare at the time' (Haskin, quoted in Hickman 1977, 65).
4. Donlevy played Professor Bernard Quatermass in Hammer's two 1950 Quatermass films, *The Quatermass Xperiment* (1955) and *Quatermass 2* (1957). The role has also been performed by various actors on television and in a third film.
5. Robby the Robot's film credits include *The Invisible Boy*, *Gremlins* (1984), *Cherry 2000*, and *Looney Tunes: Back in Action* (1999). Television credits include *The Thin Man*, *Lost in Space*, *Hollywood Boulevard* and *Wonder Woman*.
6. There is obviously an issue here with the viewing of American prints of Japanese films, not least around translation and, potentially, additions/subtractions from

the original film (as happened with the American release of *Godzilla*). Where possible, reference is made to the original Japanese release.

7. Mechanical motion control was used in *2001* to allow cameras to repeat specific movements, an essential factor to build up the multiple layers needed for special effects shots. ILM computerized a similar system for *Star Wars*.

Chapter 6

1. *The Towering Inferno* and *Earthquake* both have tangential links to the science fiction genre: *Inferno* directly references the uncertain (and potentially) lethal properties of advanced technology, while both films present their view of a possible (dystopian) alternate future through spectacular state-of-the-art effects technologies.

2. This is restricted to science fiction films, obviously. In genre television, and literature, alien invasion continued to be a popular theme. Between 1970 and 1980 *Doctor Who*, for example, dealt with invasions from Daleks, Cybermen, Sontarans, Giant Spiders and the Autons/Nestene Consciousness.

3. Yvonne Tasker offers a useful criticism of a similar Britton-esque Vietnam allegory in relation to *Rambo: First Blood, Part II* (Tasker 1993, 105).

Chapter 7

1. There is, unfortunately, not space within this chapter – or book – to offer a detailed assessment of Japanese anime and its growing contribution to, and influence on, international generic production (not simply science fiction). Rayna Denison's forthcoming book *Anime: A Critical Introduction* (Berg 2012) will offer a more concerted examination.

2. The *Monsters vs Aliens* characters and the 1950s creatures that likely inspired them are Ginormica (*Attack of the Fifty Foot Woman*), B.O.B. (*The Blob, It Came From Outer Space*), Dr Cockroach PhD (*The Fly, Wasp Woman*), The Missing Link (*The Creature From the Black Lagoon*) and Insectosaurus (a combination of many 1950s giant insect and monster movies, most notably the Japanese *Mosura/Mothra*, 1961)

3. Sequels, despite being an essential part of the film industry since the silent era, have been seen as a necessary evil within recent science fiction genre production. The 1990s began with a flurry of sequels to 1980s successes (*Gremlins 2: The New Batch* (1990), *Robocop 2* (1990), *Predator 2* (1990), *Terminator 2: Judgement Day* (1991), and *Alien 3* (1992); *Star Trek* continued on with four television series, and five additional cinema outings before the part-prequel, part-'reimagining', *Star Trek* (2009); while *Star Wars* re-released 'special editions' of the original

1977–83 trilogy, and three prequels, starting with *Star Wars Episode 1: The Phantom Menace.*

4. *The Day After Tomorrow* (2004) can be seen (and was, by many critics) as an attempt to destroy New York (and other international locations) without causing physical destruction: hence, the CGI effects work in the film emphasized frozen landmarks such as the Statue of Liberty. By 2008, attitudes appeared to have reverted to type, with the same landmark beheaded by the unnamed alien monster of *Cloverfield.*

Chapter 8

1. This process continues during theatrical and DVD releases, as well as subsequent television and Internet screenings: this chapter, however, focuses only on the prerelease construction of this identity.
2. Unless otherwise noted, all press books discussed in this chapter were accessed via the British Film Institute library, in either paper or microfilm versions.

Chapter 9

1. Further work on the display of visual spectacle in science fiction trailers can be found in my 2009 book *Coming Soon: Film Trailers and the Selling of Hollywood Technology.*

Chapter 10

1. In one sense, such videos were simply an online version of earlier 'making of' VHS and television programmes and were often repurposed as DVD Special Features.
2. Another Web site (www.jamieandteddy.com) featured an apparently unrelated video diary between a girl (Jamie) and her boyfriend (Teddy). By the fifth video, it was clear that Teddy had also taken a job with Tagruato and had now disappeared. The main link to the *Cloverfield* film narrative was a photo of Jamie (from Rob's leaving party) on www.1-08-08.com. Post-film and before the DVD release, www.MissingTeddyHansen.blogspot.com offered a further narrative extension.
3. The example of *Superman* continues to apply into the 1990s, when the marriage of Clark Kent and Lois Lane occurred in TV series *Lois and Clark: The New Adventures of Superman*, alongside the comic books and animated cartoons.

Annotated Guide to Further Reading

Altman, R. (1999) *Film/Genre*. London: BFI and Neale, S. (2000) *Genre and Hollywood*. Abingdon: Routledge.

While neither book can conclusively corral the different genres under consideration, both offer useful analyses of the processes by which film genres were constructed and altered through the twentieth century. Industrial and textual foci are paramount here, alongside useful expansions into the role of marketing and critical reviews. There is, however, little sense of the audience's place in genre definition in either book.

Biskind, P. (1983) *Seeing is Believing: How Hollywood Taught Us to Stop Worrying and Love the Fifties*. London: Bloomsbury.

Although only a quarter of this book engages with science fiction, it offers an early attempt to examine the interplay of genres and American culture. One of the most accessible pieces of critical writing on this period, its major failing is the common assumption that films only represent one perspective on culture.

Brooks, M. and Barker, K. (1998) *Knowing Audiences: Judge Dredd, Its Friends, Fans and Foes*. Luton: University of Luton Press.

One of the few in-depth studies of the blockbuster audience, this comes with a science-fiction case study. Its exploration of the pleasures of viewing (including spectacle and genre), and the varied responses a single film can elicit, necessarily complicates any definition of genre that is solely based on textual evidence.

Cornea, Christine (2007) *Science Fiction: Between Fantasy and Reality*. Edinburgh: Edinburgh University Press.

A historical and cultural study of science-fiction films, this offers useful developments in often overlooked areas, most notably gender, the Orient and performance in science-fiction films. Strong analysis of individual films is supported by fascinating interviews with many key genre figures.

Jancovich, Mark (2002) '"A Real Shocker": Authenticity, Genre and the Struggle for Distinction', in Turner, G. (ed.), *The Film Cultures Reader*. London: Routledge, pp. 469–80.

Like Brooks and Barker, or Tulloch and Jenkins, this essay raises a necessary complication around audiences and genre, namely how audiences use and adapt specific canons to create their own genre hierarchies. Given the focus of genre studies has largely seen academics policing artificial borders, this article demonstrates how audience members and groups contribute to generic definitions and discourse.

Kuhn, A. (1990 and 1999) *Alien Zone: Cultural Theory and Contemporary Science Fiction Cinema*; *Alien Zone II: The Spaces of Science Fiction Cinema*. London: Verso.

There are many strong edited collections of essays on science fiction 'out there' but the essays collected together in these volumes represent some of the best critical writing on the genre. Both are products of their time: the psychoanalytic and postmodern emphasis of *Alien Zone* is a fitting summary of the 1980s, while the sequel's 1990s focus gives increased space to fandom and cross-media genre relationships.

Pierson, M. (2002) *Special Effects: Still in Search of Wonder*. New York: Columbia University Press.

This in-depth look at special effects considers how they are produced, what meanings have been associated with them, and how they have been used across a variety of genres, though with an emphasis on science fiction.

Sontag, S. (1965) 'The Imagination of Disaster', *Commentary* (October): 42–8.

The essay from which all other science fiction genre criticism grew, Sontag's work is problematic (see Chapter 3) but still engrossing. Its focus on spectacle, special effects, alien figures and dehumanization remains engaging and pertinent.

Sobchack, Vivian (1988) *Screening Space: The American Science Fiction Film*. New York: Ungar.

As relevant as Sontag's early essay is, this is an engaging attempt to encapsulate the formal properties of the science-fiction film. The argument for the visual building blocks varies but the discussion of music, dialogue and sound effects has rarely been surpassed.

Telotte, J. P. (2001) *Science Fiction Film*. Cambridge: CUP.

Exploring how the genre has consistently redefined itself, this book borrows from Telotte's other (more in-depth) studies while trying to trace a wider textual and cultural history. The use of Todorov's theories of 'the fantastic' is interesting but the move into film analysis is less persuasive than the work on contexts and history.

Tulloch, J. and Jenkins, H. (1995) *Science Fiction Audiences: Watching Doctor Who and Star Trek*. London: Routledge.

The authors may have (individually) published other work on the topic but this collection of approaches to studying fandom represents a central source book about how to apply specific methodologies to the study of genre audiences. The centrality of the audience to genre discourse has never been clearer.

Selected Filmography

Abyss, The. USA; Lightstorm Entertainment; 20th-Century Fox. Cameron, James, dir. 1989.

Adventures of Pluto Nash, The. USA; Warner Bros. Underwood, Ron, dir. 2002.

Aelita. USSR; Mezhrabpom-Rus. Protazanov, Yakov, dir. 1924.

Aeon Flux. USA; Lakeshore Entertainment; MTV Films; Paramount. Kusama, Karyn, dir. 2005.

A.I.: Artificial Intelligence. USA; Dreamworks SKG; Warner Bros. Spielberg, Steven, dir. 2001.

Akira. Japan; Bandai; Kodansha; Toho. Ōtomo, Katsuhiro, dir. 1988.

Alien. USA; Brandywine; 20th-Century Fox. Scott, Ridley, dir. 1979.

Alien Nation. USA; American Entertainment Partners; 20th-Century Fox. Baker, Graham, dir. 1988.

Alien Resurrection. USA; Brandywine; 20th-Century Fox. Jeunet, Jean-Pieree, dir. 1997.

Aliens. USA; Brandywine; 20th-Century Fox. Cameron, James, dir. 1986.

Aliens in the Attic. USA; 20th-Century Fox. Schultz, John, dir. 2008.

Alpha Incident, The. USA; Studio Film Corporation. Rebane, Bill, dir. 1977.

Alphaville, une étrange aventure de Lemmy Caution. France; Athos Films; Chaumiane; Filmstudio. Godard, Jean-Luc, dir. 1965.

Altered States. USA; Warner Bros. Russell, Ken, dir. 1980.

Amazing Transparent Man, The. USA; Miller Consolidated Pictures. Ulmer, Edgar G., dir. 1960.

Andromeda Strain, The. USA; Universal. Wise, Robert, dir. 1971.

Année dernière à Marienbad, L'/ Last Year at Marienbad. France; Cocinor. Resnais, Alain, dir. 1961.

Apollo 13. USA; Imagine; Universal. Howard, Ron, dir. 1995.

Appurshido/Appleseed. Japan; Appleseed Film Partners; Toho. Aramaki, Shinji, dir. 2004.

Ataque de Pánico/Panic Attack! Uruguay; Paris Texas Casa Productora. Alvarez, Federico, dir. 2009.

Avatar. Lightstorm; 20th-Century Fox. Cameron, James, dir. USA; 2009.

Back to the Future. Amblin; Universal. Zemeckis, Robert, dir. 1985.

Back to the Future 2. Amblin; Universal. Zemeckis, Robert, dir. 1988.

Barbarella. France/Italy; Dino de Laurentiis Cinematograpfica; Paramount. Vadim, Roger, dir. 1968.

batteries not included. USA; Amblin; Universal. Robbins, Matthew, dir. 1987.

Battle beyond the Stars. USA; New World Pictures. Murakami, Jimmy T., dir. 1979.

Battlestar Galactica. USA; Glen A. Larson Productions; Universal. Colla, Richard A., dir. 1978.

The Beast from 20,000 Fathoms. Mutual; Warner Bros. Lourié, Eugène, dir. 1953.

Beneath the Planet of the Apes. USA; 20th-Century Fox. Post, Ted, dir. 1970.

Beware! The Blob. USA; Jack H. Harris Enterprises. Hagman, Larry, dir. 1972.

Biggles. UK; Compact Yellowbill; Tambarle. Hough, John, dir. 1986.

Bill and Ted's Excellent Adventure. USA; De Laurentiis Entertainment Group; Nelson Entertainment. Herek, Stephen, dir. 1988.

Blade Runner. Ladd Co.; Warner Bros. Scott, Ridley, dir. 1982.

Blob, The. Fairview Productions; Paramount. Yeaworth Jr., Irwin S., dir. 1958.

Body Snatchers. Dorset Productions; Robert H. Solo Productions; Warner Bros. Ferrera, Abel, dir. 1993.

Boy and His Dog, A. LQ/JAF. Jones, L.Q., dir. 1974.

Brazil. UK; Embassy International Pictures. Gilliam, Terry, dir. 1985.

Bride of Frankenstein. USA; Universal. Whale, James, dir. 1935.

Buck Rogers in the 25th Century. USA; Glen Larson Productions; Universal. Haller, Daniel, dir. 1979.

Butterfly Effect, The.USA; Benderspink; FilmEngine; New Line Cinema. Bress, Eric and Gruber, J. Mackye, dirs. 2006.

Cat-Women of the Moon. USA; Z-M Productions. Hilton, Arthur, dir. 1953.

Cherry 2000. USA; ERP; Orion. De Jarnatt, Steve, dir. 1987.

Chikyû Bôeigun/The Mysterians. Japan; Toho Company. Honda, Ishirô, dir. 1957.

Children of Men. UK/USA; Strike Entertainment; Universal. Cuarón, Alfonso, dir. 2006.

Clockwork Orange, A. UK; Warner Bros. Kubrick, Stanley, dir. 1971.

Close Encounters of the Third Kind. USA; Columbia. Spielberg, Steven, dir. 1977.

Cloverfield. USA; Bad Robot; Paramount. Reeves, Matt, dir. 2008.

Colossus: The Forbin Project. USA; Universal. Sargent, Joseph, dir. 1970.

Coneheads. USA; Paramount. Barron, Steve, dir. 1993.

Conquest of Space. USA; Paramount. Haskin, Byron, dir. 1955.

Conquest of the Planet of the Apes. USA; 20th-Century Fox. Thomson, J. Lee, dir. 1972.

Contact. USA; Warner Bros. Zemeckis, Robert, dir. 1997.

Creature from the Black Lagoon. USA; Universal. Arnold, Jack, dir. 1954.

Daikaiju Gamera/Gamera the Invincible. Japan; Daiei Studios. Yuasa, Noriaki, dir. 1965.

Daleks: Invasion Earth 2150 AD. UK; AARU Productions; British Lion. Flemyng, Gordon, dir. 1966.

Damnation Alley. USA; 20th-Century Fox. Smight, Jack, dir. 1977.

Dark Angel. USA; Vision International. Baxley, Craig R., dir. 1989.

Dark City. Mystery Clock; New Line. Proyas, Alex, dir. 1998.

D.A.R.Y.L. USA; Paramount. Wincer, Simon, dir. 1986.

Day after Tomorrow, The. USA; Centropolis; 20th-Century Fox. Emmerich, Roland, dir. 2004.

Day of the Triffids, The. UK; Security Pictures; Rank. Sekely, Steve, dir. 1962.

Day the Earth Caught Fire, The. UK; Pax Films; British Lion. Guest, Val, dir. 1961.

Day the Earth Stood Still, The. USA; 20th-Century Fox. Wise, Robert, dir. 1951.

Day the World Ended, The. USA; Golden State; ARC. Corman, Roger, dir. 1955.

Déjà Vu. USA; Jerry Bruckheimer Films; Touchstone. Scott, Tony, dir. 2006.

Demon Seed. USA; MGM. Cammell, Donald, dir. 1977.

Destination Moon. USA; George Pal Productions; Eagle Lion. Pichel, Irving, dir. 1950.

Devil Girl from Mars. UK; Gigi Productions; British Lion. MacDonald, David, dir. 1954.

Dick Barton Strikes Back. UK; Hammer Film Productions. Grayson, Godfrey, dir. 1948.

District 9. USA/ New Zealand; WingNut Films. Blomkamp, Neill, dir. 2009.

Donnie Darko. USA; Flower Films; Pandora Cinema. Kelly, Richard, dir. 2004.

Doom. USA; Universal. Bartkowiak, Andrzej, dir. 2006.

Dr Strangelove, or How I Learned to Stop Worrying and Love the Bomb. UK; Columbia; Hawk Films. Kubrick, Stanley, dir. 1964.

Dr Who and the Daleks. UK; AARU Productions; Amicus Productions. Flemyng, Gordon, dir. 1964.

Dune. USA; De Laurentiis; Universal. Lynch, David, dir. 1984.

Earth vs the Flying Saucers. USA; Clover Productions; Columbia. Sears, Fred F., dir. 1956.

Earth vs the Spider. USA; American International Pictures (AIP). Gordon, Bert I., dir. 1958.

Empire of the Ants. USA; Cinema 77; AIP. Gordon, Bert I., dir. 1977.

Enemy Mine. USA; 20th-Century Fox. Petersen, Wolfgang, dir. 1985.

Escape From New York. USA; AVCO Embassy Pictures; Goldcrest. Carpenter, John, dir. 1981.

Escape to Witch Mountain. USA; Walt Disney Productions. Hough, John, dir. 1975.

Eternal Sunshine of the Spotless Mind. USA; Anonymous Content; Focus Features. Gondry, Michel, dir. 2004.

E.T.: The Extra Terrestrial. USA; Amblin; Universal. Spielberg, Steven, dir. 1982.

Event Horizon. UK/USA; Golar Productions; Paramount. Anderson, Paul W.S., dir. 1997.

Eve of Destruction. USA; Interscope Communications; Nelson Entertainment. Gibbins, Duncan, dir. 1991.

Explorers. USA; Paramount. Dante, Joe, dir. 1985.

Fahrenheit 451. UK; Enterprise Vineyard; Rank. Truffaut, François, dir. 1962.

Fantastic Four. USA; Constantin Film; 20th-Century Fox. Story, Tim, dir. 2005.

Fantastic Voyage. USA; 20th-Century Fox. Fleischer, Richard, dir. 1966.

Final Fantasy: The Spirits Within. Japan/USA; Chris Lee Productions; Square Company; Columbia. Sakaguchi, Hironobu and Sakakibara, Motonori, dirs. 2001.

Flash Gordon. USA; King Features Production; Universal. Stephani, Frederick, dir. 1936.

Flight of the Navigator. USA; New Star; Walt Disney Pictures. Kleiser, Randall, dir. 1986.

Fly, The. USA; Brooksfilms; 20th-Century Fox. Cronenberg, David, dir. 1986.

Forbidden Planet. USA; MGM. Wilcox, Fred M., dir. 1956.

Fountain, The. USA; Regency Enterprises; Warner Bros. Aronofsky, Darren, dir. 2006.

Frankenstein. USA; Universal. Whale, James, dir. 1931.

Frau im Mond/Woman (or Girl) in the Moon. Germany; Fritz Lang-Film; Universum Film (UFA). Lang, Fritz, dir. 1929.

Futureworld. USA; AIP; Aubrey Company. Heffron, Richard T., dir. 1976.

Galaxy Quest. USA; Dreamworks SKG; Gran Via Productions. Parisot, Dean, dir. 1999.

Gattaca. USA; Columbia; Jersey Films. Niccol, Andrew, dir. 1997.

Giant Spider Invasion, The. USA; Cinema Group 75; Transcentury Pictures. Rebane, Bill, dir. 1975.

Godzilla. USA; Centropolis Film Productions; TriStar Pictures. Emmerich, Roland, dir. 1998.

Gojira/Godzilla. Japan; Toho Film. Honda, Ishirô, dir. 1954.

Groundhog Day. USA; Columbia. Ramis, Harold, dir. 1993.

H. G. Wells' First Men in the Moon. UK; Columbia. Juran, Nathan, dir. 1964.

High Treason. UK; Gaumont British Picture Corporation. Elvey, Maurice, dir. 1929.

Hitchhiker's Guide to the Galaxy, The. UK/USA; Touchstone Pictures; Spyglass Entertainment. Jennings, Garth, dir. 2005.

Hollow Man. USA; Columbia; Global Entertainment. Verhoeven, Paul, dir. 2000.

I Am Legend. USA; Village Roadshow; Warner Bros. Lawrence, Francis, dir. 2007.

Inception. UK/USA; Legendary Pictures; Warner Bros. Nolan, Christopher, dir, 2010.

Incredibles, The. USA; Pixar. Bird, Brad, dir. 2004.

Incredible Shrinking Man, The. USA; Universal-International. Arnold, Jack, dir. 1957.

Independence Day. USA; Centropolis Entertainment; 20th-Century Fox. Emmerich, Roland, dir. 1996.

Invaders from Mars. USA; National Pictures Corporation; 20th-Century Fox. Menzies, William Cameron, dir. 1953.

Invasion of the Body Snatchers. USA; Walter Wanger Productions; Allied Artists. Siegel, Don, dir. 1956.

Invasion of the Body Snatchers. USA; Solofilm; United Artists. Kaufman, Philip, dir. 1978.

Invisible Boy, The. USA; MGM. Hoffman, Herman, dir. 1957.

Invisible Man, The. USA; Universal. Whale, James, dir. 1933.

Invisible Ray, The. USA; Universal. Hillyer, Lambert, dir. 1936.

I, Robot. USA; Davis Entertainment; 20th-Century Fox. Proyas, Alex, dir. 2004.

Iron Giant, The. USA; Warner Bros. Bird, Brad, dir. 1999.

Iron Man. USA; Marvel; Paramount. Favreau, Jon, dir. 2008.

Iron Man 2. USA; Marvel; Paramount. Favreau, Jon, dir. 2010.

It Came From Outer Space. USA; Universal-International. Arnold, Jack, dir. 1953.

Je'taime, je'taime. France; Les Productions Fox Europa; Parc Film. Resnais, Alain, dir. 1968.

La Jetée. France; Argos Films. Marker, Chris, dir. 1962.

Jetsons: The Movie. USA; Hanna-Barbera Productions; Universal. Barbera, Joseph and Hanna, William, dirs. 1990.

Jimmy Neutron: Boy Genius. USA; Nickelodeon Movies; Paramount. Davis, John A., dir. 2001.

Johnny Mnemonic. USA; TriStar Pictures. Longo, Robert, dir. 1995.

Judge Dredd. USA; Cinergi Pictures; Hollywood Pictures. Cannon, Danny, dir. 1995.

Jurassic Park. USA; Amblin; Universal. Spielberg, Steven, dir. 1993.

Just Imagine. USA; Fox Film Corporation. Butler, David, dir. 1930.

Kate and Leopold. USA; Konrad Pictures; Miramax Films. Mangold, James, dir. 2000.

Killers from Space. USA; Planet Filmplays; RKO. Wilder, W. Lee, dir. 1954.

Kôkaku kidôtai/Ghost in the Shell. Japan; Bandai Visual Company; Kodansha. Oshii, Mamoru, dir. 1994.

Lake House, The. USA; Vertigo Entertainment; Warner Bros. Agresti, Alejandro, dir. 2005.

Last Starfighter, The. USA; Lorimar Film Entertainment; Universal. Castle, Nick, dir. 1984.

Last Woman on Earth, The. USA; Film Group. Corman, Roger, dir. 1960.

Lawnmower Man, The. USA; Allied Vision; Alliance Communications. Leonard, Brett, dir. 1992.

Lifeforce. UK; Golan-Globus Productions; Cannon Group. Hooper, Tobe, dir. 1985.

Lilo and Stitch. USA; Walt Disney Pictures. DeBlois, Dean and Sanders, Chris, dirs. 2001.

Logan's Run. USA; MGM. Anderson, Michael, dir. 1976.

Lost in Space. USA; Irwin Allen Productions; New Line Cinema. Hopkins, Stephen, dir. 1998.

Lost World, The. USA; First National Pictures. Hoyt, Harry O., dir. 1925.

Man in the White Suit, The. UK; Ealing Studios; Rank. Mackendrick, Alexander, dir. 1951.

Man Who Fell to Earth, The. UK; British Lion; Cinema 5. Roeg, Nicolas, dir. 1976.

Marooned. USA; Columbia. Sturges, John, dir. 1969.

Mars Attacks! USA; Warner Bros. Burton, Tim, dir. 1995.

Masters of the Universe. USA; Golan-Globus Productions; Cannon Group. Goddard, Gary, dir. 1987.

Matrix, The. USA; Warner Bros. The Wachowski Brothers, dir. 1999.

Matrix Reloaded, The. USA; Warner Bros. The Wachowski Brothers, dir. 2003.

Matrix Revolutions, The. USA; Warner Bros. The Wachowski Brothers, dir. 2003.

Meet the Robinsons. USA; Walt Disney Pictures. Anderson, Stephen J., dir. 2007.

Men in Black. USA; Amblin; Columbia. Sonnenfeld, Barry, dir. 1997.

Men in Black II. USA; Amblin; Columbia. Sonnenfeld, Barry, dir. 2002.

Metropolis. Germany; Universum Film (UFA); Paramount. Lang, Fritz, dir. 1927.

Metroporisu/Metropolis. Japan; Bandai Visual Company; Toho. Rintaro, dir. 2001.

Minority Report. USA; Dreamworks SKG; 20th-Century Fox. Spielberg, Steven, dir. 2002.

Mom and Dad save the World. USA; Cinema Plus; Home Box Office. Beeman, Greg, dir. 1997.

Monsters. USA; Vertigo Films. Edwards, Gareth, dir. 2010.

Monsters vs Aliens. USA; Dreamworks Animation. Letterman, Rob and Vernon, Conrad, dirs. 2009.

Moon. UK; Liberty Films UK; Limelight. Jones, Duncan, dir. 2009.

Moonraker. UK/France; Danjaq; EON Productions. Gilbert, Lewis, dir. 1979.

Mouse on the Moon, The. UK; Walter Shenson Films; United Artists. Lester, Richard, dir. 1963.

Multiplicity. USA; Columbia. Ramis, Harold, dir. 1996.

Next. USA; Paramount; Revolution Studios. Tamahori, Lee, dir. 2007.

I nouvi barbari/The New Barbarians. Italy/USA; Deaf International; Fulvia Film. Castellari, Enzo G., dir. 1983.

Omega Man, The. USA; Warner Bros. Sagal, Boris, dir. 1971.

On the Beach. USA; Stanley Kramer Productions; United Artists. Kramer, Stanley, dir. 1959.

Outland. UK; The Ladd Company. Hyams, Peter, dir. 1981.

Over-Incubated Baby, The. UK; Robert W. Paul. Booth, Walter R., dir. 1901.

Perfect Woman, The. UK; Two Cities Films; General Film Distributors. Knowles, Bernard, dir. 1949.

Planet 51. Spain/UK/USA; Ilion Animation; HandMade Films; TriStar Pictures. Blanco, Jorge, dir. 2009.

Planète sauvage, La/Fantastic Planet. France/Czechoslovakia; Argos Films; Krátký Film Praha. Laloux, René, dir. 1973.

Planet Terror. USA; Dimension Films; Troublemaker Studios. Rodriguez, Robert, dir. 2007.
Predator. USA; Davis Entertainment; Silver Pictures; 20th-Century Fox. McTiernan, John, dir. 1987.
The '?' Motorist. UK; Robert W. Paul. Booth, Walter R., dir. 1902.
Quatermass Xperiment, The. UK; Hammer Film Productions. Guest, Val, dir. 1955.
Quatermass 2. UK; Hammer Film Productions. Guest, Val, dir. 1957.
Renaissance. France; Onyx Films; France 2 Cinema. Volckman, Christian, dir. 2006.
Resident Evil. USA; Constantin Film; Davis-Films; New Legacy. Anderson, Paul W.S., dir. 2002.
Right Stuff, The. USA; The Ladd Company; Warner Bros. Kaufman, Philip, dir. 1978.
Robinson Crusoe on Mars. USA; Aubrey Schenck Productions; Paramount. Haskin, Byron, dir. 1964.
Rocketship X-M. USA; Lippert Pictures. Neumann, Kirt, dir. 1951.
Rocket to the Moon. UK; Jules Verne Films; Anglo-Amalgamated. Sharp, Don, dir. 1967.
Rocky Horror Picture Show, The. UK/USA; 20th-Century Fox. Sharman, Jim, dir. 1975.
Rollerball. USA; Algonquin; United Artists. Jewison, Norman, dir. 1975.
Santa Claus Conquers the Martians. USA; Jalor Productions; Embassy Pictures. Webster, Nicholas, dir. 1964.
Serenity. USA; Universal. Whedon, Joss, dir. 2005.
Short Circuit. USA; David Foster Productions; TriStar Pictures. Badham, John, dir. 1987.
Short Circuit 2. USA; David Foster Productions; TriStar Pictures. Johnson, Kenneth, dir. 1988.
Silent Running. USA; Trumbull/Gruskoff Productions; Universal. Trumbull, Douglas, dir. 1970.
S1m0ne. USA; New Line Cinema; Niccol Films. Niccol, Andrew, dir. 2000.
Skyline. USA; Black Monday Film Services; Relativity Media; The Brothers Strause, dirs. 2010.
Sky Racket. USA; Victory Pictures Corporation. Katzman, Sam, dir. 1936.
Sleeper. USA; Rollins-Joffe Productions; United Artists. Allen, Woody, dir. 1972.
Soldier. USA; Morgan Creek; Warner Bros. Anderson, Paul W.S., dir. 1998.
Solyaris/Solaris. USSR; Creative Unit of Writers and Cinema Workers; Mosfilm; Unit Four. Tarkovskiy, Andrey, dir. 1973.
Somewhere in Time. USA; Rastar; Universal. Szwarc, Jeannot, dir. 1980.
Sora no daikaijû Radon/Rodan. Japan; Toho Film. Honda, Ishirô, dir. 1956.
A Sound of Thunder. USA; Franchise Pictures; Warner Bros. Hyams, Peter, dir. 2005.
Southland Tales. USA; Darko Entertainment; Universal. Kelly, Richard, dir. 2006.

Soylent Green. USA; MGM. Fleischer, Richard, dir. 1973.

Spaceballs. USA; Brooksfilms; MGM. Brooks, Mel, dir. 1987.

Spacehunter: Adventures in the Forbidden Zone. Canada/USA; Columbia; Delphi Productions; Zone Productions. Johnson, Lamont, dir. 1983.

Space Jam. USA; Warner Bros. Pytka, Joe, dir. 1996.

Species. USA; MGM. Donaldson, Roger, dir. 1995.

Stalker. USSR; Mosfilm. Tarkovsy, Andrei, dir. 1979.

Stargate. France/USA; Le Studio Canal+; Caralco Pictures; Centropolis. Emmerich, Roland, dir. 1994.

Starman. USA; Columbia. Carpenter, John, dir. 1984.

Star Trek. USA; Bad Robot; Paramount; Spyglass Entertainment. Abrams, J.J., dir. 2009.

Star Trek: The Motion Picture. USA; Paramount. Wise, Robert, dir. 1979.

Star Trek II: The Wrath of Khan. USA; Paramount. Meyer, Nicholas, dir. 1982.

Star Trek IV: The Voyage Home. USA; Paramount. Nimoy, Leonard, dir. 1986.

Star Wars. USA; Lucasfilm; 20th-Century Fox. Lucas, George, dir. 1977.

Star Wars: The Empire Strikes Back. USA; Lucasfilm; 20th-Century Fox. Kershner, Irvin, dir. 1980.

Star Wars: Return of the Jedi. USA; Lucasfilm; 20th-Century Fox. Marquand, Richard, dir. 1983.

Star Wars Episode 1: The Phantom Menace. USA; Lucasfilm; 20th-Century Fox. Lucas, George, dir. 1997

Star Wars Episode 2: Attack of the Clones. USA; Lucasfilm; 20th-Century Fox. Lucas, George, dir. 2002.

Strange Days. USA; Lightstorm Entertainment; 20th-Century Fox. Bigelow, Kathryn, dir. 1995.

Sunshine. UK; DNA Films; Ingenious Film Partners; 20th-Century Fox. Boyle, Danny, dir. 2007.

Superman. USA; Warner Bros. Donner, Richard, dir. 1978.

Teenagers from Outer Space. USA; Tom Graeff Productions. Warner Bros. Graeff, Tom, dir. 1959.

Terminator, The. UK/USA; Hemdale Film; Cinema 84; Euro Film Funding; Orion Pictures. Cameron, James, dir. 1984.

Terminator 2: Judgment Day. USA; Carolco Pictures; Lightstorm Entertainment; TriStar Pictures. Cameron, James, dir. 1991.

Them! USA; Warner Bros. Douglas, Gordon, dir. 1954.

They Came From Beyond Space. UK; Amicus Productions. Francis, Freddie, dir. 1967.

They Live. USA; Alive Films; Larry Franco Productions; Universal. Carpenter, John, dir. 1988.

Thing, The. USA; Turman-Foster Company; Universal. Carpenter, John, dir. 1982.

Thing from another World, The. USA; Winchester Pictures Corporation; RKO. Nyby, Christian, dir. 1951.

Things to Come. UK; London Film Productions; United Artists. Menzies, William Cameron, dir. 1936.

This Island Earth. USA; Universal-International. Newman, Joseph M., dir. 1955.

Thunderbirds. France/UK; Working Title Films; Studio Canal; UIP. Frakes, Jonathan, dir. 2004.

THX 1138. USA; American Zoetrope; Warner Bros. Lucas, George, dir. 1971.

Time Machine, The. USA; George Pal Productions; MGM; Pal, George, dir. 1960.

Time Machine, The. USA; Dreamworks SKG; Warner Bros. Wells, Simon, dir. 2002.

Time Traveller's Wife, The. USA; New Line Cinema. Schwentke, Robert, dir. 2009.

Toki o kakeru shôjo/The Girl Who Leapt Through Time. Japan; Mad House; Kadokawa Pictures. Hosoda, Mamoru, dir. 2006.

Transformers. USA; Dreamworks SKG; Hasbro; Paramount. Bay, Michael, dir. 2007.

Transformers: Revenge of the Fallen. USA; Dreamworks SKG; Hasbro; Paramount. Bay, Michael, dir. 2009.

Treasure Planet. USA; Walt Disney Pictures. Clements, Ron and Musker, John, dirs. 2002.

28 Days Later. UK; British Film Council; DNA Films; 20th-Century Fox. Boyle, Danny, dir. 2002.

2012. USA; Centropolis; Columbia. Emmerich, Roland, dir. 2009.

20 Million Miles to Earth. USA; Morningside Productions; Columbia. Juran, Nathan, dir. 1957.

20,000 Leagues under the Sea. USA; Universal Film Manufacturing Company. Paton, Stuart, dir. 1916.

20,000 Leagues under the Sea. USA; Walt Disney Productions. Fleischer, Richard, dir. 1954.

2001: A Space Odyssey. UK/USA; MGM; Stanley Kubrick Productions. Kubrick, Stanley, dir. 1968.

Tron. USA; Walt Disney Productions. Lisberger, Steven, dir. 1982.

Truman Show, The. USA; Paramount; Scott Rudin Productions. Weir, Peter, dir. 1998.

Uchûjin Tôkyô ni arawaru/Warning from Space. Japan; Daiei Studios. Shima, Koji, dir. 1956.

Videodrome. Canada; Canadian Film Development Corporation; Famous Players Limited; Universal. Cronenberg, David, dir. 1983.

Village of the Damned. UK; MGM British Studios. Rilla, Wolf, dir. 1960.

Voyage à travers l'impossible/An Impossible Voyage. France; Star Film. Méliès, Georges, dir. 1904.

Voyage dans la lune, Le/A Trip to the Moon. France; Star Film. Méliès, Georges, dir. 1902.

Voyage to the Prehistoric Planet. USA/USSR; Roger Corman Productions; AIP. Harrington, Curtis, dir. 1965.

Voyage to the Planet of the Prehistoric Women. USA; Filmgroup; AIP. Bogdanovich, Peter, dir. 1968.

Wall-E. USA; Pixar. Stanton, Andrew, dir. 2008.

WarGames. USA; MGM; Sherwood. Badham, John, dir. 1983.

War of the Worlds, The. USA; Paramount. Haskin, Byron, dir. 1953.

War of the Worlds. USA; Amblin; Dreamworks SKG; Paramount. Spielberg, Steven, dir. 2005.

Wasp Woman, The. USA; Film Group Features; Santa Cruz Productions. Corman, Roger, dir. 1959.

Westworld. USA; MGM. Crichton, Michael, dir. 1973.

When Worlds Collide. USA; Paramount. Maté, Rudolph, dir. 1951.

Wing Commander. USA; No Prisoners Productions; Wing Commander Productions; 20th-Century Fox. Roberts, Chris, dir. 1999.

X-Men. USA; 20th-Century Fox; Marvel Enterprises. Singer, Bryan, dir. 2000.

X – The Unknown. UK; Hammer Film Productions. Norman, Leslie, dir. 1956.

Bibliography

AFI (2008a) 'AFI's 10 Top 10: America's 10 Greatest Films in 10 Classic Genres', www.afi.com/10top10/ (accessed 1 June 2008).

AFI (2008b) 'American Film Institute Brings the Best of Hollywood Together to Celebrate "AFI's 10 Top 10"', www.afi.com/Docs/about/press/2008/AFI10_top_10_release_June08.pdf (accessed 1 June 2008).

AFI (2008c) 'Official Ballot', http://connect.afi.com/site/DocServer/10top10.pdf?docID=381&AddInterest=1781 (accessed 1 June 2008).

Allon, Y., Curren, D. and Patterson, H. (2002) *Contemporary North American Film Directors: A Wallflower Critical Guide*. London: Wallflower.

Altman, R. (1999) *Film/Genre*. London: BFI.

Amis, K. (1960) *New Maps of Hell: A Survey of Science Fiction*. New York: Harcourt, Brace & Co.

A.W. (1953) 'It Came From Outer Space: Look Out! The Space Boys Are Loose Again', *New York Times,* 18 June, http://movies.nytimes.com/movie/review?res=9B00EEDA143EE53BBC4052DFB0668388649EDE&scp=2&sq=it%20came%20from%20outer%20space&st=cse (accessed 20 August 2009).

Banks, M. (2002) 'Monumental Fictions: National Monument as a Science Fiction Space', *Journal of Popular Film and Television,* 30(3): 136–45.

Barker, M. and Brooks, K. (1998) *Knowing Audiences: Judge Dredd It's Friends, Fans and Foes*. Luton: University of Luton Press.

Baxter, J. (1970) *Science Fiction in the Cinema*. London: Zwemmer.

Bell, D. (2009) 'On the Net: Navigating the World Wide Web', in G. Creeber and R. Martin (eds), *Digital Cultures: Understanding New Media*. Maidenhead: Open University Press, pp. 30–8.

Benson, M. (2000) *Vintage Science Fiction Films, 1896-1949*. Jefferson, NC: McFarland Classics.

Bioscope (1908) '*The Electric Hotel* review', *Bioscope,* 108 (6 November): 14.

Bioscope (1909a) '*An Extraordinary Duel* review', *Bioscope,* 150 (26 August): 25.

Bioscope (1909b) 'American Film Department Advertisement', *Bioscope,* 168 (30 December): 22.

Bioscope (1910a) '*Les Progress de la Science en l'an 2000/Life in the Next Century* review', *Bioscope,* 176 (24 February): 55.

Bioscope (1910b) 'Edison Films Advertisement', *Bioscope,* 186 (5 May): 22.

Bioscope (1910c) 'Cines-Films Advertisement', *Bioscope,* 192 (16 June): 58.

Bioscope (1911a) '*One Hundred Years After* review', *Bioscope,* 13, 260 (5 October): xxv.

Bioscope (1911b) 'Essanay Advertisement', *Bioscope,* 13, 260 (5 October): 16.

Bioscope (1912) 'Vitagraph Advertisement', *Bioscope,* 15, 290 (9 May): xv.

Bioscope (1913) '*A Message From Mars* Advertisement', *Bioscope,* 20, 353 (17 July): xx–xxi.

Bioscope (1914) 'Essanay Film Mfg. Co. Advertisement', *Bioscope,* 24, 406 (23 July): 213–14.

Bioscope (1915) 'Essanay Chaplin Advertisement', *Bioscope* 28, 450 (3 June): 24.

Biskind, P. (1983) *Seeing is Believing: How Hollywood Taught Us to Stop Worrying and Love the Fifties.* London: Bloomsbury.

Biskind, P. (1998) *Easy Riders, Raging Bulls.* London: Bloomsbury.

Bizony, P. (2001) *Digital Domain: The Leading Edge of Visual Effects.* London: Aurum.

Boswell, K. (2001) 'Artificial Intelligence – Viral Marketing and the Web', *The Marketleap Report* 1(5), 16 April, www.marketleap.com/report/ml_report_05. htm (accessed 4 June 2010).

Bould, M., Butler A., Roberts, A. and Vint, S. (eds) (2009) *The Routledge Companion to Science Fiction.* Abingdon: Routledge.

Britton, A. (1986) 'Blissing Out: The Politics of Reaganite Entertainment', *Movie,* 31–2: 1–42.

Brooker, W. (1999) 'Internet Fandom and the Continuing Narratives of *Star Wars, Blade Runner* and *Alien*', in Kuhn, A. (ed.), *Alien Zone II: The Spaces of Science Fiction Cinema.* London: Verso, pp. 50–72.

Brooker, W. (2002) *Using the Force: Creativity, Community and Star Wars Fans.* London: Continuum.

Brosnan, J. (1978) *Future Tense: The Cinema of Science Fiction.* New York: St Martin's Press.

Bruno, G. (1990) 'Ramble City: Postmodernism and *Blade Runner*', in Kuhn, A. (ed.), *Alien Zone II: The Spaces of Science Fiction Cinema.* London: Verso, pp. 183–95.

Bukatman, S. (1998) 'Zooming Out: The End of Offscreen Space', in Lewis, J. (ed.), *The New American Cinema.* New York: Duke University Press.

Bukatman, S. (1999) 'The Artificial Infinite: On Special Effects and the Sublime', in Kuhn, A. (ed.), *Alien Zone II: The Spaces of Science Fiction Cinema.* London: Verso, pp. 249–75.

Campbell, J. (2008) 'The Beast Within', *Guardian,* 13 December.

Chanan, M. (1996) *The Dream That Kicks: The Pre-History and Early Years of Cinema in Britain.* London: Routledge.

Chibnall, S. (1999) 'Alien Women: the politics of sexual difference in British SF pulp cinema', in I. Hunter (ed.), *British Science Fiction Cinema.* London: Routledge, pp. 57–74 .

Collin, R. (2009) 'Avatar', *News of the World,* 14 December, www.newsoftheworld. co.uk/entertainment/film/636026/This-live-action-3D-romantic-sci-fi-epic-really-IS-the-revolution.html (accessed 8 February 2010).

Comment, B. (1999) *The Panorama.* London: Reaktion.

Cornea, C. (2007) *Science Fiction Cinema: Between Fantasy and Reality.* Edinburgh: Edinburgh University Press.

Creed, B. (1993) *The Monstrous Feminine: Film, Feminism, Psychoanalysis.* London: Routledge.

Crowther, B. (1951) 'The Screen in Review: Emissary From Planet Visits Mayfair Theatre in "Day the Earth Stood Still"', *The New York Times,* 19 September, http://movies.nytimes.com/movie/review?res=9A07EED61031E23BBC4152D FBF66838A649EDE&scp=6&sq=the%20day%20the%20earth%20stood%20 still&st=cse (accessed 20 August 2009).

Dadoun, R. (1991) '*Metropolis*: Mother City – "Mittler" – Hitler', in Penley, C., Lyon, E., Spigel, L. and Bergstrom, J. (eds), *Close Encounters: Film, Feminism and Science Fiction.* Minneapolis, MN: University of Minnesota Press, pp. 133– 59.

Darrach Jr., H. and Ginna, R. (1952) 'Have We Visitors From Space?', *Life,* 7 April.

De Cordova, R. (1995) 'Genre and Performance: An Overview', in B. Grant (ed.) (2003), *Film Genre Reader II.* Austin, TX: University of Texas Press.

Dean, J. (1998) *Aliens in America: Conspiracy Cultures from Outerspace to Cyberspace.* New York: Cornell University Press.

Dervin, D. (1991) 'Primal Conditions and Conventions: The Genre of Science Fiction', in A. Kuhn (ed.), *Alien Zone.* London: Verso, pp. 96–102.

Dixon, W. (2003) *Visions of the Apocalypse: Spectacles of Destruction in American Cinema.* London: Wallflower.

Duncan, J. (2000) 'A Look Back', *Cinefex,* 80 (January): 15–18, 161–3.

Easthope, A. (1979) 'Notes on Genre', *Screen Education* 32/33.

Elliot, A. (2009) '10 Amazing Augmented Reality iPhone Apps', *Mashable/Mobile,* 5 December, http://mashable.com/2009/12/05/augmented-reality-iphone/ (accessed 1 July 2010).

Franklin, H. (1990) 'Visions of the Future in Science Fiction Films from 1970 to 1982', in A. Kuhn (ed.), *Alien Zone,* London: Verso, pp. 19–31.

Geraghty, L. (2006) 'A Network of Support: Coping with Trauma Through *StarTrek* Fan Letters', *The Journal of Popular Culture,* 39(6): 1002–24.

Geraghty, L. (2009) *American Science Fiction Film and Television.* Oxford: Berg.

Geraghty, L. and Jancovich, M. (2008) *The Shifting Definitions of Genre: Essays on Labelling Films, Television Shows and Media.* Jefferson, NC: McFarland.

Gledhill, R. and Lister, D. (2008) 'Cardinal Keith O'Brien Attacks "Monstrous" Human Embryo Bill', *The Times,* 22 March, www.timesonline.co.uk/tol/ comment/faith/article3597851.ece (accessed 12 June 2010).

Grainge, P. (2008) *Brand Hollywood: Selling Entertainment in a Global Media Age.* London: Routledge.

Grant, B. (ed.) (2003) *Film Genre Reader III*. Austin, TX: University of Texas Press.

Grant, B. (2006) *Film Genre: From Iconography to Ideology*. London: Wallflower Press.

Gunning, T. (1986) 'The Cinema of Attractions: Early Film, Its Spectator and the Avant-Garde', *Wide Angle,* 8, 3–4: 63–70.

Gunning, T. (1994) 'The World as Object Lesson: Cinema Audiences, Visual Culture and the St Louis World's Fair, 1904', *Film History,* 6: 422–44.

Gunning, T. (1995) 'An Aesthetic of Astonishment: Early Film and the (In)Credulous Spectator', in L. Williams (ed.), *Viewing Positions: Ways of Seeing Film.* New Brunswick: Rutgers University Press.

Haralovich, M. and Klaprat, C. (1982) 'Marked Woman and Jezebel: The Spectator-In-The-Trailer', *Enclitic,* (Fall 1981/Spring 1982): 66–74.

Harraway, D. (1985) 'A Manifesto for Cyborgs: Science, Technology and Socialist Feminism in the 1980s', *Socialist Review,* 80: 65–107.

Hayward, P. and Wollen, T. (1993) *Future Visions: New Technologies of the Screen.* London: BFI.

Henderson, J. (2000) 'Lunar Ambition', *American Cinematographer,* 81(3): 108–12.

Hesmondhalgh, D. (2007) *The Cultural Industries.* London: Sage.

Hickman, G. (1977) *The Films of George Pal.* London: Thomas Yoseloff, Ltd.

Hills, M. (2002) *Fan Cultures.* London: Routledge.

Hollows, J. and Jancovich, M. (eds) (1995) *Approaches to Popular Film.* Manchester: Manchester University Press.

Hollows, J., Hutchings, P. and Jancovich, M. (eds) (2000) *The Film Studies Reader.* London: Arnold.

Holt, J. (2009) 'It's Not Film, It's TV: An Industrial Identity Crisis.' Paper given at the 'What is Film?' conference, University of Oregon, 7 November 2009.

Hunter, A. (2009) 'Avatar Review and Trailer: 3-D Sci-Fi Epic Simply Dazzles', *Daily Express,* 18 December, www.express.co.uk/entertainment/view/146704/3-D-sci-fi-epic-simply-dazzles- (accessed 8 February 2010).

Hunter, I. (1999) *British Science Fiction Cinema.* London: Routledge.

Hutchings, P. (1993) *Hammer and Beyond: The British Horror Film.* Manchester: MUP.

Hutchings, P. (1999) '"We're the Martians Now": British SF Invasion Fantasies of the 1950s and 1960s', in I. Hunter, *British Science Fiction Film.* London, Routledge, pp. 33–47.

Huyssen, A. (1986) *After the Great Divide: Modernism, Mass Culture, Postmodernism.* Bloomington, IN: Indiana University Press.

Irvine, L. (2008) 'Is there a Future for Science Fiction?', *Guardian* (22 March): 50.

Jameson, F. (1983) 'Postmodernism and Consumer Society', in H. Foster (ed.), *The Anti-Aesthetic.* Port Townsend, WA: Bay Press, pp. 111–23.

Jancovich, M. (1992) *Horror.* London: Batsford.

Jancovich, M. (1995) 'Screen Theory', in Hollows, J. and Jancovich, M. (eds), *Approaches to Popular Film*. Manchester: Manchester University Press, pp. 123–50.

Jancovich, M. (1996) *Rational Fears: American Horror Genre in the 1950s*. Manchester: Manchester University Press.

Jancovich, M. (2002) '"A Real Shocker": Authenticity, Genre and the Struggle for Distinction', in Turner (ed.), *The Film Cultures Reader*. London: Routledge, pp. 469–80.

Jancovich, M. and Johnston D. (2009) 'Film and Television, the 1950s', in M. Bould, A. Butler, A. Roberts, S. Vint (eds), *The Routledge Companion to Science Fiction*. Oxford: Routledge, pp. 71–9.

Jenkins, H. (1988) '*Star Trek* Rerun, Reread, Rewritten: Fan Writing as Textual Poaching', in Penley, C., Lyon, E., Spigel, L. and Bergstrom, J. (eds), *Close Encounters: Film, Feminism and Science Fiction*. Minneapolis, MN: University of Minnesota Press, pp. 171–203.

Jenkins, H. (1992) *Textual Poachers: Television Fans and Participatory Culture*. New York: Routledge.

Jenkins, H. (2006) *Convergence Culture: Where Old and New Media Collide*. New York: New York University Press.

Jenkin, H. (2010) 'Five Ways to Read Avatar', http://henryjenkins.org/2010/02/five_ways_to_read_avatar.html (accessed 1 March 2010).

Johnston, K. M. (2007) 'Selling Genre in the 1930s: The Universal Horror Trailer', *Film International*, (May), www.filmint.nu/?q=node/73 (accessed 11 April 2011).

Johnston, K. M. (2008a) 'The Coolest Way to Watch Movie Trailers in the World! Trailers in the Digital Age', *Convergence*, 14(2): 145–60.

Johnston, K. M. (2008b) '"Three Times as Thrilling!" The Lost History of 3-D Trailer Production, 1953–54', *Journal of Popular Film and Television*, 36(4): 150–60.

Johnston, K. M. (2009) *Coming Soon: Film Trailers and the Selling of Hollywood Technology*. Jefferson, NC: McFarland.

Kaminsky, S. (1989) 'Don Siegel on the Pod Society', in Lavelley, A. (ed.), *Invasion of the Body Snatchers: Don Siegel, Director*, New Brunswick: Rutgers University Press, pp. 153–7.

Kawin, B. (1995) 'Children of the Light', in B. Grant (ed.), *Film Genre Reader II*, Austin, TX: University of Texas Press, pp. 308–29.

Kernan, L. (2004) *Coming Attractions: Reading American Movie Trailers*. Austin, TX: University of Texas Press.

King, G. (2000) *Spectacular Narratives: Hollywood in the Age of the Blockbuster*. London: IB Tauris.

King, G. and Krzywinska, T. (2000) *Science Fiction Cinema: From Outerspace to Cyberspace*. London: Wallflower Press.

Kirby, L. (1997) *Parallel Tracks: The Railroad and Silent Cinema*. Exeter: University of Exeter Press.

Kitses, J. ([1969] 2004) *Horizons West: The Western from John Ford to Clint Eastwood*. London: BFI.

Klinger, B. (1989) 'Digressions at the Cinema: Reception and Mass Culture', *Cinema Journal*, 28(4): 3–19.

Klinger, B. (1994) *Melodrama and Meaning: History, Culture and the Films of Douglas Sirk*. Bloomington, IN: Indiana University Press.

Kuhn, A. (ed.) (1990) *Alien Zone: Cultural Theory and Contemporary Science Fiction Cinema*. London: Verso.

Kuhn, A. (1999) *Alien Zone II: The Spaces of Science Fiction Cinema*. London: Verso.

Lamb, P. and Veith, D. (1986) 'Romantic Myth, Transcendence and *Star Trek* Zines', in D. Palumbo (ed.), *Erotic Universe: Sexuality and Fantastic Literature*. New York: Greenwood Press.

Lavalley, A. (1989) *Invasion of the Body Snatchers: Don Siegel, Director*. New Brunswick: Rutgers University Press.

Luciano, P. (1987) *Them or Us: Archetypal Interpretations of Fifties Alien Invasion Films*. Bloomington, IN: Indiana University Press.

Maltby, R. and Craven, I. (1995) *Hollywood Cinema: An Introduction*. Oxford: Blackwell.

Maslin, J. (1984) 'The Screen: "Terminator," Suspense Tale', *The New York Times*, 26 October, http://movies.nytimes.com/movie/review?res=9D05E4D91539F93 5A15753C1A962948260&scp=11&sq=terminator&st=cse (accessed 20 August 2009).

McArthur, C. (1972) *Underworld USA*. London: Secker & Warburg.

McCarthy, T. (2001) '*Final Fantasy: The Spirits Within* review', *Variety*, 8 July, www.variety.com/review/VE1117798442.html?categoryid=31&cs=1 (accessed 8 January 2010).

Mittell, J. (2001) 'A Cultural Approach to Television Genre Theory', *Cinema Journal*, 40(3): 3–24.

Mittell, J. (2002) *Genres and Television: From Cop Shows to Cartoons in American Culture*. London: Routledge.

Monthly Film Bulletin (1936) '*The Invisible Ray* Review', *Monthly Film Bulletin*, 3(6) (February): 28.

Morris, W. (1999) '*Matrix*: An Utterly Unique Film', *San Francisco Examiner*, 31 March, www.sfgate.com/cgi-bin/article.cgi?f=/c/a/1999/03/31/STYLE7325.dtl (accessed 20 August 2009).

Moving Picture World (1916) 'Famous Players Issue Advance Film', *Moving Picture World* 29(13) (30 September): 2094.

M.S. (2004) 'The Bourne Supremacy review', *Time Out London* 1773 (August): 11–18, www.timeout.com/film/reviews/81255/The_Bourne_Supremacy.html (accessed 1 February 2010).

Neale, S. (1980) *Genre*. London: BFI.

Neale, S. (1990) 'Questions of Genre', *Screen* 31(1) (Spring): 45–66.

Neale, S. (1993) 'Melo Talk: On the Meaning and Use of the Term "Melodrama" in the American Trade Press', *Velvet Light Trap* 22 (Fall): 66–89.

Neale, S. (2000) *Genre and Hollywood*. Abingdon: Routledge.

Netzley, P. (2000) *Encyclopaedia of Movie Special Effects*. Phoenix, AZ: Oryx Press.

O.A.G. (1953) 'Invaders From Mars: Here Come Those Flying Saucers Again', *New York Times,* 30 May, http://movies.nytimes.com/movie/review?_r=2&res=9405E 4DA163DE23BBC4850DFB3668388649EDE (accessed 20 August 2009).

Parr, B. (2009) 'Top Six Augmented Reality Mobile Apps', *Mashable/Mobile* (19 August 2009), http://mashable.com/2009/08/19/augmented-reality-apps/ (accessed 1 July 2010).

Pearson, R. and Messenger-Davies, M. (2003) 'You're Not Going to See That on TV: *Star Trek – The Next Generation* in Film and Television', in M. Jancovich and J. Lyons (eds), *Quality Popular Television: Cult TV, the Industry and Fans*, London: BFI, pp. 103–17.

Penley, C. (1991a) 'Introduction', in C. Penley, E. Lyon, L. Spigel and J. Bergstrom (eds), *Close Encounters: Film, Feminism and Science Fiction*. Minneapolis, MN: University of Minnesota Press.

Penley, C. (1991b) 'Feminism, Psychoanalysis and the Study of Popular Culture', in L. Grossberg, C. Nelson and P. Treichler (eds), *Cultural Studies*. New York: Routledge.

Penley, C. (1991c) 'Time Travel, Primal Scene and the Critical Dystopia', in C. Penley, E. Lyon, L. Spigel and J. Bergstrom (eds), *Close Encounters: Film, Feminism and Science Fiction*, pp. 63-81. Minneapolis, MN: University of Minnesota Press.

Penley, C. (1991d) 'Brownian motion: Women, Tactics, and Technology' in C. Penley and A. Ross (eds), *Technoculture*. Minneapolis, MN: University of Minnesota Press, pp.135–61.

Penley, C. (1997) *NASA/Trek: Popular Science and Sex in America*. London: Verso.

Penley, C., Lyon, E., Spigel, L. and Bergstrom, J. (eds) (1991), *Close Encounters: Film, Feminism and Science Fiction*. Minneapolis, MN: University of Minnesota Press.

Persons, D. (1994) 'Retrospect: *2001: A Space Odyssey'*, *Cinefantastique,* 25(3): 32–47.

Pierson, M. (2002) *Special Effects: Still in Search of Wonder*. New York: Columbia University Press.

Pingree, G. and Gitelman, L. (2003) 'Introduction: What's New About New Media?' L. Gitelman and G. Pingree (eds), *New Media 1740–1915*. London: MIT Press, pp. xi–xxii.

Pringle, D. (1996) *The Ultimate Encyclopaedia of Science Fiction: The Definitive Illustrated Guide*. London: Carlton.

Quigley, M. (1959) 'The "Prize Baby" Remembers', *Motion Picture Herald,* 217(5), 7 November.

Rickman, G. (ed.) (2004) *The Science Fiction Film Reader.* New York: Limelight.

Rogers, V. (2009) 'Fangirl Invasion: The Changing Face (and Sex) of Fandom', www.newsarama.com/film/090827-fangirl-invasion-1.html (accessed 28 August 2009).

Rogin, M. (1987) *Ronald Reagan, the Movie and Other Episodes in Political Demonology.* Berkeley, CA: University of California Press.

Romney, J. (2009) 'Avatar', *Independent,* 20 December, www.independent.co.uk/arts-entertainment/films/reviews/avatar-james-cameron-163-mins-pg-1845569.html (accessed 8 February 2010).

Rothkopf, J. (2009) 'Film Review: *2012*', *Time Out New York* issue 738 (19–25 November), http://newyork.timeout.com/articles/film/80592/2012-film-review (accessed 19 November 2009).

Sargent, E. (1915) *Picture Theatre Advertising.* New York: The Moving Picture World, Chalmers Publishing Co.

Sarris, A. (2008) 'Alphaville', The Criterion Collection Online Cinemateque, www.criterion.com/current/posts/38 (accessed 25 June 2009).

Schatz, T. (1981) *Hollywood Genre: Formulas, Filmmaking, and the Studio System.* New York: Random House.

Schatz, T. (1993) 'The New Hollywood', in J. Collins, H. Radner and A. Preacher (eds), *Film Theory Goes to the Movies.* New York: Routledge, pp. 8–36.

Shone, T. (2004) *Blockbuster, or How Hollywood Learned to Stop Worrying and Love the Summer.* London: Simon & Schuster.

Silverman, J. (2007) 'Meet Avi Arad, the Man Who Launched the Superhero Craze', *Wired,* www.wired.com/entertainment/hollywood/news/2007/05/spider_aviard?currentPage=2 (accessed 7 May 2007).

Silverman, K. (1991) 'Back to the Future', *Camera Obscura,* 27: 108–33.

Sobchack, V. (1988) *Screening Space: The American Science Fiction Film.* New York: Ungar.

Sontag, S. (1965) 'The Imagination of Disaster', *Commentary,* (October): 42–8.

Springer, C. (1991) 'The Pleasure of the Interface', *Screen,* 32(3): 303–23.

Staiger, J. (1990) 'Announcing Wares, Winning Patrons, Voicing Ideals: Thinking about the History and Theory of Film Advertising', *Cinema Journal,* 29(3): 3–31.

Stewart, G. (1985) 'The "Videology" of Science Fiction', in G. Slusser and E. Rabkin (eds), *Shadows of the Magic Lamp: Fantasy and Science Fiction in Film.* Carbondale, IL: Southern Illinois University Press, pp. 159–207.

Stewart, G. (1998) 'The Photographic Ontology of Science Fiction Film', *Iris,* 25: 99–132.

Tasker, Y. (1993) *Spectacular Bodies: Gender, Genre and the Action Cinema.* London, Routledge.

Telotte, J. (1995) *Replications: A Robotic History of the Science Fiction Film*. Urbana, IL: University of Illinois Press.

Telotte, J. (2001) *Science Fiction Film*. Cambridge: Cambridge University Press.

Telotte, J. (2009) 'Film 1895–1950', in M. Bould, A. Butler, A. Roberts and S. Vint (eds), *The Routledge Companion to Science Fiction*. Abingdon: Routledge, pp. 42–51.

Thilk, C. (2008) 'Movie Marketing Madness: *Cloverfield*', *M3* (January 2008), www.moviemarketingmadness.com/blog/2008/01/17/movie-marketing-madness-cloverfield/ (accessed 4 June 2010).

Thompson, K. and Bordwell, D. (1994) *Film History: An Introduction*. New York: McGraw-Hill.

Thornham, S. and Purvis, T. (2005) *Television Drama: Theories and Identities*, Basingstoke: Palgrave Macmillan.

Toke, D. (2004) *The Politics of GM Food: A Comparitive Study of the UK, USA and EU*. New York: Routledge.

Total Immersion, '"I am *Iron Man 2*" Augmented Reality Experience', *Newsarama* (23 June 2010), www.newsarama.com/comics/iron-man-2-phone-app-100623.html (accessed 1 July 2010).

Tudor, A. (1974) *Theories of Film*. London: Secker & Warburg/BFI.

Tudor, A. (1995) 'Genre', in B. Grant, *Film Genre Reader III*. Austin, TX: University of Texas Press, pp. 3–11.

Tulloch, J. and Jenkins, H. (1995) *Science Fiction Audiences: Watching Doctor Who and Star Trek*. London: Routledge.

Variety (1950) 'Rocketship X-M Review', 26 May, www.variety.com/review/VE1117796306.html?categoryid=31&cs=1 (accessed 20 August 2009).

Variety (1951a) 'The Man From Planet X Review', 1 January, www.variety.com/review/VE1117792912.html?categoryid=31&cs=1 (accessed 20 August 2009).

Variety (1951b) 'When Worlds Collide Review', 1 January, www.variety.com/review/VE1117796306.html?categoryid=31&cs=1 (accessed 20 August 2009).

Vaz, M. and Duignan, P. (1996) *Industrial Light and Magic: Into the Digital Realm*. London: Virgin Publishing.

Vizzini, B. (2009) 'Cold War Fears, Cold War Passions: Conservatives and Liberals Square Off in 1950s Science Fiction', *Quarterly Review of Film and Video*, 26(1): 28–39.

Warren, B. (1997) *Keep Watching the Skies: American Science Fiction Movies of the Fifties*. Jefferson, NC: McFarland.

Warshow, R. (1970) 'The Gangster as Tragic Hero', in *The Intermediate Experience: Movies, Comics, Theatre and Other Aspects of Popular Culture*. New York: Doubleday.

Wells, H. (1967) 'Preface to the 1921 Edition', in *The War in the Air*. Harmondsworth: Penguin.

Whittington, W. (2007) *Sound Design and Science Fiction*. Austin, TX: University of Texas Press.

Wierzbicki, J. (2002) 'Weird Vibrations: How the Theremin Gave Musical Voice to Hollywood's Extraterrestrial "Others"', *Journal of Popular Film and Television* 30(3) (Fall 2002), pp. 125–35.

Williams, A. (1984) 'Is a Radical Genre Criticism Possible?' *Quarterly Review of Film Studies*, 9(2): 121–5.

Wingrove, D. (1985) *Science Fiction Film Source Book*. Harlow: Longman.

Wood, A. (2002) *Technoscience in Contemporary American Film: Beyond Science Fiction*. Manchester: Manchester University Press.

Wood, R. ([1986] 2003) *Hollywood From Vietnam to Reagan ... And Beyond*. New York: Columbia University Press.

Wooley, C. (2001) 'A Visible Fandom: Reading *The X-Files* Through X-Philes', *Journal of Film and Video* 53(4): 29–53.

Wright, Wl. (1975) *Six Guns and Society: A Structural Study of the Western*. Berkeley, CA: University of California Press.

Wyatt, J. (1994) *High Concept: Movies and Marketing in Hollywood*. Austin, TX: University of Texas Press.

Wyndham, J. (1968) *The Seeds of Time*. London: Penguin.

Index

CPSIA information can be obtained
at www.ICGtesting.com
Printed in the USA
LVOW04s1838141216
517268LV00008B/44/P